MW00571924

RIDING THE WAVE

RIDING THE WAVE

SEVEN LEADERS OF CHANGE

Mini Menon

COLLINS BUSINESS
An Imprint of HarperCollins*Publishers*

First published in India in 2013 by Collins Business
An imprint of HarperCollins *Publishers* India

ISBN: 978-93-5029-178-8

2 4 6 8 10 9 7 5 3 1

HarperCollins *Publishers*
A-53, Sector 57, Noida, Uttar Pradesh 201301, India
77-85 Fulham Palace Road, London W6 8JB, United Kingdom
Hazelton Lanes, 55 Avenue Road, Suite 2900, Toronto, Ontario M5R 3L2
and 1995 Markham Road, Scarborough, Ontario M1B 5M8, Canada
25 Ryde Road, Pymble, Sydney, NSW 2073, Australia
31 View Road, Glenfield, Auckland 10, New Zealand
10 East 53rd Street, New York NY 10022, USA

Typeset in 12/16 Minion Regular at
SÜRYA

Printed and bound at
Thomson Press (India) Ltd.

For my parents
for their love and guidance,
and Anish and Dhruva,
who make my world go round

CONTENTS

PREFACE

The idea of this book came to me in 2009 when I was doing a series of interviews with the heads of some of India's biggest companies on UTVi (now Bloomberg TV India). In the two preceding years, most Indian companies had witnessed difficulties few could fathom. The book charts the journeys of some of these companies and their heads through the ups and downs of business in India and outside.

The subprime mortgage crisis of 2007–08, triggered by overly aggressive bankers selling bad-quality mortgages and complicated financial products in the US, the collapse of Lehman Brothers, the freezing of money flows, the slowdown in the US and Europe, bankruptcies in Detroit—the list of setbacks was endless. For many of India's biggest companies, this was the first brush with the flip side of being part of a globalized economy. It hurt more because between 2002 and 2007, before the financial crisis and the subsequent recession, most Indian companies had grown exponentially. Easy access to money from across the world, since India was amongst the most sought-after investment destinations then, had made them acquire firms and grow in scale and size.

When the problem surfaced in 2008 and it became clear that

everyone would be hit, there was shock all around. But, by the end of 2009, as I criss-crossed through corporate boardrooms, I saw that many companies had managed to keep their head above water. Most were able to do so because they had also gone through a period of churn and intense learning.

The seven businessmen in this book, though not as well known as the more glamorous and headline-making business leaders, represent sectors such as infrastructure, manufacturing, healthcare and media that will play a crucial role in India's growth. They are all 'owners' of their businesses but more important, each has a fascinating story to tell, one that is deeply interwoven with the postmodern history of India.

There are many others who could have been in this book. However, in hindsight, I couldn't have chosen a more exciting set of men. Because between 2010—when I first approached them for this book—and 2013, when it was done, each of them consistently made headlines.

Some were in the eye of a storm, while others were selling their businesses to start anew. Some were witnessing the failure of their best-laid plans while others were courting controversies like never before. But there was one thing in common to all of them: each of them had bounced back despite the odds. The challenges they faced made them recalibrate their strategies and helped them focus their energies on the opportunities that came their way.

This book offers a ringside view of these men and how they conduct their business. I hope you enjoy reading it as much as I did writing it.

Mumbai,
August 2013

INTRODUCTION

The old adage that change is the only constant is as true of business as it is of life.

Many Indian businessmen have learnt this the hard way, especially over the last two decades. And, in many senses, this is but the beginning.

Before 1991, for nearly half a century, India's business landscape had been almost static, characterized by slow growth. A controlled economy in which the state determined everything—from what you made to how much, and who you sold it to—meant there was little incentive to do anything but lobby for licences, jostle for space and scrounge for access. The term 'entrepreneurship' as we know it today was unheard of.

In 1991, as the curtains came down on the ubiquitous licence-permit raj, everything changed. The economy opened up after a series of external crises, triggered by a spike in oil prices and the collapse of trade with India's biggest partner, the erstwhile Soviet Union—all of which led to a balance of payments (BoP) crisis. After this, over the next few years, it was almost as though every businessman was put on a giant roller coaster. The world's biggest companies made a beeline for India; those who had survived began to put serious money into the market here; and most of India's old business houses went through a period of deep churn. If companies were wracked by internal convulsions, externally things looked even worse as the opening up was followed by a series of economic lows and highs that continue even today. Many Indian companies survived despite these uncertainties and spread their wings far and wide.

Riding the Wave is the story of seven businessmen who grew out of this ferment. They scripted their stories on the canvas of this changing landscape. Their success is not just a symbol of enterprise in the face of many odds, it is also a testament to their ability to adapt, innovate and stay ahead of their game.

I have broadly divided these men into the 'Inheritors', the 'Builders' and the 'Outsiders'. In a country where being a big businessman was normally a factor of the community you belonged to or the connections you had, the men in the last category would never have been successful had they not risen with the tide of change in India. They are great examples of the entrepreneurship driving growth in India today. Each of these men straddle different sectors, but they also have a lot in common.

The first of these is someone who has had a pretty rough run, especially over the last three years—Hindustan Construction Company (HCC) chairman Ajit Gulabchand. Few realize that his company today is a sliver of what remains of a very substantial legacy, that of Seth Walchand Hirachand, who was among India's top ten businessmen in 1947. Biographers compare Walchand with Ford founder Henry Ford and eccentric American businessman and aviator Howard Hughes. The reason: Walchand didn't just create a business empire, he also created whole new industries in India: automobiles (Premier Automobiles Limited [PAL]), shipping (the Scindia Shipyard [now Hindustan Shipyard Limited] in Visakhapatnam) and aviation (he laid the foundation of Hindustan Aeronautics Limited). By the time Gulabchand started to manage a small portion of his uncle's inheritance, which he was to inherit later—HCC—in 1983, there was little to lord over. Walchand was a memory and HCC, the company he had started his journey with, a small contractor bleeding under mounting losses.

The next two decades saw Gulabchand build his company almost from scratch. He brought a new vitality to HCC. New technology encouraged new capabilities, and in the short window of growth that companies in India's infrastructure sector got between 2000 and 2010, he built two of Mumbai's best-known projects: the Bandra–Worli Sea Link (BWSL) and part of the expressway connecting the city to Pune.

Yet, ironically, between 2010 and 2012, HCC's next big idea, a township project called Lavasa, was caught in the eye of a national storm. Few remembered how far Gulabchand and his company had actually come. Instead, for a little while, he became a public symbol of all that is wrong in Indian business and its connections with politics.

The second inheritor has a lot in common with Ajit Gulabchand, though they are a decade apart in age. Gautam Thapar (GT) is the grandson of another businessman who was in India's top ten list in 1947. GT's grandfather, Karam Chand Thapar, like Walchand Hirachand, was a self-made man whose journey started in the collieries of Jharia in Jharkhand. But he worked his way up, suffered a severe financial reverse twice between the two World Wars and went on to create an empire comprising banking, paper, ceiling fans, textile and several other businesses. By the time GT got to manage a small arm of what had been a big group, there was little to build on and too much to handle. But he managed it well, taking the two Thapar heirlooms—papermaker Ballarpur Industries Limited (BILT) and engineering firm Crompton Greaves—to the top of their league, only to be caught by a long and painful global slowdown between 2008 and 2012. This slowdown forced him to rewrite his story.

While neither Ajit Gulabchand nor Gautam Thapar have been able to match up to the men whose legacies they inherited, they have done a lot more in other ways. It speaks volumes of their business acumen that they were able to capitalize on what they got. What makes these two stories even more interesting is that neither was the obvious choice as the heir. They just stumbled upon the remnants of their legacy, most of which had been lost either to the government, which nationalized whole sectors through the 1960s and '70s, or whittled down by the family.

Which brings us to the two 'builders' in this book.

Baba N. Kalyani is by far one of India's most famous businessmen overseas. In the early 1970s, Kalyani walked into a small forging workshop that his father, Dr Neelkanth Kalyani, had started in Pune to help make agricultural equipment for the Kirloskars. Today, it is estimated that every passenger car sold by the big auto giants across the world has been fitted with some part, be it big or small, built by Bharat Forge. The company has several plants across cities like Germany's Stuttgart to China's Changchun; at one time, it was also one of the three largest forging (metal-casting) companies in the world.

Most people said India would never be able to manage high-quality manufacturing, but Kalyani has proven everyone wrong. In 1989, a little before the opening up of the Indian economy, he earmarked Rs 150 crore to rehaul his factory. By the time the economy opened up, Kalyani was already on the road, travelling across the US, briefcase in hand, selling auto parts he made to truck-makers there. By the time the first slowdown hit the Indian automotive industry in 1997–98, Kalyani had made inroads into Germany, the Mecca of high-end engineering. Few people have been able to stay ahead of change like him.

If Baba N. Kalyani excelled in the world of automotive engineering and beyond, Ajay Piramal did so in pharmaceuticals. After building an empire, he is starting from almost scratch today, to write his story anew.

But beyond all the business success, Ajay's story is also one of triumph against destiny and personal tragedy. He has come a long way from the time his family owned one of the old, decrepit textile mills of central Mumbai which were forcibly shut down by the longest labour strike in history. Ajay didn't just steer his textile mill—the oldest in the city—out of that crisis, he built a pharmaceutical empire from scratch, acquisition by acquisition, only to sell part of it for a massive profit, an amount that made every businessman in the world sit up and take notice.

Today, Ajay, the man they call India's shrewdest deal maker, is on to even bigger things. It is a reiteration of his success that in 2010, when US President Barack Obama came to India's commercial capital, Mumbai, it was Ajay who sat next to him. Scientists in his state-of-the-art R&D centre, in what was once a tyre factory, are working on the next big billion-dollar drug. He has far bigger ambitions and he is scripting a role for himself and the Piramals on the international stage, be it through the corridors of Harvard, or through his string of new acquisitions across the world.

Both Baba N. Kalyani and Ajay Piramal have shown an astuteness and vision few in India can boast of.

The inheritors and the builders may have had a template to work on but the next three businessmen started with a blank slate and their stories are equally spectacular. Take GMR Group chairman G.M. Rao. Till his early twenties, this builder of India's swanky new airports, notably the T3 of Delhi's Indira Gandhi International Airport, spent hours cycling on the hot and dusty roads around his home town, Rajam, in Andhra Pradesh. The son of a trader, Rao has come a long way since he began his journey with nothing but an education. But he did have the gumption to get off that cycle to become a small-time factory owner, then a small successful businessman, and then a regional player, a banker and an industrialist.

If G.M. Rao's journey has been awe inspiring, Ronnie Screwvala's has been equally so in a different line of business. The founder of UTV, Screwvala is considered to be one of India's smartest media moguls—the man who got the better of even Rupert Murdoch! He started as a youngster who dabbled in theatre in the comfortable confines of old-world Mumbai. Though his journey to become one of India's coolest film producers took him less than a decade and just a few kilometres north from where he started out—from south Mumbai to Juhu, the heart of India's film industry—it was a road no one had taken before. In the vibrant world of satellite television and blockbuster films, Screwvala brought a new sensibility that ensured that he was always a step ahead of the audience. Isn't that a good place to be, in a business that is notoriously fickle?

From hosting the first English talk show on Doordarshan to setting up the first cable network, albeit a small neighbourhood one, from making India's first daily soap to bringing in the first serious private equity investment (global private equity firm Warburg Pincus's first bet in India was UTV), the media mogul not only helped bring in a new edginess and structure to the world of make-believe in India, he also cannily steered his way through some tough turns.

Amid these profiles, there is one story that stands out in more ways than one, that of Rajeev Chandrasekhar, the original young Turk of telecom and founder of BPL Mobile. Rajeev may have achieved success early, but few men have seen such trying times as he has. Going bankrupt twice, making a mess of his business, taking up a new enterprise only to be, as he puts it, stabbed in the back, this man has seen the seedy side of Indian business and the corruption that stalks it. But he survived all that and did it, as singer and actor Frank Sinatra would say, 'his way'.

And today, after publicly proclaiming that he would never touch a business where the government has any role to play, Rajeev continues to surprise all those who have tracked him by being a member of Parliament. In his second term as member of the Rajya Sabha, he has driven the debate on the collusion between politics and business in ways no one else has.

A lot was stacked against these businessmen: history, policy, mindset and even destiny. But they managed to deal with the adversities and stay ahead in the game. All of them have an uncanny ability to look ahead, lift themselves from the present and gauge what's coming. It is this mindset that has helped them every step of the way along their journey.

Between 2010 and 2012, each of these seven businessmen has had to start all over again, but they have managed to do so successfully in a tough environment.

PART I

THE INHERITORS

AJIT GULABCHAND

It was biting cold even under the noonday sun and walking on the wet, slippery road wasn't easy as Ajit Gulabchand, one of the delegates, headed to the World Economic Forum (WEF) convention centre in Davos.

The other delegates mostly travelled in the WEF vehicles that ferried attending CEOs and dignitaries to meetings held in different pockets of this quaint Swiss town during the annual business summit, one of the most important events of its kind since it was conceived in 1971. But old hands such as Gulabchand, who had been coming to this small resort to attend the summit for decades, preferred to be on their own, enjoying the relative privacy they had here.

Gulabchand remembered his meeting with old friend Rahul Bajaj while walking in a lane like this one just two days ago. The two were close pals even though Bajaj was a decade older than Gulabchand, who was sixty-one, and both of them had been coming to Davos since the latter was in his thirties. Bajaj was always zipping about, living life to the fullest, especially in Davos. Gulabchand chuckled, thinking of the lively times they had had in Davos over the years.

They had been such nonentities when they had started coming to Davos. Nobody had even heard of them, or any Indian businessman for that matter. Truth be told, the world's top CEOs, who had begun to throng the summit over the years, often had difficulty placing India on the map. India was insignificant, a write-off in a world dominated by free-market capitalists.

How things had changed over the last ten years. Gulabchand and Bajaj were now the senior citizens of corporate India. India was the flavour of the last couple of years, and as if to underline its growing clout that year, the arrival of the largest-ever delegation from India was also marked by a campaign talking of 'Inclusive India'. Gulabchand thought it ironical, given what was happening back home. Despite a plethora of scams and a floundering government, India was still the most sought-after destination for setting up business.

Things had changed fast here and faster back home. The year 2010 had been a bittersweet one for Gulabchand and his company, Hindustan Construction Company (HCC), one of India's oldest construction companies.

He had seen everything that year: from heady highs to depressing lows.

In May 2010, HCC entered the big league in the construction world by acquiring a Swiss construction company, Karl Steiner AG, for 35m Swiss francs (roughly, Rs 150 crore). This was the first big international acquisition by a construction company in India. That this company had built the WEF headquarters in Zurich added to its appeal.

If this was a colourful new addition, back home, his company's high-profile masterpiece, the Bandra–Worli Sea Link in north Mumbai, had been commissioned the previous year, after nearly a decade of delays, making HCC a household name in his beloved city.

But he had hardly had the time to enjoy the satisfaction of a job well done.

The bridge, which had become a landmark representing a new, resurgent Mumbai, had barely begun to be used when a lot of things started going wrong. So, on that crisp afternoon in Davos, on 30 January 2011, bitterness was all Gulabchand could feel. His year of glory and recognition in India and on these Alpine slopes was marred by problems, particularly one that could destroy everything he had built through the last two decades and make him bankrupt. His dream of creating a whole new city, an urban paradise, a close replica of Davos, at Lavasa in the Sahyadri Hills, had run into trouble.

The Swiss-style chalets, Davos-inspired convention centres, the recreation facilities to provide a quick weekend getaway, the pristine green-swathed slopes and the villas for the well-heeled were partly ready in the new hill station Gulabchand had created and called Lavasa. But no sooner had he unveiled his ideas and city to the world with lofty plans to raise Rs 2,000 crore (the project was valued at Rs 15,000 crore) through a listing on the Indian stock exchanges, than things had started going wrong.

The green lobby in India, led by none other than Environment Minister Jairam Ramesh, had accused him of flouting laws and destroying the region's fragile ecosystem.

His friends and family were being targeted and attacked. No one had been spared. Soon, all construction had come to a halt in Lavasa. It became as silent as the hills around it.

Gulabchand was aware of the impact of all this. Because as he sat here and spoke about growth with a heart, 'sustainability', as it was dubbed, and developing the green agenda, a campaign he was heading at the World Economic Forum this year, he knew some of the delegates from India were asking whether he was the right man to lead the debate. Worse still, back home, his entire company was struggling, hundreds of people had been laid off, creditors were at his door, investors were edgy, and it seemed as though everyone had lost a lot of money betting on him.

Gulabchand was a fighter and had fought many battles, each one bigger than the last, with a lot more at stake each time. The one thing he was certain of was that tomorrow was another day, one full of opportunities.

For now he decided to just soak in the debates. Economists Joseph Stiglitz, Nobel laureate, and 'Dr Doom', Nouriel Roubini, who had predicted the 2008 US subprime mortgage crash, were discussing the state of global recovery. His own future could wait.

He wasn't to know how bad things would get in the months to come. He had no inkling that he would find himself on a cliff edge, struggling to hold on while staring into an abyss, the Davos days a fond memory.

THE INHERITANCE

Hindustan Construction Company (HCC) underwent several changes in 2010. Amid the highs and lows, the curves and cliff edges it navigated through, HCC also changed headquarters, from an old-world functional, bland, blocky grey building to a swanky new chrome-and-glass high-rise. The distance between the old office and the new one was barely a few hundred yards, but the change it represented was enormous. The offices belonged to two different eras. The new one was an unmissable landmark glinting in the sun, rising above Mumbai's grubby suburb Vikhroli. The location, 247 Park Mumbai, was worthy of HCC's new focus: to be a builder of modern cities.

But both the old building and the new had one thing in common: the turbaned, larger-than-life bust of the group's founder, Gulabchand's uncle, Seth Walchand Hirachand, at the entrance. The sculpture was of a swarthy man whose most striking feature had to be the piercing and watchful eyes behind the glasses, which made one take another, closer look. The bust was reminiscent of another audacious businessman, Reliance founder Dhirubhai Ambani. But few people would draw that parallel, save perhaps Gulabchand, who had been close to both men.

Like Dhirubhai Ambani, Walchand's story was also one of sheer chutzpah and enterprise. He started with nothing but guts as a small-time contractor latching on to petty construction jobs handed out by the British army and government in pre-Independence India. But like Ambani, his ambition was insatiable, and he grew from making barracks to building some of modern India's most enduring monuments—its biggest dams, tunnels and railway lines.

Even today, India's commercial capital Mumbai gets its water through the pipeline HCC built, from the nearby Tansa Lake, one of the city's three main reservoirs. Travel to Pune to the south and you will pass through the Bhor Tunnel Walchand built through the Western Ghats.

The list is long, but Walchand's legacy was not limited to the many monumental projects he executed; it extended to many sectors he virtually created. He built India's first shipyard, Hindustan Shipyard Limited; the country's first aircraft factory, Hindustan Aeronautics Limited; and its first car plant, Premier Automobiles Limited, the maker of Premier Padmini (based on an old Fiat design), still seen on Mumbai's crowded roads in the form of the ubiquitous cabs.

Walchand not only created these companies, he was the pioneer in each of these industries. It is a little-remembered fact that even today, the day his company Scindia Steam Navigation Company Limited's first liner sailed—after he fought the British to get rights for Indians to conduct commercial shipping internationally—is celebrated as India's Maritime Day. Yet, as his biographers point out, even this was not where the real genius of the man lay.

Business historian Gita Piramal writes in her book *Business Legends*:

> Walchand did all of this [built companies] often without a silver rupee in his pocket. Just a burning ambition that saw him trying to be a car maker like Henry Ford, an aircraft manufacturer like Howard Hughes, and a shipping magnate, all rolled into one ... That was also his failing ... While Walchand built an empire, one of the ten largest in India, he wasn't able to hold on to it.

Like his peer Karam Chand Thapar, who was the founder of the Thapar Group of Companies, Walchand first lost most of what he had built (shipping and aeronautics) to the government, and what was left behind—Premier Automobiles, HCC and interests in sugar—was distributed between his brothers and their children (he was heirless), who weren't able to add anything to what he had created.

Seth Walchand Hirachand (*extreme left corner, in white*) at the inauguration ceremony of the Bhor Tunnel in the Western Ghats

HDFC founder H.T. Parekh summed up Walchand's legacy in *Business Legends*:

> The unique success of Walchand in keeping the flag of India's merchant marine flying against heavy odds was tarnished in the evening of his career by knotty day-to-day problems of internal management, right personnel, a rigid economy and [inability] to check internal dissension, to which he paid scant attention and which created a crisis within the company.

Walchand was a dreamer and a builder but he didn't bother with the minutiae of everyday management—that, in a nutshell, is the general conclusion.

Ajit Gulabchand, who was barely five when Walchand died in 1953, has a different take on the man. He doesn't remember him for his shortcomings but for his charisma, which evidently grew on him. 'You know, he never went back to his office after the day he fainted there, after his heart attack. He was a proud man.' After that, for a year before he died, every evening, Walchand would get into his Chrysler and go for a drive around Marine Drive with Gulabchand. Trips that he remembers fondly. 'I would always climb in, enjoy the wind against my face and watch the silent man beside me. He would never speak. But what stood out always were those piercing eyes.'

At that time, Walchand was just an old uncle who took him for a nice car ride each evening. But this changed the day Walchand died. 'There was a swarm of people around our house. All the roads were choked. I remember standing on the terrace, peering through the railing at the crowd below. I realized that Walchand Kaka was someone of great importance,' Gulabchand remembers. As he grew up, his fascination with the man and what he had created grew. He would read every article about Walchand he could lay his hands on and lap up every bit of information on him. Over the years, the obsession turned to admiration and ambition.

Gulabchand wanted nothing more than to follow in his uncle's footsteps and perhaps live up to the legacy he had created. In his new office, one can see Gulabchand's life-size portrait smiling down, longish hair combed back, a glint in the eye and head tilted to one side. One could almost be looking at the face of Walchand Hirachand, many decades on.

GROWING UP

With his casual elegance, his collection of antiques, his Bentley, Porsche, his uncle Walchand's old Chrysler, a helicopter and airplane, Ajit Gulabchand fits well into the stereotypical image of the rich old industrialist who has had money for a few generations.

And nowhere is this more keenly felt than within the company. Many of the older company retainers still refer to him as Seth-ji. It's a tag Gulabchand is embarrassed about. Others who have watched him from the outside say he represents all that old-world money in India does. For example, connections, because the success he has made of HCC could have come only with the political patronage he enjoys.

But for all his easy charm and polish, Gulabchand is uncomfortably candid for an Indian businessman and has no qualms about speaking his mind on a host of issues. He doesn't play safe. He is not politically correct, something which has got him in trouble several times. 'You can't be an activist and a businessman in India and Ajit should remember that,' an old friend said. 'He just doesn't know when to stop. Some of his views are so rigid, it's a wonder he has survived for so long. He should have been a journalist, not a businessman,' another commented.

When asked why he believes that socialism has hurt the country and that India needs a right-of-centre view on almost everything, Gulabchand said, 'Till well into the 1980s, I would tell any youngster asking me for advice that his best bet would be to go outside India. You will be able to succeed here only if you have money and family wealth. This was not the place to make something on your own.' Not surprisingly, Gulabchand is a die-hard capitalist. If in a reflective mood, he will even tell you that after the dust has settled and his company is back on track, he wants to do nothing more than create a platform, a think tank or an academy, for ideologues like him.

But, ironic as it may sound, there is another side to the man. All the way from 1978 to '91, he wore plain white, hand-spun cotton or a khadi kurta and pyjama, the de facto uniform of most Indian politicians. So, was it symbolic that he changed around the same time that India's economy opened up?

There are few Indian businessmen who have embraced change as readily as Ajit Gulabchand and he also knows just how long the road ahead is. His father, Gulabchand, was Walchand's younger brother and almost as headstrong as his sibling. If Walchand was a maverick and a gutsy businessman, Gulabchand was a fiery nationalist. An active member of the über right-wing Hindu Mahasabha, he was involved in the early, more militant phase of the freedom struggle and the Civil Disobedience Movement in the 1940s.

Ajit Gulabchand proudly says, 'My father was imprisoned twice and almost hung with his colleagues [who were] for a bombing case in Sholapur.' Always ready with a quip, he jokes, 'He would have been one of the statues in Sholapur [bronze statues were erected in honour of these martyrs] had he not escaped to Goa and remained incognito for months after the incident.'

The more the senior Gulabchand got into trouble with the British authorities, the more his brother Walchand tried to rein him in. He finally succeeded after years of trying, when Gulabchand decided to give up politics for business.

One of the reasons was probably his second wife and Ajit Gulabchand's mother, Dr Shanta Saptarshi, who was a woman far ahead of her times, the likes of whom he had never met before. 'She was the first Indian woman to be a fellow of the Royal Medical Society, Edinburgh. She practised medicine in Vienna but returned to India when Hitler invaded the city. My parents met and got married. She was a very modern and educated Maharashtrian woman, a breath of fresh air in the traditional Gujarati household we lived in,' Gulabchand remarks.

He attributes a lot of his success to his mother. For instance, at a time when most of his cousins were in vernacular schools, she insisted that Gulabchand get an English education and exposure to a world outside the traditional Gujarati household he grew up in. In reality, Gulabchand seems far more Marathi than Gujarati. Many even joke that Marathi is the official language in this old Gujarati company, thanks to him. He often falls back into chaste Marathi mid-sentence, when he has to elaborate a point.

By the time Ajit Gulabchand was born, in 1949, the family was quite large. He himself was the eighth son of Gulabchand, the first from his second wife, and between his half brothers and cousins, there were enough young men waiting to acquire and manage a piece of their uncle Walchand's vast empire.

Gulabchand's first go at work came when he was twenty-two. His father passed away and just out of college then, he got his first business assignment in far-off Delhi as a manager at the Indian Hume Pipe Co. Ltd, a Kolkata-based company Walchand had acquired in 1926.

In 1920, angry at the way things were going with his partners—the Tatas—in the construction business (Walchand had hit the big league after merging his small construction companies with the Tatas to form Tata Construction, HCC's precursor), Walchand decided to pack his bags and move to Kolkata. The idea was to go to the centre of the jute trading business to try his hand at jute. But instead of becoming a jute trader, Walchand spotted an opportunity when he heard about an interesting company that was doing some cutting-edge work in the pipe business.

Indian Hume Pipe (formerly the Calcutta Hume Pipe Company) made high-intensity, taut, concrete pipes for transportation of water. Founded by a Melbourne-based entrepreneur and inventor, Walter Hume, the company had pioneered the creation of a new reinforced cement concrete (RCC) pipe that was sturdy and cheap to make. In a short period the Hume pipes, still the default name for RCC pipes in the market today, became a rage across Australia and Asia (where it was made under licence) and transformed the way pipes were made and laid.

Gulabchand realized two things during his stint as manager in Delhi. First, that he wasn't a numbers guy, a guy who 'sat at the till'. 'I realized I was far better at creating an idea, making a plan and getting it implemented. For me, business wasn't just about the money, it was about creating something.' The other thing he realized was that he could be quite popular in Delhi's social circles. When he had moved to Delhi, both he and his wife, actor Meera Joglekar, were very young and they didn't know many people in the city. But old connections helped—among them Yashwantrao Chavan, the Maratha strongman who was finance minister at the Centre and their local guardian—and soon the young couple became popular and started hanging out with a young set of the power brigade.

The days in Delhi were mostly fun for Gulabchand. But life was also a series of business lessons. At the Indian Hume Pipe factory, he was assigned to manage its Badarpur plant near Faridabad that made a range of products, including the higher-end 'pre-stressed' concrete the company had started producing.

Even so, Gulabchand realized the potential of this new form of concrete, the strength and flexibility it offered.

Technically speaking, pre-stressing enabled concrete to overcome its natural weakness in tension or under pressure by using steel cables or rods to provide a 'clamping load', or stress, so that the concrete could deal with high pressures by countering it. Pre-stressed concrete is now an essential part of building bridges and high-pressure water pipes.

Gulabchand's job was to streamline operations in the factory he was in charge of. He did that but also created a new market for this very profitable product. 'This business was already there within the company, I simply helped market it better. I also streamlined operations in the factory and over the months I was there, we could quote far better rates to our buyers.' Soon the factory began to make higher profits and his elder brother, Bahubali, who was MD of the company, put him in charge of all the factories of the company across north India.

But just as things were looking up, in 1975, Gulabchand was called to Mumbai and given a new assignment: heading the family's sugar mill in Ravalgaon. It was here that Gulabchand would have his first real brush with politics and embark on building the associations that would stand him in good stead in the years to come.

THE PAWAR CONNECTION

Apart from being a pioneer in shipping and industry, Walchand Hirachand was a man who believed that the use of modern technology would be essential to transform the face of agriculture in India. And Ravalgaon, known today for the candy it makes, such as Coffee Break and Pan Pasand, was to be his test case. He brought high-tech machinery into the existing sugar mills to modernize them. These high-tech sugar factories marked a coming together of two of Walchand's obsessions: agriculture and industrialization.

Gulabchand was rather upset when he was asked to move from Delhi to Ravalgaon. He would have preferred going to Walchandnagar, where he grew up. But Ravalgaon gave him a sense of the real world and threw him into the midst of a politically sensitive and significant face-off. Over time, it also won him some very powerful political friends.

To understand the close connections between sugar and Maharashtra politics and what a young Gulabchand found when he reached Ravalgaon, one has to travel back in time.

The sugar belt of western Maharashtra, where Ravalgaon is located, not only forms the nerve centre of India's sugar industry, it is also the base of the state's political power as it was the stage for one of socialist India's biggest dream projects—the sugar cooperative movement.

In the 1920s, the development of canal irrigation by the British in the otherwise dry western Maharashtra belt had attracted hordes of migrants, all Marathas, to the area. Most of them had been gardeners and land tillers and they had been called in by the British because they were among the few people who knew how to grow irrigated crops. With water, sugarcane plantations proliferated in the dry belt and, gradually, the area between the canals saw a tapestry of big and small cane farms.

But abundance gave rise to a problem between those who produced the sugarcane—the farmers—and those who processed it, the private sugar factory or mill owners. Cane cannot be transported over long distances, and the farmers, especially the smaller ones, were dependent on the sugar mills to buy their cane at the price the local mill owner fixed for their produce. As a result, exploitation set in and the farmers were caught between a rock and hard place—the moneylenders and the sugar-mill owners.

Most small cane growers began to transform the cane into a crude form of sugar—jaggery—at home. The overproduction of this, in a good year, often meant that prices regularly hit rock bottom and the farmers were pushed to penury. It's against this backdrop that a local farmer, Vitthalrao Vikhe Patil, initiated a cooperative movement that was inspired by the collective farming experiment in the erstwhile Soviet Union. All the way from the early 1930s, the Communist regime in Russia had encouraged small farmers to come together and pool their resources to create collective *kolkhozy*s or farms, which characterized Soviet agriculture. In India, the concept received much support from Congress leader and economist Dr D.R. Gadgil, and, in 1948, the first such cooperative farm in Maharashtra's Pravaranagar village came up.

The cooperatives gave small owners some say in their fortunes, ensured there were economies of scale in sugarcane cultivation and brought the exploitation to an end.

So successful was this early experiment that by the 1950s, these sugar cooperatives started dominating the industry. In the decades that followed, they changed the face of the politics of Maharashtra. Kumar Ketkar, editor of the Marathi newspaper *Dainik Divya Marathi*, explains how the sugar cooperative came to form the edifice of the state's politics, dominating discourse and policy making. According to Ketkar, who has reported for some of India's biggest national dailies for over three decades, one has to look at the transformation of this swathe of western Maharashtra over the decades to understand the evolution.

'Even fifty years ago, a major part of the rain-shadow areas was barren and farmers lived in penury. There has been a complete transformation there, something that happened largely due to the rural cooperative movement,' Ketkar says. Travel there and the prosperity is evident. The rich fields are complemented by scores of factories and industrial hubs.

The rise of the west, economically and politically, also led to the emergence of strong affiliations between the politicians and businessmen of the region. Gulabchand's close association with Sharad Pawar, the Nationalist Congress Party (NCP) founder and current agriculture minister at the Centre, and one of the most powerful political leaders to emerge from the area, began in Ravalgaon. Gulabchand represented the clutch of factory owners who had been upstaged by the cooperative movement and were now dependent on it for survival because the price at which the factories bought the sugarcane from the farmers was determined by the state and the powerful political leaders from here.

Gulabchand arrived in Ravalgaon in the eye of a storm. 'The year I arrived in Ravalgaon, we incurred severe losses. The year after, we made record losses.' Presiding over what looked like a one-way slide, he was at his wits' end.

'See, when you have a sugar factory, you can't just go out and buy sugarcane from anywhere. It has to be cane from within the area. There is no sugar factory in the world that doesn't have some kind of a lock-in on the supply pipeline. Between 1975 and '77, when I became the managing director, Maharashtra State Farming Corporation, the cane farmers' association representing the farmers, simply refused to give it to us. As a result, the factories faced huge losses.' Ravalgaon was caught in such a bind that a major part of Gulabchand's five-year stint in Ravalgaon was spent lobbying with politicians to convince the Maharashtra State Farming Corporation (MSFC) to restore the cane supply.

One thing that helped him was his friendship with Pawar, then an upcoming politician from Baramati, in the heart of the so-called sugar belt. The connection between the two, to begin with, was their wives; both were Maharashtrians whose families had known each other in Pune.

'Sharad Pawar was [Yashwantrao Chavan's] blue-eyed boy in those days because he was a bright fellow, not powerful then, but influential nonetheless. In 1977–78, he helped me lobby with Vasantdada Patil, who was the chief minister of Maharashtra.'

The period between 1975 and '78 was tough. 'In 1975, the MSFC that supplied the majority of the cane refused to do so. In 1976, prices of cane, dictated by the government, shot up, and in 1977, prices of sugar were finally decontrolled.'

In 1978, Gulabchand managed to wrest price and supply concessions not just for himself but for all sugar mill owners across western Maharashtra. 'There used to be a big purchase tax on buying cane. It was a huge sum if you looked at the volume of cane we bought each year. I used my influence to get it waived. For eight years at that. I made them realize how this was wrong as a practice in the long run and how it was hurting us.' This proved to be a lifesaver for the sugar producers. Suddenly, the old sugar families in the region, like the Ruias, Ruparels and Agashes from Pune, started to take notice of the young Gulabchand.

But to his credit, he quickly began to change things around within the mill as well. After his experience with Indian Hume, he was quick to realize that there were a lot of problems. The first was that the sugar mill was run, like most other companies managed by the family, with very loose controls. The entire produce was sold to a wholesaler, who made all the money. Gulabchand realized that this had to be changed. So they began a weekly auction to get the best price for sugar. This was just one of many initiatives. He went on to redesign the entire organizational structure within the company and divided the business into smaller, more manageable parts. In the confectionery business, initially set up to ensure that the excess produce was not wasted, he decided to take on distribution as well, since this was where a lot of the profits were licked off.

'When the confectionery division began, it was as an offshoot of sugar. We had so much sugar that we would boil it. That's what most confectionery actually is. Before I came, they looked at it as just that—boiled sugar, with some value added. I looked at it as a consumer product that could be branded and marketed.'

For this, Gulabchand not only rejigged the processes within the company, he also raised money to modernize the sugar factory. By 1980, the company had managed a turnaround. The five years he spent at Ravalgaon gave Gulabchand a sense of the realities of doing business in India. While most of the private sugar mills have disappeared from the region, Ravalgaon is very much there, still a brand to be reckoned with. It is managed by Gulabchand's nephew, Harshal.

The five years in Ravalgaon set the stage for things to come. First, it built Gulabchand's reputation as a man with strong political connections. Second, it laid the foundation of a close friendship between him and Sharad Pawar. They hit it off so well that almost immediately, Gulabchand believes, this equation soured relations between him and the nephews of Seth Walchand Hirachand.

People who know Gulabchand say that his most striking quality is that he can hit it off instantly with anyone. He himself claims that people often get it wrong when they write him off as a Sharad Pawar loyalist. Gulabchand jokes that he had never voted for the man or his party, the NCP. 'We are just good friends. In fact, he always tells me to go abroad during the elections so that I don't vote for the BJP.'

Gulabchand has been close to other leaders from the BJP and Congress parties. And, even now, the children of powerful Congress leaders at the Centre refer to him as 'Ajit Kaka'.

THE BIG FIGHT

As with most large Indian business families of the time, there was disquiet within the Walchand household through the 1980s over control and inheritance.

While Ajit Gulabchand was Walchand Hirachand's second brother and the man in charge of the business, on his death, Gulabchand's sons were not seen as the most favoured within the group. Lalchand, Walchand's youngest brother, had been like the son he never had, and it was to Lalchand's sons that the prime spoils of the Walchand empire—Premier Automobiles, Walchandnagar Industries and Hindustan Construction Company—went. Ajit Gulabchand and his brothers were given the peripherals like the Indian Hume Pipe Co. and Ravalgaon, of which the eldest brother, Bahubali, was made managing director.

Much of this disquiet came from the fact that both Ravalgoan and Indian Hume Pipe had begun to expand rapidly under Ajit Gulabchand and his brothers. 'They found out that we had a disproportionate distribution. The four of us—Bahubali, Arvind, Rajas and me, all Gulabchand's sons—owned 80 per cent of the group through Indian Hume and Ravalgaon. I think they got a little afraid and packed me off to manage a small metal fabrication company, Acrow India Limited, in Vikhroli, on the outskirts of Mumbai ,' Gulabchand remarks.

It was an attempt to sideline Gulabchand, but it would turn out to be the launch pad of a far bigger battle. The Acrow India plant, which was a virtual dump in 1981–82, would go on to become the site of Ajit Gulabchand's swanky high-rise headquarters one day.

But the trigger came from an unlikely place.

The first chapter of the big battle within the Walchand group was written in Kolkata, in the house of the Goenkas, amidst another family squabble.

The Goenkas, who were considered the doyens of Kolkata's Marwari business community, were going through a period of strife in the late 1970s. After a series of acquisitions that had transformed the family from one of traders and moneylenders to industrialists and plantation owners, Keshav Prasad Goenka, the patriarch of the family, was forced to divide his companies with a combined net worth of Rs 150 crore between his three sons, Jagdish, Gauri and Rama Prasad (RP) Goenka.

The cause of the division was the growing bickering between his sons and RP's political ties with former prime minister Indira Gandhi.

Those were politically turbulent days. The Morarji Desai government that came to power in March 1977, after the Emergency, had begun to breathe down on old Gandhi loyalists. Many within the Goenka family believed that they had willy-nilly become victims of the 'vendetta'.

R.P. Goenka was of the view that over the years he had been sidelined within the family. He was adamant about securing the future of his sons, Harsh and Sanjiv, both young at the time. This provided the backdrop for RP to create a new empire—the RPG group.

The strategy at the heart of this new empire-building exercise was acquisitions. Sitting on a large amount of liquid cash after the split, RP's first purchase was Ceat Tyres in 1981, at a time when it was India's third-largest tyre company. This was followed in quick succession by a series of acquisitions: a major engineering procurement and construction (EPC) company, KEC International, in 1982; Searle India, now RPG Life Sciences, in 1983; Dunlop, a year later; Bayer after that (this was sold later); and music company HMV in 1988.

By the last one, RP had officially become India's 'takeover king' and his subsequent acquisitions of Kolkata's power company, Calcutta Electric Supply Corporation (CESC), and Harrisons Malayalam Limited (HML), the tea plantation company, only underlined this. But there were setbacks as well, the most famous being his thwarted attempt at trying to buy the blue-chip Bombay Dyeing. This was by far the most audacious attempt by RP, who was high on his earlier successes.

He wasn't ready, though, for the way the old Mumbai business families closed ranks around one of their own, the young Nusli Wadia. Nusli had fought hard to save his company and inheritance even though his father, Neville Wadia, had nearly sold Bombay Dyeing to Goenka. Those were tense times in Mumbai's business circles. A corporate raider had shaken up the calm of Ballard Estate and every big promoter was trying hard to ring-fence his company. It was in the middle of this, in June 1982, after that initial, very public setback, that RP made a last-ditch effort to make his group even bigger.

Canny and street smart as he was, RP decided to turn his attention to one of the other marquee blue-chip companies—Premier Automobiles Limited (PAL). The problems within this company were obvious. While there are different versions of what happened next, what stands out is Gulabchand's role in it.

Premier Automobiles was an easy target. The Doshis, who were Lalchand's side of the family, managed the affairs at the company, and the family's stake in Premier Automobiles, one of the two carmakers that enjoyed a free hand of the Indian marketplace, was a paltry 7 per cent.

The idea of acquiring Premier Automobiles came after a chance meeting Harsh Goenka had with the head of Fiat (Premier's partner) in Turin, Italy. Harsh was there to meet the top bosses at Ceat (also headquartered in Turin). The Fiat chairman, apparently unhappy with his partners in India, offered Harsh the prototype of a new car that Fiat was developing. Excited at the opportunity of getting a foothold into the exclusive club of Indian carmakers, Harsh apparently returned with a letter from the Fiat chairman promising support, and he and RP worked out the modalities of how to get into the company.

With mounting debts, losses and nothing but an outdated two-decades-too-old 1960s car on the roads, it was not difficult. Institutional investors like state insurers LIC and IDBI, who held a majority stake in the company, were only too happy to oblige and pump in new money into PAL.

It was only a matter of time before the Goenkas began to garner more shares, mostly from the stock markets, and within a few months of spotting an opportunity in PAL, there was a full-fledged and very public hostile takeover battle on the cards.

Gulabchand's side of the story is different. He was in London when the first rumblings began. By the time he came back, he was appalled to see the gloom at Construction House, PAL's headquarters in Ballard Estate. 'It was most frustrating. We were clueless about how to deal with the problem. Everyone was simply wringing their hands. I told Vinod [Doshi], "Let's start buying stock from the marketplace . . . Let's take on RPG".' Heated arguments followed. Not one to give up, and angry at the way the family's fortunes were being squandered, Gulabchand decided to up the ante and whip up sentiment against the aggressive Goenkas.

'It was obvious that R.P. Goenka was trying to carve out a fortune for his son Harsh in Mumbai. By now it was clear that Sanjiv would remain in Kolkata and Harsh would move to Mumbai. What better way to make him matter than by getting him a nice blue-chip company,' Gulabchand remarks.

As the battle lines were drawn, Walchand's nephews also united, for the first time. Gulabchand was given the task of ensuring that RP didn't get enough stock in PAL from the stock markets. He also took the help of his powerful circle of friends to exert pressure and win support. He had seen the same drill play out in Bombay Dyeing, albeit under different circumstances, and he was adamant that he wouldn't let the Goenkas get a toehold.

Three factors helped swing things in favour of the Walchand family. First, as the takeover battle got to fever pitch, there were articles in the press against the aggressiveness of the Goenkas. Full-page advertisements began appearing underlying the role and contribution of Seth Walchand to Indian business. Next, Gulabchand turned to old friend Rahul Bajaj for support. Bajaj, a fellow Marwari, reportedly advised Goenka to abstain from an aggressive stance and takeover. His argument was that the Walchands were a local family (though Gujarati) with strong roots in Maharashtra. The powerful unions in PAL would never let an outsider come in. Finally, it was Sharad Pawar, an important voice, who put pressure on the Congress leadership and Prime Minister Indira Gandhi.

After months of high drama and brinkmanship, the Goenkas retreated and suddenly there was an eerie calm. Things went back to normal almost as suddenly as the problem had surfaced. Gulabchand believes that RP gave in to the pressure in the face of criticism from the press and Mumbai's business circles. He hadn't anticipated the reaction would be so strong. 'He didn't want to settle his son Harsh in Mumbai amid such hostilities. He was a canny old man. He realized how difficult it would have been for Harsh in the long run. You know, RP and I became very good friends after all this happened. He was an admirable man. I was even on the board of one of his companies.'

THE SPLIT

R.P. Goenka's takeover attempt of Premier Automobiles turned out to be the proverbial last straw.

Ajit Gulabchand has always been an impatient man, full of ideas, be it about the new opportunities ahead, the economic policy, the state of the world, or how to run the country. Even now, in his mid-sixties, he seems like a man in a hurry. Looking at him, it's not difficult to imagine the energy he must have exuded when he joined the family enterprise in his twenties. 'I grew up on stories of Walchand Kaka. I remember the drives I would go on with him, when he was ailing. He was a striking man and there was an intensity even in his silence.'

It's no wonder then that Gulabchand entered the Walchand group as a young intern in the accounts division with stars in his eyes and more than his fair share of idealism and ambition. This is what he had wanted to do all his life. He wanted to emulate his uncle. But he was in for a rude shock.

'I was taken aback by what I saw around me. People used to walk in to work after a leisurely Gujarati breakfast, at ten thirty in the morning. There was no enterprise, no vision. There was none of the greatness of ideas that marked out Walchand and what he did.'

Not surprisingly, Gulabchand was chafing at the bit. He wanted a clear mandate to run things his way, even if it meant doing so in a small section of the group and even if it came at the cost of breaking away.

Soon after the RPG crisis had blown over, he initiated a family split. It was a long process and a group of mediators and well-wishers, including Rahul Bajaj and Sharad Pawar, were brought in to facilitate it.

'Both sides possibly felt short-changed. But to be fair to Ajit Gulabchand, he was a sport. He said he would go with whatever came his way,' someone who followed the split closely said.

What came his way was the by-now very small Hindustan Construction Company.

But the company was symbolic for Gulabchand. After all, it was from here that Seth Walchand Hirachand had begun his entrepreneurial journey.

'My biggest regret is not about the share I got but the fact that it took so long. No one seemed to be in a hurry except me. It took from 1984 to 1994 and the last bit fell into place in 1998 [after Bahubali passed away, the Gulabchand branch holdings were further divided]. We could have closed it in the first year itself,' he recounts.

The final settlement was what the Gulabchand side of the family had proposed upfront, but by the time it happened, the group had let go of many an opportunity. It had missed out on almost all of the first decade of liberalization and many of the companies, including Premier Automobiles, were beyond redemption.

When the first tranche of division happened between the Lalchand and Gulabchand factions in 1994, there were some who went so far as to comment that this was the end of the Gulabchands in business.

BUILDING UP

In the well-stocked library of the fortnightly *Business India*, in Mumbai, a vestige of a bygone era when news organizations still stored physical clippings of articles and editorials (a lot of the material is also online here), the story of the Doshis and

Gulabchands is captured in a series of small articles strewn across files, categories and years. The story that emerges is telling and reiterates the changing fortunes within the two arms of the family.

In the new headquarters of HCC in Vikhroli, a sizeable portion of a floor is devoted to an exhibition of what the company has built so far. Blow-ups of old sepia-toned pictures of some of the most famous building works and infrastructure projects of the country—the Farakka Barrage in West Bengal, the unique double curvature dam at Idukki in Kerala, the RCC chimney in the Bhabha Atomic Research Centre in Trombay, the country's first metro rail in Kolkata and four of the six nuclear power plants in India—all built by the company, are on display.

But the pedigree and legacy aside, when Gulabchand came on board as MD in 1983, the big challenge for the company was survival.

Unprecedented construction by the Iraqi government under Saddam Hussein in the mid-1970s had seen a series of small Indian construction companies heading to Baghdad. While HCC had been one of the beneficiaries of this boom there (it built thirty-eight bridges in a matter of four to five years), its focus outside India meant it was gradually beginning to lose out at home. A host of new aggressive construction companies like Jaiprakash Associates began to challenge the dominance of HCC in the domestic market.

As the 'Iraqi Banquet' (the term used to describe the opportunities Iraq offered) ended by the early 1980s, when Iraq and Iran went to war with each other, these companies turned their attention back home.

In those days, in India, the government was the only entity

that used to hand out construction contracts. So what followed was stiff competition and undercutting for new contracts.

The war in Iraq also meant that a lot of the payments that were due were held back. When Gulabchand took charge of HCC, a lot of the company's money was stuck in projects across Iraq and with almost no business in India, the company incurred losses for the first time in its history. In 1984–85, the company secured only ten contracts totalling Rs 44 crore out of the 116 tenders it submitted. Gulabchand found himself at the helm of a loss-making company, in a business he had no clue about. After years of complaining about old mindsets and slow pace of change, this was his chance to prove himself when it mattered the most.

Gulabchand was determined to earn his inheritance and fortune.

THE TURNAROUND

The balance sheet of HCC gives a fair inkling of how things turned around for it. In 1984–85, the year HCC went public, it clocked a profit of Rs 2.31 crore, thanks to some of the residual payments from the Iraq contracts. Over the next two years, profits plummeted. It incurred losses of Rs 1.95 crore in 1985–86 and the next year, this figure went up to Rs 3.46 crore.

Five years after Ajit Gulabchand took charge as MD, the company turned profitable, in 1988, and it continued to grow till it faced a crisis in 2011.

So how did he do it? He worked out a multi-pronged plan to change the working of the company. The first step was to get leaner. Gulabchand trimmed the organization. He introduced a voluntary retirement scheme, bringing down employee overheads from 32 to 21 per cent of the company's turnover.

He also brought down costs. A close watch was kept on raw material, for instance. A retired project manager at HCC says, 'For the first time, we got a commercial angle into our contracts. Earlier, the focus was to get a job done on time. Now, the emphasis was on the fact that we are in business to make money and we had better make it!' He explained what else changed.

HCC had for long been a bloated, overly centralized company with hardly any focus on profitability. While excessive control from the headquarters in Mumbai meant that projects in far-flung corners of the country were inadvertently delayed, it also meant leakages in the supply chain, through procurement prices which were higher than necessary and inventory pile-ups. This meant even greater losses.

Under Gulabchand, project managers were given more autonomy to manage their finances and their working capital requirements. Also, the company decided to renew its focus on the Indian market and bid more aggressively for projects. This was crucial because the post-Iraq era had seen far more competition from the new companies that had sprung up. That apart, even between projects, Gulabchand mandated that HCC look at higher end, more complex projects that required specialization. This was an astute move because it helped the company in many ways. It made sure HCC did bigger, more high-profile projects, which in turn helped ward off competition. It meant higher profitability since the company could charge a premium for its 'expertise'.

'We decided that we would do projects of only Rs 20 crore and above [this was big money in the 1980s because the government was the primary client and construction contracts were usually much smaller]. We were among the handful that could execute these orders and we also developed areas of specialization like hydro power projects and dams. We had a lot to show here, because we had done so much of it in the past.'

Gulabchand's was clearly a canny, long-term vision even if it meant additional costs in the short term.

Among other things, HCC decided to 'own' all the equipment it needed for building work. Until then, the equipment was leased on a project-by-project basis. The reason for this change was practical. A former deputy general manager, K.V. Mehta, explained, 'Most of the equipment we need for big projects is not on hire in India and the equipment that is, is not worth hiring! Moreover, for big building projects where work can go on for as long as three to four years, the cost of hiring is very high.' Owning equipment made sense, and though the costs were higher in the beginning (some of the equipment bought by HCC had import duties of 80 per cent), the purchases made managers go after projects to justify the expenditure. Costs over time turned into savings, giving HCC an edge over competitors.

All this was slow, painstaking work but there were steady returns. Between 1984 and '87, out of 297 tenders HCC had submitted bids for, it got only twenty-three. Between 1988 and '89, it got nearly half the contracts it bid for. These were worth a neat Rs 232 crore.

Success made the company even more ambitious and in the next few years, HCC bid for some of the biggest contracts given out by the Government of India. Most of these were funded by the International Monetary Fund (IMF) and World Bank, the biggest lenders to the cash-strapped government.

As the business landscape changed, Gulabchand and HCC kept pace. He realized that companies like his were outdated when it came to technology and expertise, the biggest determinants of success in the future. This made HCC foray into another area—partnerships. It formed joint ventures with international majors. In 2000–01, it bagged a contract with Korean major Hyundai, which is a heavy engineering firm apart from being a well-known automobile manufacturer, to build a bridge across the Yamuna river in a suburb of Allahabad in Uttar Pradesh. It also partnered with Chinese sub-contractors to bid for the Bandra–Worli Sea Link.

However, even as Gulabchand was strengthening HCC, Premier Automobiles was slipping into an abyss from which it could never quite get out.

To be fair, the problems started in the 1970s itself, when the virulent trade union leader Datta Samant, a doctor by profession, led an agitation in PAL. The deal he negotiated with the PAL management would set the stage for his rise as the man who led one of the biggest trade movements of our times and, eventually, the slide of PAL.

Samant's biographers say a great part of his success came from PAL. He managed to negotiate a lucrative deal for the workers even as the management failed to hold its own in a difficult time. As a result of this, by 1985, expenses on wages and salaries as a percentage of sales were at 20 per cent in PAL.

Attempts were made to get PAL back on track. In 1985, for instance, faced with competition from Maruti, PAL launched a fairly successful car, the 118 NE, even managing a record advance booking, but this too proved futile. PAL was just not able to stand up and be counted as Maruti arrived and took over the Indian car market, changing it forever.

A lot has been written about what went wrong. At the heart of it, experts point out, was the problem that PAL had not kept pace with the competition. The management was weak. There was no planned programme for capital infusion and there was no modernization. For instance, the company still had an operational paint shop from the 1940s.

Comparisons with its peers underlined the crisis. As one critic put it, 'Telco [Tata Motors in Pune] and PAL began at roughly the same time. But whereas in Telco, the head, Sumant Moolgaonkar, had the vision to develop and improve upon the products that the government allowed them to make, the vision in PAL died with Walchand Hirachand. The second generation did virtually nothing to consolidate and improve upon what the great man had created.' By the mid-1990s, Gulabchand and his cousins, the Doshis, who had inherited the cream of Walchand's empire, were walking very different paths.

NOT AN EASY ROAD

The year 1991 brought about many changes in the Indian economy, and even though the benefits of liberalization took time to filter through to HCC and infrastructure spending picked up only a decade later, in 2001, when Atal Bihari Vajpayee was the prime minister, HCC was ready for the opportunity when it came.

It became a name when it constructed a section of the Mumbai–Pune Expressway, the first tolled, modern expressway in India.

For Gulabchand, it also opened up a tantalizing new prospect. Till 2000, when the expressway was opened to traffic, the drive between the two cities, which an estimated 100,000 passenger cars undertake each day, took four to five hours on tough and dangerous roads. An initial study in 1990 showed that the Mumbai–Pune stretch of the old NH4, connecting Mumbai

The Mumbai–Pune Expressway; a major section was constructed by Hindustan Construction Company in 2000

and Chennai, was one of the three busiest stretches of highway across India.

HCC was one of the many construction companies that were given the contract to build a major chunk, the stretch between Pune and the hill township of Lonavala. The contract was substantial, worth over Rs 190 crore, and the job tough, because the 16.6-kilometre Chowk to Adoshi section was nothing but a forest that had to be cut through.

But HCC did it. Not only did it build the road on time, it also cashed in on it by having the foresight to stake claim and earn acclaim for the work it had done.

While at least five other construction companies had built the expressway, few remember the others. For the first time, an old-world construction company was making headlines for the work it had done. A year later, by 2001, Gulabchand was already on to his next big idea—the Bandra–Worli Sea Link.

THE BRIDGE THAT TOOK SO LONG

Drive over the sea link and there are two giveaways on who built it. First, the blue colour painted on the roof of the toll point, the same blue as in HCC's logo, and the second, a small one-storey building where the bridge starts, which talks of the project and the legacy of Walchand Hirachand, the man who established the company that built it.

Few enter this makeshift museum, but it is an important statement, strategically placed. For HCC, it is worth the effort, given that the bridge has become such an important modern landmark. But it took a long time coming.

In 1999, Bal Thackeray, supremo of the Shiv Sena (the nationalist political party founded in 1966), had laid the foundation of the project, which was part of a larger plan to build sea links or road bridges connecting different ends of the island city to ensure a line running parallel to the choked roads. But it was only a decade later, in 2009, that the bridge became functional. By then it was apparent that thanks to the issues this bridge had raised, a similar bridge would probably take double that time, if it ever did come up.

Seen from ashore, the sea link, with the shimmering suspension bridge at the centre of it, looks like an imposing structure. This wasn't the way it was envisaged and there are different views on how a simple bridge became a national landmark. While the clearances for the sea link took time to fructify, the biggest hurdle the bridge faced was from environmentalists, who claimed that the bridge violated environmental norms and would disrupt the flow of the Mithi river, and villagers in the fishing hamlet in the rocky outcrop behind the Indian Coastguard base in Worli.

In 2004, villagers from this fishing village led others along the coastline encompassing the Bandra, Mahim and Worli fishing settlements on a series of protests against the construction of the link, claiming that it would make fishing along the coastline impossible and destroy their livelihood. Their logic was that their boats would not be able to pass under the proposed structure. The protests went on for months and finally forced the Maharashtra State Road Development Corporation (MSRDC), for whom HCC was executing the contract, to undertake a full overhaul of the project. This included reworking most of the bridge design and realigning it 200 metres away from the coastline.

This not only changed the project's dynamics, it also sent the cost of the bridge skyrocketing.

Originally estimated to cost Rs 600 crore, by the time the bridge was made after all the delays, the cost at Rs 1,600 crore was more than double.

As the project changed dimensions (spanning a much longer 5.6 kilometres in length and 413 ft in height at its tallest) there were hints of foul play. There were accusations that HCC had instigated the fishermen to create a stand-off that forced the MSRDC to resize the project and thus make it more lucrative for HCC. Gulabchand brushes off the accusations, saying it was part of the propaganda against the project. 'Look at the bridge. It is the new landmark of Mumbai. Shouldn't we be proud of it? Could we have compromised with it?'

Driving across the bridge each day, and saving an hour at the least if you are travelling to the old business hub of Nariman Point via Worli, it's hard to imagine a time without it and hard not to appreciate its beauty as the sunlight filters through the cables that hold the bridge together.

But the long wait and the many controversies surrounding the bridge that took too long to build must have seemed like nothing compared to what Gulabchand and his company were up against next: HCC's most ambitious project till date, the hill township Lavasa. Lavasa was to bring him and his company down on their knees.

LAVASA

Drive up the winding roads into the Western Ghats and you will be amazed at just how far a three-hour drive can get you from the crowded, noisy city of Mumbai. Through 2008–09, Lavasa, a small hill town, was being marketed as a quick weekend getaway for weary city slickers. But by November 2010, it resembled nothing short of a ghost town. There were barely a handful of people at the city centre, the small restaurants on the artificially created pier were empty and the picturesque chalets looked more like a beautiful but unfinished painting. Months down the line, things looked even worse as many of the last workers, building what was claimed to be India's first planned hill city, put down their drills for good.

At the messy flat-turned-office just off Mumbai's Marine Drive, activist Y.P. Singh, a former policeman, has a different take on why the multi-billion dollar hill station project came to a grinding halt in 2010. Singh is a familiar face on the many

TV debates across news channels and the man behind some of the big headline-grabbing corporate cases, including those filed against the Government of Maharashtra and the MSRDC over the Bandra–Worli Sea Link controversy, and the more recent Lavasa case.

Singh, who has never met Ajit Gulabchand, blames him for what happened. 'If Ajit Gulabchand hadn't been so strident, he wouldn't have gotten into so much trouble.'

Just when HCC started the roadshow to meet a cross section of investors across India around the ambitious IPO of Lavasa, social activist Medha Patkar, a campaigner for the rights of locals to their land and habitat, reached the township. She accused HCC of forcibly acquiring land from the people living there. Given that work had started in 2004, and there had been no major problem around the acquisition of land since then, Gulabchand had a show-cause notice slapped against Patkar, prohibiting her from instigating the locals.

It was after this that Medha Patkar approached Singh. According to him, 'Medha-ji wanted to meet me for months, and I finally said okay, let me go through the files. I actually took time off from the other work I was doing and studied the files for a month. That's when I came across the Achilles' heel.'

In most such cases, Singh usually tried to find the key, the weak point around which he could build his argument. Here, it was very simple. 'The key was the fact that there wasn't an environmental clearance. There is no law on how to plan and create new hill stations and this is what businessmen like Gulabchand and politicians exploit to make millions in profit. In the case of Lavasa, there was another motive,' Singh claimed.

It was 14 July 2007. The venue was a peaceful resort

overlooking the Lavasa valley, aptly named Ekant. It was far simpler than the frillier, more colourful buildings being built in the valley below. While its entrance was unassuming, it led to a hill and from there to narrow lanes that drew trekkers looking for a break.

But on this day, there was a lot of noise in Ekant. The team responsible for building Lavasa, headed by none other than the chairman, was making a presentation to a powerful panel. In attendance was Maharashtra chief minister Vilasrao Deshmukh, Union agriculture minister Sharad Pawar, his nephew, Maharashtra irrigation minister Ajit Pawar, and other dignitaries.

All of them had come to see the plans for the much-publicized hill town. Gulabchand and his team spoke about the tie-ups and the facilities and asked the powerful guests for quick clearances of building permissions and new roads that would make the town come alive. According to the minutes of the meeting later submitted in the court, a lot of time was spent discussing the need to permit construction of taller buildings in the area and whether it was in keeping with the guidelines of the Ministry of Urban Development. The team also wanted permission to lease an 800-acre stretch of government-owned land adjoining their development area.

Few would have noticed the fine print of the minutes of a meeting like this. After all, it was the then (and now Opposition) Shiv Sena-BJP government which had invited the private sector, in this case HCC, to develop the township in a bid to promote tourism in the state. But three years down the line, this document became a crucial cog in the wheel of the case against Lavasa and its chief promoter. All of it hinged on one question: What was the country's agriculture minister doing in this meeting in Lavasa? What was his locus standi? Was he there to help old friend Gulabchand get the clearances he was asking for? As the case against Gulabchand and Lavasa built up, the fact that Pawar's daughter Supriya Sule and her husband were big stakeholders in the project between 2002 and '04 made things worse.

The connection between Lavasa and Sharad Pawar ran even deeper. The idea to create the lakeside city was first mooted by Sharad Pawar when he was the chief minister between 1993 and '95.

There was a lot to prove Y.P. Singh's theory right: there was a close connection between Pawar and Gulabchand in the Lavasa project.

So how does Gulabchand justify the Pawar connection? 'You must remember that it was the state government that wanted this project. It declared that it wanted to develop a few areas in the region and one of them was Mose Valley in Lavasa. The other was Sahara City near Lonavala. There were six such places demarcated and if it was supposed to be a public–private initiative, what was wrong with the state leaders being involved in it?' He believes that a lot of the problems around Lavasa stemmed from misreporting. For instance, while everyone reported that Pawar visited Lavasa and was taken through the project, step by step, they didn't mention the visit of several other politicians, from Vilasrao Deshmukh to one of the Shiv Sena's prominent leaders and former CM Manohar Joshi. Moreover, as Gulabchand points out, the actual issues that Lavasa raises are far more complex: there are no clear title holdings for land in India. This means that even if land has been bought from an individual, anyone from his family can raise questions and stall work on it years later. This is a problem faced by every private company building an infrastructure project or trying to expand a factory, anywhere in India.

'You know, none of the charges of corruption stuck. We had opened our books completely when we filed for the initial public offering. I think a lot of issues got confused with Lavasa,' Gulabchand says.

LAVASA VS THE MINISTRY OF ENVIRONMENT AND FORESTS (MoEF)

Within a year and a half of taking over, by December 2010, Union Minister for Environment and Forests Jairam Ramesh had become the most talked-about minister in the UPA Cabinet and the most feared man in the country's business circles.

For the first time ever, the ministry was standing up against 'unbridled development' that was putting the environment at risk. Ramesh had managed to stall some very big projects in India. For at least the two years that followed, it seemed as though 'green tape' had replaced the 'red' one that India was famous for.

Of the numerous causes the MoEF took up, three stood out. The first one was the most high-profile: the $12bn steel plant to be set up by South Korean major POSCO in Odisha. This was a project that Chief Minister Naveen Patnaik and Prime Minister Dr Manmohan Singh were adamant about taking forward, but nothing moved for a long time, till Ramesh drove in the last nail.

Though the MoEF had cleared the setting up of the firm's integrated steel project in Jagatsinghpur in 2007, Ramesh stalled the clearance three years later, saying that the company had not submitted a comprehensive environment impact assessment report. He also pointed out that the company hadn't informed the ministry that there were tribals living in the project area. Though his ministry finally handed out clearances, with a list of sixty conditions, in May 2011, there has been little progress since then because in March 2012, a judicial body—the National Green Tribunal—ordered a suspension of the project. Now it has gone back to yet another committee which has raised more concerns. Meanwhile, the original environmental clearance for the project granted for a five-year period lapsed in 2012 and now the company will have to rework its proposal based on the recommendations of the committee. The project is still in limbo.

All this made national and international headlines.

In August 2010, Ramesh stalled another project, this one by UK-based Vedanta Resources Corporation, a mining and metal giant founded by Anil Agarwal, also in Odisha, in the Niyamgarhi Hills. Vedanta wanted to mine bauxite from the hills, for which it had clearance, but the ministry under Ramesh cancelled this on charges that mining was in violation of the Environment (Protection) Act among others, and the $1.2bn investment was stalled. The company was criticized as its operations were a threat to the lives of the Dongrea Kondh tribe and the wildlife in that region.

In November 2010, the MoEF forced the closure of all work in Lavasa. Even though the Department of Environment of Maharashtra gave its final clearance to Lavasa under the Maharashtra Hill Station Regulation of 1996, Ramesh's ministry said Lavasa should have approached it for clearances since the area it covered was above 1,000 metres in altitude and cost more than Rs 5 crore. The ministry issued a show-cause notice and an order to stop work, saying that the developers were guilty of violating the Environment (Protection) Act. The ministry also demanded a fresh environment plan from the company and an assessment by a group of experts. The show-cause notice, besides instructing Lavasa to stop all construction work, also ordered the demolition of all developmental work undertaken since 2004–05 for violations that 'it may have committed'.

A long legal battle followed. Lavasa immediately filed a writ petition in the Bombay High Court stating that the MoEF notice was issued with malafide intentions and under pressure from political activists.

It was finally in 2011 that Ramesh's successor at the MoEF granted conditional environmental clearance to the project.

Gulabchand wonders if Ramesh's personal ambitions had any bearing on the crisis. POSCO, Vedanta and Lavasa were only a part of a larger agenda to take on corporates. There were sixty other projects that were blocked. Ramesh's ministry raised other issues too, from mining in forests to development of coastal zones. By the end of 2011 every Indian business group was facing the heat from the green ministry.

As far as Lavasa is concerned, Gulabchand proudly points out that villagers from the eighteen villages in the Lavasa region supported the project, through its court battles, even filing their own petition in the Bombay High Court and petitioning the MoEF.

Between November 2010—when all work in Lavasa was stopped—and November 2011, when the MoEF under its new minister, Jayanthi Natarajan, of the Congress, gave the go ahead to start work, the Indian economy, and with it every sector and company, faced difficulties. Buffeted by a series of scams, ranging from those surrounding the Commonwealth Games held in New Delhi in October 2010 to the 2G scam, it was almost as though the entire government decision- and policy-making machinery had come to a standstill.

Infrastructure projects were stalled, inflation was hurting everyone and delays in projects sent costs through the roof. 'If you see my speech to shareholders in 2011, the problems were descending upon us very fast: the claims, mounting from Rs 700 to Rs 2,000 crore, the suddenly ballooning interest burden and, on the other hand, a slowdown in orders, creating a squeeze,' Gulabchand explains. In Lavasa alone, it was estimated that the company was losing Rs 2 crore per day for every day that it couldn't carry out any construction work.

What HCC was facing was common across the infrastructure space and it taught Gulabchand an important lesson: sticking to one core business is not the right strategy. 'It's okay to stick with your core in a country like the US where everything is private but here, when you have twenty sectors opening up for the first time, why shouldn't you think of moving to others?' At the heart of the logic is perhaps his belief that if he had had another business to fall back upon, the pain might not have been as acute. Ironically, while he was facing the heat in India, the only place where he seemed to be making money was Switzerland—he had Karl Steiner AG there, the Swiss construction company HCC had acquired in May 2010. Even a Eurozone financial crisis hadn't affected business in Switzerland.

Now Gulabchand has bigger plans. 'For example, if mining is opening up, why shouldn't HCC think of it, because one of the key aspects of mining is quarrying and tunnelling. That's why all the big hydroelectric power companies in Canada moved to mining—because they had huge machinery.'

A fighter to the last and a die-hard optimist, Gulabchand is looking ahead. But before he goes on to other things, there is still a lot of cleaning up to do.

As company CFO Praveen Sood explains, 'Normally, he leaves the numbers to us and looks at the overall vision for the group, but these days the balance sheet is the only thing he is looking at.' 'Operation consolidation' is on at HCC and there is enough reason for it.

The one-year delay in Lavasa has cost the company a lot of money and time. With mounting debts and most of its other projects slowing down, business has been tough. 'We need to inject about Rs 1,500 crore into the company to get it back on track,' says Sood. It was with this target in mind that the company got into a CDR (corporate debt recast) with its bankers to rework the over Rs 7,000 crore of debt it had accumulated.

Starting 2013, HCC started to sell some of its assets, reduce costs, and consolidate operations (something it had been doing for some time). It has already sold a 70 per cent stake in the building that houses its corporate park. It has scaled back its teams and collapsed some of the five business verticals it had set up. But it will take a couple of years for things to stabilize.

FULL CIRCLE

Two decades after taking over as the head of one of India's oldest construction companies, Ajit Gulabchand and his firm seem to have come full circle.

In 2011–12, HCC incurred its first loss in twenty-three years. Also, for the first time, the focus shifted from the engineers in charge of commissioned projects and building works to the legal team, which was busy ensuring that the company was ready to fight for claims as projects got delayed by months. Ironically, this had been the situation when Gulabchand took charge of HCC in 1983. The legal team in the 1980s, he jokes, was bigger than the team of engineers and in the closed economy, where the government was the only client, a lot of time was spent getting claims for the inevitable delays that came with government-funded construction contracts. Thirty years later, sadly, there is a sense of déjà vu as the biggest infrastructure projects remained stalled or delayed because of the slowdown in the economy and the delays in government policy making.

All through 2010 and well into 2012, as the Lavasa saga played out, HCC turned to its lenders for help even as Gulabchand began focussing on resurrecting the company's finances. It was evident that he would have to apply the brakes on some of the more ambitious plans he had drawn up. Expectations of the great build-up of an India that HCC would be part of had to be moderated.

His take is simple. 'I have been through problems before, but this time the stakes are higher.' A passionate free-market proponent, Gulabchand is frustrated at how things have turned out, especially when there is potential for more. 'There is no businessman in India who doesn't wish he was ten years younger. Ask Ratan Tata and even he will agree. My generation has spent so much time waiting for change that we are now running to catch up.'

Gulabchand with grandson Varun

This is true for Gulabchand, now

in his mid-sixties, because not only did he spend most of his working years doing business within the confines of a closed economy, like many others of his generation and background, he also lost nearly a decade getting his inheritance in order and waiting for the infrastructure sector to open up. And, today, the wait for the great build-up of India's infrastructure continues.

So, after all this, is he still as optimistic and enthusiastic about business as he was earlier? 'You know, in many ways, the last couple of years were also my best. My grandson Varun was born. There is never a completely bad or a completely good year and I think we went through some challenging times, but we will get back on our feet.'

For Gulabchand, the transformation of his legacy and having been able to change the contours of the small construction company he inherited to make it a big conglomerate with far more capabilities and operations beyond India is a matter of pride.

The next thing on the agenda, according to him, is getting the company back in order and then, perhaps, doing the things he has always wanted to do. For one thing, he wants to spend more time in Lavasa, developing a classical arts centre and setting in place a think tank to study a more right-of-centre approach to development.

Gulabchand always carries with him a classic quote by Goethe: 'Whatever you can do or dream you can, begin it. Boldness has genius, power and magic in it.' He reads it every time he is depressed. He believes in what the quote stands for. And why not? It has seen him through the many ups and downs of the last few years.

GAUTAM THAPAR

Gautam Thapar, GT to his friends and employees, doesn't seem like someone who needs to prove anything to anyone in the world. Always preferring to keep a low profile, he has this quiet, measured way of talking, and a soft-footed yet purposeful stride. In less than fifteen years, he has done enough to earn all the attention he commands.

GT has always stood out in the crowd. The year 2002 was no different. His company, Ballarpur Industries Limited (BILT), the flagship of the $4bn or Rs 24,000 crore Avantha Group, was sponsoring a big tournament at the sprawling DLF golf course in Gurgaon, featuring Fijian golfer Vijay Singh. Despite the sensation he was in those days, while the tournament was in progress and afterwards, during the press conference, it wasn't Vijay who stole the limelight but the distractingly good-looking young head of the company.

By this time, GT had become the toast of Delhi's business

circles. People were talking about how he had turned around the fortunes of two Thapar Group heirlooms—the paper company BILT and power transformer maker Crompton Greaves, which had almost collapsed in the 1990s.

In the years following Independence, the group, founded by GT's grandfather, Karam Chand Thapar, or KCT as he was known (all the Thapar men are referred to, in the company, by their initials), had been among the top five industrial houses in India with interests in businesses like mining, paper, power equipment, banking and insurance. But by the late 1960s, as the Indian government began its nationalization programme, gaining control of most of these sectors, the group lost almost two-thirds of its business. Of what remained, the biggest were paper (BILT), textiles under the JCT brands, and Crompton Greaves, which was one of the biggest players in the Indian power-equipment market, selling transformers and ceiling fans.

Each of these companies dominated the markets they were in. The licence-permit raj, through which the state dictated the production of a majority of goods, had created monopolies while also killing enterprise. The opening up of the Indian economy in 1991 changed the marketplace forever as protection gave way to competition, leading to trouble in most big businesses run by families. The Thapars were also on the verge of being wiped out till GT came into the picture.

Not only did he engineer the turnaround of BILT and Crompton Greaves that he had been given charge of, by 2002, he had also begun to focus on a new theme—acquisitions.

Sadly, while this should have aroused a lot of positive interest, people were still talking about how GT was not supposed to be the Thapar who would lead the group into the future.

GT, however, had a plan and a vision in mind, one that

would change the contours of his group. Over the years, not only did he help these companies regain their top ranking in India, he also realized that in the new, open-business landscape, the world was the stage and it was essential that his group be able to compete with the best in the world.

To understand the future that GT is scripting, it is important to understand where he came from and how he began.

According to Rajeev Vederah, vice chairman of BILT, GT's makeover was indeed a feat. When Vederah met him for the first time, GT was a happy-go-lucky youngster with no experience in business.

Today, that same guy is the boss.

NOT THE HEIR APPARENT?

Gautam Thapar can throw people completely off guard with his candour when he decides to open up and speak about life while he was growing up.

The Thapars were one of the wealthiest—and classiest—industrial families of first Kolkata and then Delhi, where they moved a few years after KCT's death, in 1963.

KCT founded the Thapar empire in the early twentieth century. Like most businessmen of his time, he bet on every sliver of opportunity the British offered. His first big breakthrough came after the First World War, when he entered the coal business. The war had triggered a coal (aptly referred to as black gold) boom in India, and to cash in on the opportunity, KCT shifted base to Kolkata, the epicentre of the coal trade, in 1920.

Within a few years he became one of the biggest players in the business and came to be known as the 'coal king', rubbing shoulders with the clique of Marwari traders—the Birlas, Poddars and Goenkas—who controlled the purse strings of the commodity-trading business at that time. Kolkata was the trading hub, the commercial heart from where raw material like coal and jute were shipped to other parts of the country.

The fortunes of KCT, like many traders of the time, depended on British contracts. Life was chequered with many ups and downs. KCT's biographer, Arunabha Dasgupta, points out that he lost all his money when he dabbled in jute, in the early 1930s. It took years for him to bounce back, thanks to the next war.

GT remembers the lavish lifestyle of the family. Though he and his siblings shared the Thapar name with his cousins, that was the only thing they had in common. He recalls, 'We were Thapars, but we were not the at-par Thapars. We had the name but not the money, and that's my memory of growing up. I remember I got my first pair of jeans when I was a teenager and I first went abroad only when I was in college.'

His earliest memories of the old man are from the days when the family lived in the landmark Thapar House on Kolkata's Ballygunje Circular Road. What GT remembers about KCT is the way he used to throw him up in the air as a kid in the garden of their house. To him, KCT was a larger than life figure.

Just when KCT was ready to pass on the baton to his first-born from his second wife, Mohini, the son, Brij Mohan, GT's father, shocked the old man by saying that he was not interested in the business or his inheritance. He just wanted to break free.

'I just had to. Till then I had only been exposed to the business world and suddenly the Moral Rearmament Army opened my eyes,' Brij Mohan recalls. The brainchild of British thinker Frank Buchman, the Moral Rearmament Army (MRA) was set up in 1938 when Europe was rearming militarily before the Second World War. The idea was to rally the youth to work for world peace and unity as the road to progress. Many prominent thinkers and writers of the time, including novelist Daphne du Maurier, supported the movement and wrote about it. British tennis star H.W. Austin edited a book, *Moral Rearmament (The Battle for Peace)*, which sold half a million copies.

An avid tennis player himself, Brij Mohan probably read about the MRA in Austin's book and, much to his father's chagrin and despite his mother's tears, left home in 1955 to follow a path of discourse, debate and discovery with the MRA. While the 'experiment' was to fail, forcing a disappointed and disillusioned Brij Mohan to return to his parents' house within months, life was never the same again.

Once Brij Mohan had decided to pass on the baton and, in his father's eyes, shirk the responsibility of managing the family affairs, the business went to Brij Mohan's younger brother, Lalit Mohan Thapar. Several years passed before Brij Mohan was able to make peace with his father, but he did so on KCT's deathbed.

Brij Mohan, who is eighty plus now, still remembers everything that happened so many decades ago in minute detail. Records of the time have been unkind to the man and few have given him credit for his real achievement—setting the stage for what GT did many years later.

GT is extremely fit despite being in his fifties. He was the quintessential jock during his tenure at Doon School, Dehra Dun. If life at home was stifling, school evidently made up for it and he came into his own on the sports field. 'I had little real interest in academics. It didn't fire me up enough, but I was good at most sports. I really enjoyed the strategizing, planning and the spirit of every game.' Today, he is as passionate about golf as he is about business.

Sports and his successes on the field may well have laid the foundation for the hard-nosed, aggressive ambition he was to display later on in life. At that time, however, he had only one burning ambition in his heart. 'I just wanted to get out of the country as soon as I could. So, the moment I passed out of Doon School, I went to my father and told him I wanted to go abroad. He flatly refused.' There was simply no money and even getting an education loan from a bank was not easy.

In desperation, GT turned to his uncle, Lalit Mohan. He wasn't sure if he would agree, but he did have a convincing plan in case the answer was in the negative. 'The one thing that I was certain about was that he would never say no to an engineering degree. He would never have sponsored me had I wanted to do something else! But the ticket to the US and admission to pursue a chemical engineering degree in Purdue University came with a rider. My uncle said he would give me a one-way ticket and enough money to live there. If I wanted to come back, I would have to do so on my own.' GT was so thrilled, he didn't mind at all.

He wanted to enjoy life and that's what he did. 'Life then was about the next party. By month-end, I and my friends would have wiped out our allowances. Stretching the dollar took on a whole new meaning!' To make his way back to India each year and spend time with his family during the vacations, GT worked part-time—he ferried cars for companies from New

York to California each year he was there. And he rounded it off with a summer job at his uncle's friend's trading company on the West Coast.

In his last year of college, in 1983, he decided to try and get a job in the US.

But this was easier said than done. When he went to his summer employer for help, his answer was, 'Check with your uncle and I'll give you a job only if he allows it.'

GT met his uncle with his proposition but was quite taken aback when Lalit Mohan exploded, livid. What followed was a vicious verbal duel, ending with his uncle yelling at him: 'You will end up being a waiter in the US!' GT's answer, 'At least I will be a happy one!' was the last straw. GT and his uncle didn't speak to each other for years after this incident.

Luck was not on GT's side either. 'The US economy had slowed down at the time. Companies were cutting back and it had become impossible for anyone to get a visa and work permit. Under these circumstances, I had no option but to return to India.'

THE FIRST TURNAROUND

For a full year after his return, Gautam Thapar simply moped around. There was nothing to do, no dreams to fulfil. He would spend hours locked up in his room, only to get out, play a game of squash and spend a night out with friends.

Alarmed at how he was drifting, and painfully aware of the consequences, his father was forced to step in and turn to someone he had struck up a warm friendship with inside Thapar House—Brij Mohan Bakshi, a dynamic vice president in the group. Bakshi had been brought in to set up a joint venture the Thapars were planning with Dupont and he and Brij Mohan would often discuss business for hours on end.

Bakshi was entrusted with the task of mentoring GT. Brij Mohan remarks, 'Bakshi was the right man to work with and to learn from. I just had this feeling about it and when Bakshi came to me and said, "Sir, do you trust me?" I said, "Yes, 110 per cent." "I'm going to take your son under my wing and let me tell you, we employees are better judges of sons' abilities than parents. I promise you that your son will be ready to replace your brother in two years."' Unlikely as it appeared then, that is what happened, though it took a little longer.

A year after GT returned, desperate to get him 'to do something, anything', Brij Mohan sent him off to meet Bakshi.

After a lot of nagging by his parents, GT finally made it to Thapar House, but with some reluctance. He had met Bakshi a couple of times in New York while he was studying and had intended to stick around for just a few minutes. Instead, the meeting went on for a couple of hours.

'As we chatted, he constantly challenged my views, questioned all the assumptions I made,' GT recalls. They were talking of what the young man wanted to do with his life. GT was in no mood to take anyone's advice, especially that of an outsider. Not only did the half-hour-long encounter get Thapar all worked up, Bakshi also forced him to sit in his office and wait as he wrapped up a meeting with representatives from Dupont. Though GT was seething with anger and frustration by now, to his surprise, he realized that he was not only finding the conversation fascinating, he was even picking up points and he had a great discussion with the vice president on these afterwards.

GT's meeting with Bakshi opened up a whole new world to him. He found an area—chemicals—he was fascinated by as an engineer. That the two men shared a strong bond is evident from GT's statement: 'He was a great guy. He was larger than life, outgoing, and a great leader. He always made me think.' Bakshi was also responsible for GT mending fences with his uncle.

GT was quickly absorbed into the Thapar fold. His first assignment was a short stint in one of BILT's biggest manufacturing plants—the Yamunanagar facility near Delhi—in 1985. The man who was to become the managing director of BILT, Rajeev Vederah, was then in charge of the plant. He mentions how Thapar, an unsure youngster, would spend hours in his office, absorbing what he saw. For GT, the few months he spent there were an eye-opener. He came out of his internship disenchanted and disappointed. 'There was absolutely no passion, no vision there; they were just doing a mundane job and it was very depressing.'

That was when GT decided he had far more to learn under Bakshi's tutelage. Between 1985 and '90, GT assisted Bakshi as he turned around a bleeding subsidiary of BILT, Andhra Pradesh Rayon (APR), which supplied rayon pulp to Grasim. The factory, which was located at Kamalapuram, a small village near Warangal, Andhra Pradesh, turned wood into pulp for Grasim's rayon production.

Rayon ('ray of light', because of its sheen) is a synthetic fibre, one of the first to be manufactured by man. In 1664, British naturalist Robert Hooke argued that artificial filaments could be spun from a substance similar to what the silkworm secreted to make silk, for example, gummy wood. It took two hundred years for the actual production of the commercial rayon fibre to begin. Over time, scientists developed the viscose-processed fibre that is so commonly used today in textiles and home furnishings.

The Aditya Birla group company Grasim Industries is one of the world's largest producers of viscose-stable fibre (VSF). When GT joined Bakshi in 1985, the Kamalapuram plant was supplying rayon pulp to one of Grasim's three VSF factories, in Harihar, Karnataka. By the time Bakshi took charge of it, APR had already run into losses of Rs 170 crore because Grasim, its only client, was refusing to pick up material from the plant because of a disagreement. Bakshi stepped in and, within a few years, managed to script a transformation.

GT got his first taste of 'turnaround management' in the years that followed. 'The lessons were basic. What surprised me was how BILT could have allowed things in its subsidiary to come to such a pass,' he remarks.

APR was one of the several small acquisitions that BILT had made over the years. Like many industrial groups of the time, BILT was an umbrella organization. Government policies and the stringent Monopolies and Restrictive Trade Practices (MRTP) board had ensured that no company with scale and size could expand beyond a point. This meant that businessmen were forced to try and get every licence that was available in order to diversify into new businesses (also acquiring small 'in trouble' companies in the process), even if it meant modest returns.

While this was the only recourse for growth, the problem was what happened after the acquisition. 'The main paper business at Ballarpur was always making so much money that the managers thought these newly acquired companies were a major drain on their resources. Also, nobody tried to rectify the problems that had led to losses for these companies in the first place,' GT says. The result was a maze of small firms—subsidiaries—draining cash.

APR faced another predicament. It didn't produce anything that could be utilized by the parent company, BILT. It made rayon pulp instead of paper pulp and actually depended on BILT's chemical plant for chlorine, an important ingredient in making rayon pulp.

So how was the turnaround of APR scripted? The first step was to woo back Grasim, upon whom the company was wholly dependent. It was a long wait for GT outside Aditya Birla's office as Bakshi remained closeted inside, mending fences with him. The relationship between Grasim and APR had soured after differences between the managements of the two companies and things got into such a logjam that Grasim refused to buy rayon pulp from APR. With no buyer, the Kamalapuram factory came to a standstill, worsening the losses at APR. Finally, Bakshi came up with a deal which had Grasim promising to buy rayon and even fund APR's much-needed modernization and expansion plans.

'Between 1985 and '90, we shuttled five to six times a year to the factory at Kamalapuram.' It was a hot, difficult and bumpy drive from Warangal, a district headquarters in Andhra Pradesh. The area, which is at the heart of the Telangana region, had made headlines in 1969, when the first major protests for a separate Telangana state had surfaced there. Spearheaded by students, it ended with a bloody police suppression that killed hundreds.

The exposure that this on-the-ground exercise in Kamalapuram gave GT couldn't be compared to anything else. 'Each visit opened up a new facet of the problem. The apathy was appalling, as was the fact that this subsidiary was an outpost no one within Ballarpur gave a fig about, even though it was burning such a big hole in the balance sheet!'

Over the next few years, with Bakshi at the helm and through rapid improvement in efficiencies, deft management of inventories, better production and technology, not only did APR turn itself around, but it also started making profits.

Just when APR's comeback story was being scripted, GT faced a major personal setback. Bakshi passed away after a massive heart attack and he was left holding the reins of APR and the tie-up with Dupont, which was stuck in complicated licence issues.

By now, APR's turnaround had not just given GT a worm's-eye view of what was wrong with the business, it had also taught him how it could be made to work. But he was yet to prove his mettle. It would take a hearty fight to do that.

TAKING OVER

The year was 1992. Thapar House was shaken out of its inaction. And this had nothing to do with the opening up of the Indian economy or what it would mean for paper-maker Ballarpur, which had ruled the Indian market for decades.

The corridors were buzzing with rumours about how there was a rebellion in one of the outposts of the company in Andhra Pradesh. Adding masala to the gossip was the fact that the rebellion had been initiated by a young Thapar boy. The young man had the audacity to question the way things had been done in the company for years. He had created such a stir that Lalit Mohan Thapar was forced to summon him to his office one day.

'The problem in being a small offshoot of a big parent company is that you often get walked all over and that's exactly what happened to APR. The company had become a "dumping ground" for the Ballarpur chemicals business. APR picked up ingredients such as chlorine used in the rayon pulp bleaching process from the chemicals division at market prices but it had little control over its supplier. When prices crashed and the chemicals division could not sell chlorine in the market, APR would have to pick up the entire lot at high prices. On the flip side, when the markets picked up, APR was left scrambling for material and a hefty bill at the end of it.

'Chlorine would come in big cylinders and suddenly you would have a stockyard full of cylinders. At other times, there would be such a shortage that the plant wouldn't function,' GT says. Emboldened, perhaps, by the financial turnaround of APR, one day he flatly refused to give back the chlorine cylinders that had piled up to the chemicals division until APR's dues were cleared.

'This completely shook the Ballarpur management. Never before had there been such defiance; nobody had questioned how things were being run.'

Of course, adding another dimension to the shock within the group was that this could lead to a run-in between GT and his cousin, Vikram Thapar, who was the man in charge (after all, the grapevine suggested that Vikram, the son of KCT's eldest son, Inder Mohan, and the old man's favourite, would inherit BILT).

But that confrontation was fight two; the first one happened in the chairman's office.

As GT dug in his heels, the CEO of the chemicals division marched straight to Lalit Mohan. The younger Thapar was hauled up. Instead of being apprehensive about 'what next',

GT stood his ground. He had prepared well for the meeting and had facts and figures to buttress what he had done. Nevertheless, GT was surprised when Lalit Mohan took his side.

As news that he had won the war against the CEO spread, there was a subtle change in the way people began to relate to him. For starters, he was put in charge of the chemicals business. It was a chance to prove his mettle as a chemical engineer, and he took up the challenge immediately. After the public pat on the back he was unstoppable.

BILT Chemicals manufactured products like caustic soda and specialty chemicals used in paper manufacturing. It had four factories, in Karnataka and Gujarat.

Soon GT began to question a lot of things about the way these factories were run. He travelled to the Dupont factories in many parts of the world and studied their systems and processes. He realized there was a vast difference in how things were being done back home and often wondered why Dupont processes couldn't be replicated.

A BIGGER PROBLEM AND A MATTER OF SURVIVAL

It was a summer weekend in 1997 and as head of BILT's chemicals arm, Gautam Thapar decided to go ahead with a plan whereby McKinsey & Company, the consultants he had roped in, would check the calibre of his top brass.

The consultants had planned a two-day intensive, closed-door off-site session at Pataudi, 60 kilometres from Delhi, during which the team would be taken through a module to help them work out their plans and check the viability of each based on a template set by some of the biggest global conglomerates. It was an easy enough task and would have been a routine feel-good exercise had it not been for the outcome.

When the plans were presented, though, everyone was in for a shock.

'As each senior manager and department head made a pitch, it was clear that none of the lofty plans and projections they had made seemed to float. Forget workability, each plan was ripped apart and it seemed as though the very basis of the business was being questioned. Most plans seemed to have been built in the air,' GT remarks.

Lalit Mohan, whom he had brought along for the final session, was very upset. While GT was thinking of what to do next, his uncle was obviously wondering how things had come to such a pass.

After this incident, despite his nephew's pleas, Lalit Mohan refused to allow the consultants into Ballarpur's offices. While his uncle resisted a larger audit of his ace teams' calibre, GT was quick to heed their advice and worked out capital-investment plans based on the viability of the strategies. Business heads who proved their worth were given money to expand; others whose divisions were draining resources were eased out.

REBUILDING BILT

The 1990s were a period of highs and lows for India's then largest paper company, BILT, which accounted for nearly 85 per cent of the group's overall revenues.

As long as the Indian economy was closed, companies like BILT had enjoyed a free hand. Since supply determined demand and not vice versa, there was hardly any incentive to improve the quality of paper produced, or invest in better technology. As a result, the quality of Indian paper was poor. The industry was also marked by shortages made worse by the dealers who controlled its trade. The problems persisted well into the '90s, with many companies refusing to read the signs. Experts point out that this is perhaps why even today, twenty years after liberalization, though the marketplace has changed, India is still constrained by the amount of, and the kind of, paper it produces.

Despite being one of the fast-growing economies of the world, India accounts for barely 2 per cent of the world's paper production. Most of what is produced is also of a very basic quality. As a result, hundreds of thousands of tonnes of high-end paper, used in a host of modern-day commodities such as digital paper and even tea bags, is imported from the US and Europe.

Andhra Pradesh Rayon in Kamalapuram, one of BILT's several acquisitions

'Between 1991 and '99, we had virtually no capacity increase. We went through eight to nine years [of liberalization] selling and making the same amount of paper we had been making ten years earlier!' But even as this happened, costs were going up, a lot of the company's cash was going into funding loss-making subsidiaries that didn't have any hope of a turnaround, and the balance sheet was a mess.

'The business cycles of many of the businesses in the company were very different. The paper collection cycle may have been thirty days, for instance, but the glass collection cycle, a business BILT had entered into in 1975, when it acquired JG Glass Industries that supplied glass containers to pharmaceutical and beverage companies, was a couple of months at the least. This BILT arm, at its height, was the second-largest player across India. Also, if many businesses were pulling in different directions, the main one was literally being controlled by outsiders. The most profitable part of Ballarpur was controlled by its distributors. In fact, this web of middlemen not only seemed to have licked away all the cream over the years, it was they who determined what products were to be made and sold in which market,' GT remarks.

As competition grew stronger, it was evident that BILT couldn't afford the status quo. The opening up of the Indian economy had brought with it a reduction in duties and new foreign direct investments in many sectors, including paper. Many of the big international paper companies, including one of the biggest in the region, Indonesian competitor Sinar Mas, owned by one of Asia's largest paper players, Asian Paper and Pulp, was making aggressive plans to enter the business in India. The first step to implement its strategy was to poach managers who had worked at BILT.

In 1993, over a dozen of BILT's top brass, including Rajeev Vederah, walked across to the other side. Ironically, since that was the year of spectacular profits, with paper prices going up all over the world, the exodus didn't really worry anyone. But things changed over the next few years, as import duties on paper crashed and better quality paper started entering the market.

The inefficiencies in Ballarpur's management had also skewed the prices in the paper market. 'Since it was the largest player in the business, BILT decided the price. Others simply bettered it because they used it as a benchmark, a top band of the price—if they improved their efficiencies internally, they could sell at the same price and make far more money, while our profit margins were capped because of serious inefficiencies,' GT explains.

As the market's dynamics changed, BILT started to go downhill. Probably frustrated by the company's inability to respond adequately to the looming challenges, the CFO, Hemant Luthra, who had been the quintessential insider within the company for years and Lalit Mohan's right-hand man, resigned. Lalit Mohan refused to accept Luthra's resignation for months. Finally, with no choice left, the competition gnawing at his heels and the company hurtling towards a crisis, he made GT, who had proved his mettle by now, the CFO of the company, though he did not have any real experience in finance.

What do you do when the chips are down: stand up, take notice and splurge to outdo the competition, or regroup, work on what's right and get rid of what's not working? This classic dilemma was doing the rounds of the corridors of power in 1995, at Thapar House, a landmark on Delhi's Janpath, in

Connaught Place. Vikram Thapar, the man in charge of BILT's day-to-day affairs, opted for the first. His response to the problem seemed to be, 'let us spend our way out of it'. GT, the man who was entrusted with the purse strings and a messy balance sheet, chose the second.

Vederah explains how, by now, time was running out for BILT as well.

In 1993, after poaching the company's top managers, including Vederah, Sinar Mas was planning a massive state-of-the-art paper production facility in Bhigwan, near Pune. The facility was completed in 1997, and it looked like it would challenge and maybe even usurp the comfortable corner BILT had enjoyed for so long.

One of several articles in international newspapers of that time quotes Sinar Mas officials as saying, 'We want to make coated paper India has never seen before!' Juxtapose this with the state of BILT, a company that had not seen any new investment or expansion in its core paper division for years. All through the 1990s, not a single new machine had been added at Ballarpur, and when plans were finally put in place, it involved a massive outlay of Rs 550 crore, to be raised mostly through debt. This was not just too much. It was also too late.

Vederah, who had kept an eye on BILT even after leaving it, explains that no single person could be blamed for the failure of the plan, which, in hindsight was inherently flawed. 'However ill-conceived this plan was, it was discussed all through 1994 and given approval by the board.' And in 1995, the first tranche of money started making its way into the company's factories. Sadly, the move's timing could not have been worse!

By the time more than half the money was pumped into the

company, in mid-1996, international paper prices, on an upswing till now, began to crash and BILT walked headlong into a crunch. The fact that most of the company's top brass had left didn't help.

'By the end of 1997, we thought it was over for us, and if we didn't take corrective measures, we would be sure to default on the convertible bond issue [made as part of the fund-raising for investments] that would come up for renewal in 1998,' Vederah recounts.

It was a make-or-break situation for the Thapars. But the problem in BILT had been long in the making and the crash only made the situation worse. The one thing GT noticed as he began attending BILT's board meetings as head of the chemicals business was how, by the time the various subsidiaries of BILT put together the results of the year gone by and their projections ahead, it would be well into the next year. Even though the financial year ended on 31 March, the board meeting to discuss these results happened months later. By then, there was really no way the results could be gauged. Also, projections and investment plans were often off the cuff. In fact, the biggest problem the company faced was that investment decisions were taken based on the big plans that managers thought up. As GT says, it was telling that the weakest divisions often made the largest investment requests, in an attempt to cover up their own mistakes. They blamed everything and everyone else for the losses they were incurring.

'By 1997, money simply ran out for BILT. A lot of the money that had been raised for long-term plans had been put to use for immediate capital needs. The paper cycle, which had been on an upswing in the first half of 1996, turned suddenly. Prices crashed, and we had raised so much debt to fund the expansion plans by then that banks started calling in to take back the money,' Vederah remarks. He wasn't with BILT then, but the market was rife with reports of how the Thapar flagship was in dire straits. It was going to default on a payment.

Lalit Mohan turned to GT for advice, since he had proven his worth with the turnarounds of APR and the chemicals division.

GT had to manage the finances to pay back the loan and he had just a few hours to do so, but he seemed to work some magic and pulled it off by getting international investors to bail out BILT in the nick of time. 'Gautam proved himself to be the right man for the group, otherwise we would have been on the road,' says Brij Mohan, his voice quivering, even now, with excitement as he thinks back on the crisis.

As news spread that he had managed to save the company from an embarrassing default and collapse, GT became a hero across the company's far outposts and there was little doubt of what was to follow.

The change of guard at the top was, however, gradual from then on. GT began taking most of the crucial decisions while cousin Vikram, more than a decade his senior, slowly bowed out.

Starting 1997, GT first got the team he was comfortable with together. Vederah, the man who had set up most of the factories on the ground for BILT through the decades, and who knew Gautam well, was brought back in. GT also brought in the CFO, B. Hariharan, with whom he had worked closely while he was turning around APR. A new man, Yogesh Agarwal, who is MD of BILT, was put in place to handle the sales. Over time, Agarwal managed to work his way out of the tight grip of the countless distributors who had ruled BILT for so long and changed the way business was done.

The rest of the team had its work cut out too. By 1998, the clean-up had begun. A team was deputed to go around the world cancelling a lot of the orders that had been given out when the company had decided to go in for massive investments.

Every non-core business was sold, including the residual stake in the glass business the company had, the shares in the BILT–Dupont joint venture, and the *Pioneer* newspaper. The company's IT arm was spun off into a separate company, the chemicals division where GT had honed his management skills was hived off to form Solaris Chemtech, and BILT was made to refocus on its core—a pure paper company.

Re-energizing the Thapar flagship took two long years of painstaking work and, internally, efforts were made to ensure that the mistakes of the past were not repeated. For instance, the framework that McKinsey had worked out to determine the viability of the business plans and cost structures in the chemicals arm was reintroduced. Costs were brought down, inventories were managed. Money was pumped back into business, and all this was made possible with the help of a clear strategy and a team that could deliver at the helm. On the ground, too, a clean-up was carried out.

BILT was rebuilt from scratch. It helped that it was such a well-established paper brand.

This was also the time of the family settlement, a process which had started in 1998. By 2000, everything was amicably settled. Under the plan, Lalit Mohan Thapar retained control of Ballarpur, which GT was managing by now. Vikram and his family got the real-estate portfolio, and the corporate headquarters—Thapar House—for which GT still pays Vikram rent; Brij Mohan Thapar got Crompton Greaves and Greaves

Cotton (he split the two between sons Gautam and Karan); and the third brother, Man Mohan Thapar, got JCT and a host of other concerns.

When GT got Crompton Greaves, Lalit Mohan feared that his nephew would turn his attention away from BILT. His fear was justified because the power transformer company had also run into trouble by this time (it had just made a massive loss, the first in its history).

Given the odds, the crucial stage BILT was in, and the fact that no one else could be trusted, Lalit Mohan decided that BILT would also be handed over to the younger Thapar.

The prodigal nephew had earned his way to the top; he had saved his grandfather's company and, by engineering its turnaround, he had proved he was cut out for bigger things. And this was only the start.

For GT, the big turning point in the Ballarpur story came in 2001, when an investment banker approached him, asking whether he would be interested in buying Sinar Mas's new facility in Bhigwan. This was the same facility that had given the Thapars so many sleepless nights. After a mere twenty-minute meeting, GT said, 'Of course!' Within two months, in record time and at a great price, 'a steal' at $114m, half the amount it had taken to build the plant, the deal was done. The factory was his now!

This acquisition was the biggest that any company in India had made in the sector. It did a lot for the company, apart from sending out an important message: Ballarpur was back in business. 'The perceptional value this acquisition gave us was far greater than any other. Everyone started believing that they were winners as the acquisition helped boost the morale within the company,' GT recalls. This was a good thing considering how badly the company had been bruised and battered, first by the competition and then by the aggressive restructuring over the last few years. It was a fitting response, too, to anyone who had written off Ballarpur and the attempts by a forty-one-year-old to resurrect the company.

But even after all the good this acquisition did, few realized that it could open up a new world of opportunity for the company.

CROMPTON GREAVES

As BILT marked its turnaround and first acquisition, Crompton Greaves, also in GT's charge by now, was facing a complex set of problems, though the company had products that were brands in their own right. And most of the solutions for turning the company around came from within, mostly from Sudhir Trehan, the company's MD.

GT allowed Trehan to take decisions and backed him at all times, but from a distance. Having worked in BILT when times were tough, he had learnt some hard lessons, most importantly, that the best an owner could do was give a free hand to the head in taking tough decisions when required. Lalit Mohan had given his nephew that support. Now it was the nephew's turn to do so. And he knew this: 'Remove the gloss of success and power, and the CEO's job is actually a very lonely one.' GT had experienced this first hand when he had sold a lot of what BILT owned, including the newspaper. This had meant people losing their jobs and a lot of criticism that came with it. But he simply had to.

In Trehan's case, the task was so tough that he became the most hated man in Crompton Greaves within the first few months.

Trehan began his career in Crompton Greaves as a management trainee and worked there all through his thirty-year career, save for a short stint at Alstom, a competitor.

Like Ballarpur, Crompton Greaves was also witnessing a massive reversal of fortunes by 2000, when Trehan took over as the company's MD. One has to get a sense of what the company is all about to understand what went wrong.

Crompton Parkinson came into the Thapar fold after KCT acquired Greaves Cotton in 1947. Greaves manufactured a wide array of products in the engineering sector, such as diesel generation sets. Crompton initially made motors for the textile industry, centred in Mumbai. The two companies were brought together as Crompton Greaves in 1966. Interestingly, Crompton Parkinson itself was formed by Col R.E.B. Crompton, who is credited with bringing electricity into India—in Kolkata—in 1899. The company was British-owned and when Crompton Greaves was formed, Crompton Parkinson held a 40 per cent stake and the Thapars owned 25–27 per cent, with the rest held publicly. Over the years, the Thapars increased their stake in the company, even as the British parent ran into trouble and changed hands a couple of times.

Today, Crompton Parkinson, the parent company, doesn't exist. But Crompton Greaves has a thriving international business and a subsidiary in the UK.

It is also a household name in India. Crompton Greaves makes motors used in fans (every third fan sold in India still runs on Crompton Greaves's motor) and power transformers (it is the largest power transformer company in certain categories in the country). The bulk of its revenue comes from the power business and, for decades, its biggest clients were the state electricity boards, which were mostly in a mess. At the household and consumer level, Crompton Greaves is still one of the major players in the ceiling-fan market, otherwise dominated by a clutch of unorganized and unbranded players. In fact, it's a testimony to the complexities of the Indian marketplace in appliances that fans, the hottest selling among them, are dominated by old Indian manufacturers, decades after the opening up of the economy. Experts say it is difficult to survive here because of the competition from fakes and unorganized players and the dominance of old hands like Usha, Bajaj and, of course, Crompton Greaves.

Seeing the success of the company today, it's hard to imagine how dismal the situation seemed just a decade or so ago.

Trehan explains how the story went sour for Crompton Greaves. 'Right from the beginning, Crompton Greaves competed with the Indian arms of the biggest power-equipment players of the world, Swiss-Swedish multinational ABB and French Power company Alstom, but this didn't matter before liberalization. These companies [ABB and Alstom] were like regular Indian companies. They competed for the same government orders.' If the market was the same, so were the products they offered and the technology they used. Instead of using the high-tech wares that their parents introduced in the West, what came into India were old, outdated hand-me-downs.

'But to be fair to the competition, there was hardly any incentive to spend on technology or improve products before 1991. The prices were fixed, as was the output, and all the players knew exactly what orders and what margins they could hope for,' Trehan adds.

In a nutshell, Crompton Greaves and its biggest competitors were in the same boat, business was determined by the state, and there was really no scope of doing anything more—a story that resonates across industrial segments in pre-liberalization India.

All this was, however, to undergo a major overhaul in 1991. The opening up of the economy resulted in a sharp fall in import duties and the entry of aggressive Japanese manufacturers like Mitsubishi into the power-equipment market in India. They came in with the latest technology and soon, as duties fell, it became apparent that their products were often not just better, but much cheaper.

As often happens with big change, this was also the time when the market for these companies began to change. First, the state electricity boards went in for an overhaul, a desperate attempt to plug the massive transmission losses because of outdated technology in an already power-deficit country. Second, the private sector provided an opportunity as new factories were set up, often with captive power plants, and massive capacities were built up.

As the market dynamics within the business changed, the Indian arms of ABB and Alstom were quick to gear up, moving into full throttle with the help of their parent companies. At this juncture, Crompton Greaves was left standing alone, totally unprepared to face the changing scenario.

The result was that, within years, the company lost a lot of business, profits and goodwill. Starting 1995, the fall was drastic and, in 2000, for the first time in its sixty-three-year-old history, Crompton Greaves made a huge loss of Rs 147 crore.

For someone like Sudhir Trehan, who had spent a lifetime at Crompton Greaves, these were terribly frustrating times. 'My rise within Crompton Greaves had been spectacular, but as I was moving up, I was also being made painfully aware that a lot was wrong with the company. Crompton Greaves still believed it was great and showed little regard for the customer. We would tell him how he should run the equipment. The belief was that our equipment was right, even if there were complaints,' Trehan says. While this was the public manifestation of the company's attitude, internally too the company had very little drive and was slow to change.

There were other serious problems. By the mid-1990s, Crompton Greaves, like most companies owned by families in India, had diversified in a big way. Restrictions on scale and the barriers to entry led companies to widen their businesses rather than deepening and strengthening their core.

At its height, for instance, Crompton Greaves was a partner in twenty-four joint ventures, many of them extremely small, sometimes selling only a single product. And several were making losses.

It was on 19 April 2000 that Trehan took over as MD of Crompton Greaves, and from the very next day he got down to sorting the mess. According to him, 'The first tough thing to deal with was the people. There were 10,500 of them in the company. The number had to be brought down to 5,000.' This would have been a tough call, especially towards the end of the twentieth century, because many industrial sectors were coming out of a slowdown and unions were powerful entities.

But Trehan had little choice and his first target was the primary factory, located in Chembur, Mumbai. It was an expensive place as it was inside the city, and that was where the axe was to fall first.

Trehan sacked thirty-four general managers, vice presidents and divisional presidents. The next day, he called the union leader, who controlled most of the unions in the city, and told him that the company would double its losses if drastic steps were not taken soon. People would be asked to go. Trehan had an ace up his sleeve. 'I told him we will have to sack people if we are to survive but I can assure you that it won't be just your people, senior managers will also be axed,' he told the union leader. That this was not an empty promise had already been proven the day before, when Trehan had walked the talk.

The fact that senior executives, who worked out of plush offices, were also being asked to go only underlined the gravity of the situation. He not only won the support of his people by sacking these employees first, he also convinced them that change was necessary.

'It was obvious that our plants were overstaffed. Productivity was so poor that workers used to work for just two and a half hours a day. Also, their sheer number meant that there was shortage of work and managers purposely overstaffed their factories because they wanted to cover their backs,' Trehan explains. This problem was a legacy of the past. It had already sounded the death knell for entire industries like the once-bustling textile mills of Mumbai, where similar issues and a fiery union had spearheaded one of the longest shutdowns in the history of industry.

Taking a cue from what was happening on factory floors everywhere, Trehan came to the conclusion that buttressing the system with excess labour meant that, no matter what happened, productivity would suffer and losses would mount.

Second, the facility in Chembur cost too much money. Land and labour were expensive and high duties (the infamous octroi, a toll tax to be paid at the time of crossing borders while entering or exiting Mumbai) ensured that products weren't competitive even as they came out of the factory gate.

The argument was won not by the facts that Trehan put on the table but by a formula that he had worked out in his head.

He promised the union leader that the first 2,000 employees to be sacked would be white-collar executives. This would give the workers time to absorb the changes. Subsequently, 3,000 employees would be given the pink slip, with a VRS package.

With a nod from the union leader, Trehan and Crompton Greaves crossed the first big hurdle on the long road to a turnaround. Numbers were reduced drastically within the same year, the facilities and plants in Mumbai were shifted to Goa and Ahmednagar, and new working norms were laid down.

'Everyone had to come out of their comfort zone. We worked out strict eight-hour shifts on the factory floor with a ten-minute tea break in the morning and evening and a thirty-minute lunch break,' Trehan recalls. The unions refused to be bound by schedules at first but eventually agreed.

'Our own senior team believed that the drastic changes and cuts were a foolhardy thing, but as things started falling into place, support started coming in.'

The other big cost-cutting exercise came through inventory management. 'We decided that we will not outsource more than 10 per cent of the material needed for production. We would use up our inventory.' The company's borrowing at that time was Rs 850 crore.

Like BILT, in the case of Crompton Greaves too, Trehan says, 'Dealers were running the business. They would sell our fans and motors and not pay for months. Sometimes they would say that they haven't sold the stuff.' Trehan got tough and asked them to return the unsold inventory.

Money was also raised by selling non-core businesses, even telecom. In the first round of telecom licensing, Crompton Greaves had been one of the winning bidders that got the Chennai circle under its belt. The licence was sold to Bharti

Televentures and the eventual hiving off and sale of the telecom company, Skycell, raised over Rs 200 crore. This single-handedly funded the aggressive VRS package the company had initiated. Small non-core arms or subsidiaries within the fold, such as the low-tension control gear business, were sold off to French electric company Schneider, along with a plant in Nashik, for Rs 76 crore.

The across-the-board tightening bore results. 'We collected money from our customers, halved our inventory and cut down our debtors by half.' From a loss of Rs 147 crore in 2000, its losses came down by 50 per cent within a year, and in 2002 the company turned in a profit of Rs 7 crore.

It had been tough. 'For six to seven months [in the beginning] I was alone, nobody wanted to see my face or share anything with me. In tough times, you are the most unpopular person in the system,' Trehan recalls. But he knew all along that he had the support of GT.

Between 2002 and '04, the company gradually built up its balance sheet, and market share and profits during the period leaped from Rs 7 crore in 2002 to Rs 50 crore the following year. Soon, that too doubled. The good run continued for a while.

GOING BEYOND THE TURNAROUND

The turnaround of BILT and Crompton Greaves is just one part of the story that GT and his team worked on. He did not intend to stop with just the turnaround.

As he got more and more involved with the business and the environment in which it functioned, he realized he could do much more. The idea of the biggest 'strategy trump card' he has used to grow his business since then came through an acquisition, that of Sinar Mas's Bhigwan facility soon after the turnaround of BILT. From the time work began on the factory in the mid-1990s, for GT, it had been a constant reminder of the threat to BILT and the failure within the company.

The acquisition opened up new possibilities. It gave BILT the kind of updated and high-end technology it had never seen before. BILT quickly replicated it to upgrade its other facilities. The better technology allowed the company to move up the paper ladder. If, until now, the company produced coarser, more basic forms of paper, the acquisition allowed it to manufacture world-class paper. Technology and new manufacturing techniques made production more efficient and this meant that, within years, BILT was ready to compete with the biggest papermakers across Asia.

GT had managed to chalk out future plans in his mind in the twenty minutes he took to decide on the deal. That's probably why Vederah says, 'When Gautam spoke to the senior managers after BILT's turnaround, he said he wanted the company to achieve a one-million-tonne capacity and a billion dollars in revenue over the next decade. The targets seemed impossible then, but he had a clear vision of how to go about achieving them.'

Both these targets were met in 2010 and GT used the opportunity to rework the numbers and once again set an impossible-sounding target.

If this was the experience at BILT, by 2002, when Crompton Greaves went out shopping, the canvas had become much larger. Once again, it was driven by a real need.

Here, too, the ever-evolving market and competition on the ground necessitated change. 'There were two major stumbling blocks for us at this time. First, the clean-up at Thapar House had taken too long and we had lost crucial time in the bargain. The acquisition of Sinar Mas's Bhigwan plant by BILT had made it only too clear that our companies were painfully behind the times as far as technology was concerned,' GT remarks.

He learnt an important lesson. 'Running a business in the new, open India is very much about second-guessing how the market and the competition will evolve and planning around it.'

The Indian customer is not driving you for a better product. 'Maybe it was a factor of their limited exposure as well,' GT says. This, he believed, made it imperative for Indian companies such as his to look outside India, at the world market, and compete in the toughest and most discerning marketplace. 'We needed to go out and do things better.'

So when it came to Crompton Greaves, GT decided that to compete with the best in the world, one would have to go out and fight the competition at their game in their market. The opportunity came in 2005, when a niche Belgian transformer-maker, Pauwels Transformers Inc., which was in trouble, came up for sale.

'When we heard about it, Sudhir and I visited the plant and it was a complete eye-opener. Even though the company was facing financial problems, there was no doubt that it had cutting-edge technology that was years ahead of anything Crompton Greaves had.'

Within days, the decision was made. After two major turnarounds back home, reviving Pauwels was simple. 'When we got there, we realized the financial problems had cropped up because of problems we were familiar with at both CG and BILT—loose money management, no focus on the core, and defunct subsidiaries.' Within months, the Crompton Greaves team split, one looking at how to revive the company, and the other trying to understand how it built transformers that were lighter (and hence far more advanced) than those built by Crompton Greaves. In a few months, the company was back on its feet; Crompton Greaves not only acquired high-end technology, it also acquired the Belgian company's additional manufacturing facilities for power and distribution transformers in Belgium, Ireland, the US, Canada and Indonesia.

In one fell swoop, Crompton Greaves had become a transnational company. The new factories brought with them new products, new customers and new markets.

Following this acquisition, Crompton Greaves went on an overdrive. Every year since then, it has shopped either for a new niche technology company or a new market and footprint. In 2006, for instance, the company took a high-voltage transformer company, Ganz, in Hungary. A year later, it bought an Irish firm, which was followed up with an acquisition in Sonomatra, France. The following year saw the acquisition of MSE Power Systems in the US. Though 2009 seems to have been a quieter year, the company made up for lost ground in 2010, buying a firm in the UK, Power Technology Solutions (PTS), and three businesses of Nelco in India.

So why has the pace been so hectic and what are GT's plans? In today's business world, geographical boundaries don't matter. What does is access to the latest technology, the most cost-efficient production, and customers. The focus on international acquisitions gives Crompton Greaves all three. In the normal course, it would have taken years for the company to have reached the level it has in six years. Also, interestingly, according to him, in a business where a lot of the products are determined by the users, it helps to cater to those who are innovating and looking at new technologies and solutions themselves. In India today, on the flip side, most of Crompton Greaves's customers are state-run electricity boards, but as and when new technology comes into India, the company will be ready with a whole suite of products.

In a sense, competition is also driving the company's aggressive international forays. GT is quite aware of the fact that despite all the passion and push, Crompton Greaves is still a small player on the global high table, compared to big boys like Alstom and ABB, but as the Indian market booms and new technology takes over, Crompton Greaves will be in the reckoning not just as the most cost-effective alternative, but also the most efficient.

GT has always looked at the bigger picture when it comes to capturing markets where competition is tough. Though located in India, where the power sector has been going through its ups and downs, he just can't ignore what's happening across the world. 'How can you sit in a market where there is going to be a lot of spending on power generation, transmission and distribution and not say one needs to be a major player?'

Acquisitions made sense for another reason: 'The Indian power transformer market in 2004 was a mere 2 per cent of the world market, and I was clear that Crompton Greaves would find it difficult to actually capture more than one-fourth of this even if it tried its best. The choice then was, do we want to saturate here, let history repeat itself, or compete for a far larger pie on the world stage?'

The logic is undeniable and quite practical, and for each analyst of Dalal Street who says that many of his acquisitions haven't totally paid off, GT's argument is an answer. He is looking way ahead and being in far-off markets is giving him a ringside view into the changes driving the power sector the world over.

'Changes in policy in the more developed markets are necessitating a fresh relook. The nature of the power industry is changing. For example, there are mandated policies of 25 per cent non-conventional energy, which is a huge challenge for static grids, and so everyone across the world will have to upgrade technology. Over the next few years, India will also have to follow the same route.'

If technology, market and footprint are the big strategy drivers at Crompton Greaves, at BILT, controlling the source of raw material—pulp—has been the biggest concern. This necessitated a second acquisition, Sabah Plantations, in Malaysia, in 2007. This came on the heels of a big capacity expansion the company undertook in its plants. It allowed BILT to access pulp for its ever-expanding Indian operations and access to lucrative markets in South East Asia, to which Sabah catered.

If the strategy at Crompton Greaves is to look at the developed market for technology, in time for the big power sector build-up in India, in the case of BILT the strategy seems to be to cash in on the global shift towards the east.

'For far too long, the rules of the game and trade [prices] in the paper and commodity business have been set by the developed markets. Today, for the first time, with India and China emerging as the fastest-growing consumer markets, these countries will, over the next decade or so, lay down the rules of the game,' GT explains.

If CG and BILT have their plans in place, so does GT, beyond these two companies. His new group, Avantha, formally christened in 2007 to carve out a new identity, has an interesting portfolio of investments that include the old—chemicals, power transformers and, soon, power generation, and the new—IT and gourmet food. Take, for example, Global Greens, a specialty foods division that has farms across Belgium and India. The company cultivates gourmet vegetables like gherkins, jalapenos and cherries and is already exporting these to more than fifty countries.

GT has nurtured and built an interesting portfolio of companies and each has two themes in common. First, the fact that today geographical boundaries really don't matter, and second, over time, the biggest market for almost everything he is building is going to be India.

But while the focus is on the horizon, the ground realities have not been ignored, and the journey has had its ups and downs, which were most evident in 2011.

UPS AND DOWNS

For much of 2010 and 2011, for stock market pundits on Dalal Street, Crompton Greaves was the stock to hold. Brokerage had put out 'buy' recommendations on CG in an otherwise lacklustre market. Lacklustre, thanks to the concerns around inflation and a series of interest-rate hikes that had seen the Indian markets emerge as the worst performing till S&P decided to downgrade US debt, creating a storm in the global markets in August 2011. Till even a month before that, Crompton Greaves had been 'outperforming' the markets, giving better returns because of the revenues here and globally it had been generating—$2,223m for FY 2010–11. With the kind of build-up the government was planning in power—Rs 140,000 crore in the Eleventh Five Year Plan alone, till the end of 2011—

expectations were that CG would be one of the biggest beneficiaries. That the company was getting nearly a third of its revenue from developed markets where governments were initiating a massive upgradation of power grids meant even better tidings. Analysts were quick to opine that there was little doubt that Gautam Thapar's go-global programme had worked.

But within weeks, the sentiment changed.

On Dalal Street, analysts who cover companies and sectors for brokerages, who in turn recommend them to their clients—either small investors or big institutional buyers—are proud of the way they can predict, almost to the last decimal, what a company's earnings will be every quarter, quarter on quarter, as listed companies are bound to report it.

As it is in financial centres everywhere, there is an art and a science behind this.

The projections are always a product of painstaking analysis based on detailed meetings with the management, close tracking of business orders and wins and plant visits. They rarely go wrong because of the dexterity with which every number is put under the lens and the fact that often millions of dollars can be lost because of a wrong call.

This is what happened with Crompton Greaves on 19 July 2011. A simple press release declaring the statement of accounts, addressed to the exchanges, announced that the company's net profits had fallen 59 per cent in the first quarter of FY 2011–12, the quarter from 1 April to 30 June.

Analysts were shocked as they were expecting a sharp rise in profits as per their projections. As they took a closer look at the numbers, they realized that the drop had come within the company's core power-systems segment, the centre of most of the excitement over the last few years. The crisis across Europe, financial and growth pangs in Spain, Italy and Portugal had had an impact—no government was willing to place orders for the upgradation of their power grid. In India, there were bigger problems. Raw material costs had gone up and the state electricity boards and the government, amongst the company's biggest clients, were not giving business.

By the end of the day, Crompton Greaves, until then the darling of the markets, was down 14 per cent. Investors had lost a fair bit of money and foreign institutional clients, by far the most important, were calling from New York and Hong Kong to find out what had gone wrong. In the confusion that followed, charges of insider trading and stock rigging were made and the company's stock price continued its downward spiral. While many of the allegations were subsequently refuted, the company's woes did not end. Over the next few months, troubles seemed to mount for Crompton Greaves as it became evident that the slowdown in Europe and its core business here in India would impact the company in the future.

In the volatile Indian stock market, where extreme euphoria and optimism are often followed by nervousness and pessimism depending on how the headwinds are blowing, the curious case of what happened at Crompton Greaves will take time to unravel as the charges made (Avantha filed a case with market regulator SEBI, claiming that someone had purposely crashed the stock) are probed. What can't be denied is that for a company that has worked so hard to get where it has, it will be a constant reminder of how careful it needs to be as it charts the next leg of its journey.

TOWARDS THE FUTURE

Despite the many ups and downs, it is obvious that GT has come a long way from being an uncertain outsider inside the Thapar family, to the rightful heir who saved, revived and renewed the legacy he inherited. Over the years, he has transformed himself into a savvy businessman, and the rechristening of his group as Avantha only underlines the new identity: AVAN comes from the word avant-garde, which means introducing new ideas or being innovative, and the THA has been borrowed from the Thapar surname.

While old-timers feel anguish at the end of an era and the Thapar name in Indian business, by renaming it, GT seems to have reiterated the point that he has moved far beyond the Thapar name and legacy.

But it is not easy to completely shake it off and often comparisons are drawn, within the family and among the old hands who worked with them, between Karam Chand Thapar, the patriarch who built the business empire, and Gautam Thapar, who transformed it.

Brij Mohan Thapar knows the difference between the two entrepreneurs. 'You know, there is no simple rule for success. There are about five million ways of being successful. I feel those were different times. My father was a man of his times. Gautam, god bless him, seems to be the right man for our group. We are lucky.

But 'there is an invisible intuitive something that runs in the blood from generation to generation. You know, I always was worried about a little thing. That Gautam's ambition might be too great to achieve. But then [as I watch him] I have always been reminded of Robert Browning's words: "Ah, but a man's reach should exceed his grasp, or what's a heaven for?"'

GT has been pushing the limits in more ways than one. Today, Avantha has operations in twenty countries and a 22,000-strong workforce. He intends to more than double that size over the next five years.

Senior managers in the company, and those who have worked closely with him within or outside the group, say the next five years will be crucial for GT. The general sense is that if he manages to steer his way through these, the successes so far will pale in comparison to what can be.

Gautam Thapar (*extreme right*) with his uncle, Lalit Mohan Thapar, and aunts

According to Vederah, 'The biggest challenge is going to be sustaining this growth. Gautam has also made some seriously large projections. He has gone on record to say that he wants Avantha to be a $10bn group by 2015. That's more than double the current size of the company.' While the deadline for this has undoubtably been extended, Vederah is clear that all of this can't be done without a massive scale-up or acquisitions. Each business head is only too aware of that.

'I am pretty unemotional about it [companies and businesses] now. I tell my managers that if you want to be part of the Avantha Group, you need to perform. There is no free lunch. Of course, one has to invest in a young business, but there is an opportunity there as well!'

At a juncture when Crompton Greaves is global in its operations, a strong need for a business head who could showcase a much larger canvas of experience was felt. Which is probably why Sudhir Trehan was replaced by Laurent Demortier, the new man at the helm of CG. Demortier has worked with Alstom and Areva, some of the biggest companies in the power equipment space in the world.

This need for global talent is not limited to the top, according to GT, with more and more revenue for the group coming from overseas. The biggest challenge the group faces is training its team to think global and be comfortable across geographies.

So, has he made many mistakes along the way? 'Most of the mistakes I made have been around people, getting the wrong person for a position that didn't suit him. This has a far-reaching impact. Not only does it hurt the business, it also ruins the morale and the career of a perfectly good professional!'

While the journey so far has been eventful for him, GT agrees that it hasn't been a bed of roses either. Doing business in India is tough.

The biggest problem is that while everyone is talking about the larger picture and the potential for growth, there seems to be no plan for how to achieve this. It is a complaint that is commonly voiced at a time when the biggest investment plans in India have been stalled because of policy bottlenecks and little seems to have been done to address structural changes required to ensure sustainable growth.

'We have a whole system focussed on trying to achieve a big growth number, but how do you get there when you have not fixed basic issues like arriving at some kind of a consensus between ministries. You have to have the ports ministry, the mines ministry, the railways, all of them talking and working with each other even to transport basic material,' he reiterates.

Then there is the issue of accessing crucial raw material like coal for the many power projects that promoters like him are initiating. Access to local resources has become so difficult that promoters keen to set up power generation units (given the massive power deficit and obvious demand) are being forced to acquire mines overseas. This might seem like a trend now, but over time, it could spell disaster because it would mean far more expensive raw material and hence higher costs of production.

These are some of the many hurdles that businessmen face today.

At another level, GT's biggest ambition is to create a group that doesn't need him at the top as a hands-on manager, something not many businessmen say. His logic is, however, simple: 'I will be a truly satisfied man the day I can kick myself out of the CEO's chair, assured that the ship is running smoothly and Avantha is comfortably climbing up an aggressive growth trajectory.'

The rationale is clear. With his family settled in London and GT shuttling around the world, he believes the best he can do for Avantha is to rise above the day-to-day and work on looking at the horizon, where the opportunities are immense and the path to get to them complex. He is also adamant that his children shouldn't be forced to wear the mantle of inheritors, or, in other words, to take on the reins.

He wants them to join the group only if they are inclined to. He and his father have, after all, lived by the rule, 'Take your own path.' But history aside, ensuring that all the companies within Avantha run in a corporatized way will also mean longevity and reduce dependence on a single person at the top.

GT himself is almost dismissive of the high expectations from people around him. He is too independent to let anyone else define success for him, or the goal he has to achieve to prove that he has made his mark.

The last couple of years have been tough for him, both in business and at home. He lost his mother, and a lot of his plans got delayed as global markets slowed down and the bets he made on power, and the growth it would see in the West and India, failed to fructify. In Ballarpur Industries Limited, this slowdown meant the delay of any plans for expansion.

All through this tough patch, one hardly heard of GT. It was as if the chairman of the Avantha Group had closed the door to the world outside and was focussing on rebuilding his team, recalibrating strategies and retooling the group. After all, after a clear ten-year run, it was time to take a pause before the next leap that he is poised to make. The last word probably belongs to his father when he says, 'Gautam has done a great job, but in my heart, I believe that the best is yet to come.'

PART II

THE BUILDERS

BABA N. KALYANI

It was a November morning in 2003, a day Baba Neelkanth Kalyani will remember all his life. And why not? He had been working towards this for over a year now. But seeing the group of tense and solemn-faced German factory workers assembled at the entrance of the Carl Dan Peddinghaus (CDP) plant in the small town of Ennepetal, an hour's drive from Dusseldorf, he couldn't help but think of the road he had travelled and the longer one ahead. Imagine what would have happened if he had told these highly skilled technicians and engineers present here that his company, Bharat Forge, which was officially taking over theirs, had started as a small hammer shop, supplying small parts to automobile companies. That he had spent most of the last few months living out of a suitcase, trying to convince German bankers, politicians, CDP customers and virtually everyone who had an interest in the company why he should do the takeover.

But no matter how compelling the journey so far had been, these were the last things Kalyani was interested in sharing with those present. The local press had created a furore over how an Indian company was trying to enter Germany, targeting a firm that represented all that was good about the famed German 'Mittelstand' (small and mid-sized high-tech companies) that formed the core of the country's technological and industrial prowess.

It didn't help that the 150-year-old family-owned company Kalyani was taking over was well known across the region. But he knew that the men around him were aware of what they were up against. All through 2002, there had been a collapse across Mittelstand. An estimated 37,700 of these companies had gone under due to the high value of the Euro and lack of credit availability that had hurt exports, the livelihood of most of these firms. And companies like CDP employed 70 per cent of the country's workforce.

But the men needn't have worried. Kalyani had a watertight plan and an ace up his sleeve. He managed to engineer a remarkable turnaround within six months of the takeover. Between 2004 and '06, he went on an acquisition spree, spreading his wings from Michigan in the US to Changchun in China, and creating one of the world's biggest forging companies in the process.

The events of that morning at the CDP headquarters were a follow-up of something that started in 1972, when Baba Kalyani first walked into the Bharat Forge shop floor in Mundhwa, Pune. The company has continued to script its success story on the world stage, not just in the business of automotive forgings but even beyond. Most of this spectacular success can be attributed to the company's chairman, who has consistently been able to second-guess change and stay ahead.

THE FARMER CONNECT

As you drive through Pune towards Kolhapur, along the sugar-rich belt of Satara in western Maharashtra, you will come across a small village called Kole, near a slightly larger town, Karad. It is here that the Kalyani story began. A lot has changed since the days Kalyani and his family lived there. It is partly Kalyani's grandfather Annappa Kalyani's enterprise that helped his family prosper.

A self-made man, Kalyani's grandfather started off as a postman who would collect mail at the Karad station, walk with it 16 kilometres to the village, and go door to door distributing it. After years of doing this, he landed a job at the local zamindar's office, and that's where he learned about 'trading' and decided to venture into it.

Annappa Kalyani's journey is well known around the villages of Karad. 'My grandfather started off with one can of oil and made money selling it. He bought some more oil and trade picked up, eventually spreading across all agricultural commodities grown in the region,' Kalyani says. He was obviously good at what he did, because in a few years, he became one of the biggest traders the region had ever seen. He was dubbed the 'turmeric king' because he virtually controlled all trade of the yellow powder in the region. But despite the seemingly effortless success, trading must have been tough and before Kalyani's grandfather died in 1954, he made his son, Kalyani's father, promise that he would never make a living out of it. 'My grandfather lost his entire fortune at least three times in his life and he was adamant that my father shouldn't have to live a life of ups and downs.'

Interestingly, Annappa Kalyani had also started other

ventures alongside trade and those were doing well. The family ran the local electricity company, supplying power to Karad, though this was nationalized later. Kalyani's father, Dr Neelkanth Kalyani, shut down the trading business and focussed on the land the family owned. He was one of the region's first farmers to cultivate sugarcane and lay the groundwork for sugar cooperatives in Maharashtra. This, in turn, gave him a foothold in local politics and the all-powerful sugar lobby. Though his father was never an active politician, he was always deeply involved in politics. He was a member of the Congress party and a close friend of Karad politician Yashwantrao Chavan, who was not only the first chief minister of Maharashtra after the division of Bombay State but also a powerful Congress leader who held important portfolios including defence, finance and home at the Centre. For over a decade, Dr Kalyani was the chairman of the influential Maharashtra Cooperative Land Development Bank, which lent money to farmers across the state.

While Baba Kalyani was growing up, his father, spotting a sliver of opportunity, started a small manufacturing unit that made gears and auto parts in Karad. This company supplied products to the Walchand-group-owned company Cooper Engineering. But the idea of Bharat Forge came from a casual conversation between the founder of the Kirloskar Group, S.L. Kirloskar, and his father.

The Kirloskars and Kalyanis have been close family friends for five generations and Kirloskar would always drop by every time he made his way out of his village, Kirloskarwadi, near Kole, into Pune or Mumbai. On one such occasion, just when the Kirloskars were planning to set up an engine-manufacturing unit in Pune, SLK (as he was known) suggested the idea of setting up a small forging company that could supply material to his plant. The decision was taken in a matter of hours and Dr Kalyani decided to relocate to Pune with his family and set up the unit there.

But raising money and acquiring licences were difficult in those days, so he approached the region's farmers, who knew him and the family well, and borrowed money from them, instead of going to the commercial centres like Mumbai and Ahmedabad. 'Even today, the big farmers around Kole, Karad, Satara and Baramati own a stake in Bharat Forge,' Kalyani remarks. Another close family friend, the maharaja of Kolhapur, helped out. His father managed to raise a princely sum of Rs 25 lakh in the process. But money was just the first step; the bigger challenge was to get started. Consultants were brought in from Cleveland in the US, because forging was a new business and Dr Kalyani wanted to get everything right. The last of the Cleveland consultants left the company only in the 1980s and Kalyani still visits one of the engineers, an old friend, every time he goes to the US.

The first forged metal part left the Pune factory in July 1966.

ENGINEERING THE CHANGE

Baba Kalyani was sent to study at King George's Royal Indian Military School (now Rashtriya Military School) in Belgaum at the age of six. His military connection comes through when you meet him. There is a certain stern formality to the man, an intrinsic sense of authority. 'The school was very military-like, and the morning started early. There were tough exercise regimes each day and lots of sports, besides gruelling studies, through the year.' Kalyani hated it in the beginning, but began to enjoy it soon because the regimen, he believes, was designed to bring out the best in everyone.

His decision to get into mechanical engineering was taken during his summer vacations, when he would spend days demolishing and rebuilding his cycle, or later, when the Bharat Forge plant was being built. He says, 'I was fascinated by all the big machines being set up and the work they were doing.' In 1966, he headed to BITS Pilani for an engineering degree, but the big trigger that fired his imagination and ambition seems to have come when he was at the Massachusetts Institute of Technology (MIT) in Boston. Kalyani thanks SLK for convincing his father to allow him to go to the US.

'I had never been outside India and it took me two to three months to get over it. What hits you is the competition when you get to an institute like MIT,' Kalyani recalls. 'It is tough and you realize you have to work hard each day to keep pace with your classmates, who are among the best in the world. The years there gave me the ability to think in a very different manner and, after going through MIT, I came out with the belief that nothing was impossible.'

As was expected of him, he joined the family enterprise as an engineer on the shop floor in 1972 for a princely pay of Rs 500. What he saw there shocked him. 'People were just not organized. There was no discipline, no organization, no leadership. There were no systems, no processes, none of the essential things. When you live in the US for even two years, you learn to follow a process, be disciplined. You quickly learn that you can't go anywhere without that,' Kalyani explains. This bothered him so much that he complained about it to his father. One day, tired of his cribbing, his father simply marched him to SLK, who was the chairman of the company, and someone the family obviously looked up to. SLK said, 'If he has such a problem, let him fix it. Throw the kid into the water.'

So, within months of joining Bharat Forge, Kalyani was given the job of a sales manager because he believed that the company's sales team wasn't pushing the products and getting new business. But when he started interacting with the clients, the companies that Bharat Forge was supplying to, it didn't take much time for Kalyani to realize that the problems here were similar to those on the shop floor. 'Within three months, I dramatically increased the sales. It was done by putting basic systems in place, simple things like making sure delivery was done on time and ensuring that we were in constant touch with our buyers,' Kalyani remarks. In just a couple of years, Bharat Forge was supplying material to two companies based around Pune, Bajaj Auto and Tata Engineering & Locomotive Company (TELCO, later Tata Motors).

Meanwhile, other manufacturers like the Mahindras had also begun giving contracts to Bharat Forge, but the scale was small. The company Dr Kalyani had set up was little more than a small forging unit, one among the many ancillary companies that had cropped up around Pune. Kalyani's father ran into another problem during this time. 'With sales picking up rapidly, the problem was of producing enough to meet the demand.' Kalyani realized that the problem actually stemmed from the shop floor itself. And that's exactly where he stayed put for the next twenty years.

The old forging shed he first started out in is nothing like the automated plants around the Bharat Forge facility today, but work still goes on here, and one can't help but feel that it has more to do with the nostalgia attached to it. The old-fashioned hammer press is where Kalyani's morning tour of the plant begins, informs shop-in-charge Ramanujan, a cheery engineer who has been with the company for the last thirty years and who knows how significant this shop has been to the fortunes of the company.

For the next decade, all the work the company did was out of here. And from the day he joined work till the time he started spending far more time in the corporate office, strategizing, in 1992, Kalyani was among the first to come in every morning.

'Everyone would know when he entered. Each morning, he would be here sharp at 7, and spend the day overseeing the production line. He knows every machine here. Give him any problem, any faulty machine, and he will fix it or at least know how to, within minutes,' Ramanujan says. The transformation of Bharat Forge from an old hammer shop to the new, fully automated software- and robot-driven plant was not an easy one.

'In the licence-permit raj, every time you needed a new machine, you would have to make five trips to Delhi to convince some babu why you needed it.' Imports were next to impossible. 'First, you would have to get an import licence, which was tough [and took a minimum of two years] in itself, and if you had one, you almost never could raise the foreign exchange for it,' Kalyani says. As a result, manufacturing units like his depended more on brawn or manpower than technology. 'The entire business model for manufacturers like us was a low-technology high-labour one, but that was slow to produce results.' The success of any company under such conditions depended on one's ability to motivate the workforce. That's probably why wage agreements and productivity clauses—laying out sops for so many hours of work—were so important.

But it is commendable that even within this set-up, Kalyani managed to improve things. The annual reports for the period from 1972 to '80 show that sales at Bharat Forge doubled each year. Innovative ways were found to deal with the growing demand.

The successes aside, this period was largely frustrating. 'While I knew we had to improve efficiencies and this was the direction to take, most of my big ideas were bottled up.' Nor was this a situation unique to him. 'The whole environment was like you had been put in a bottle with a nice big cork on it. You couldn't move or do anything.'

But Kalyani did find some ways around the many problems that came his way. For one, the company turned to the government departments for equipment. 'We bought our first open die forging press from the ordnance factory near Kolkata.' The railways and defence ordnance factories were the best bet for companies like Bharat Forge because only they did such heavy work. If the environment was tough, competition was tough too. At that time, the world's largest forging company, Wyman Gordon, was the big competitor for Bharat Forge in India. Kalyani says, 'We had the world leader right in the backyard, competing with us for fifteen years before it went bankrupt.' It was ironical that after fighting to survive in the closed economy for years, the company simply shut shop. But all through those years, the two firms competed head to head across products, keeping Kalyani and his company on their toes. 'I guess we did a better job. At least, I would like to think that we did.'

After over a decade of surviving the system and growing in

the face of many odds, the next big turning point for him came in 1983, when the policy environment began to change and a new people's car, the Maruti 800, drove out of a factory in a place called Gurgaon, on the outskirts of New Delhi.

OPENING UP

The liberalization of 1991 tends to overshadow the years that preceded it, but it was an interesting period in its own right. Faced with fast-depleting foreign exchange reserves and a soaring fiscal deficit situation, Rajiv Gandhi's government began the process of opening up the economy and exports in 1985. Many manufacturing companies were encouraged to look at overseas markets and get partners from abroad.

Meanwhile, the arrival of Suzuki opened the floodgates for other Japanese automobile majors. But companies like Mitsubishi, Nissan, Mazda and Toyota (in partnership with Indian companies like Eicher, Allwyn, Swaraj and DCM) did not bring new orders with them. 'Since this was the first time that a very high level of automotive technology had come into India, these companies began to bring their own auto component suppliers with them and with good reason. Technology in India was outdated and even basic operational costs were high, which made Indian manufacturers inefficient. Japanese auto companies would do business with you only if you had a partner they had worked with,' Kalyani says.

It was at this time that Bharat Forge, like other Indian companies who were forging partnerships with Japanese companies for technology, formed a joint venture with a US company to make brake systems for Maruti. The company was called Kalyani Brakes. But as in many technology-driven joint ventures, problems related to intellectual property rights emerged over time and Kalyani Brakes was sold to Bosch in 2000.

The arrival of the Japanese created a furore across factory floors in India. They were the best in manufacturing and they were teaching the entire world how to run a plant. This propelled Bharat Forge to explore other tie-ups and a new one with a company called MetalArt followed.

Always ready to latch on to an opportunity and quick to spot a trend, Kalyani did three important things during this period. First, he decided to consciously look beyond the commercial vehicles his company had always supplied forgings to. Second, he realized that the advent of Maruti Suzuki would revolutionize the passenger-car segment, and it was something that he should focus on, which meant that he would have to expand his product suite and work. A lot of the learning came from actually visiting Suzuki's plants in Japan. 'The application of technology was amazing. The level of automation, the quality of products—we had seen nothing like it before. In the 1970s and '80s, India was forty years behind the rest of the world. Perhaps more!' Kalyani says.

The new wave of opportunity and competition made him sit up and take notice. Exposed to the best practices on the shop floor, this period also saw companies like Bharat Forge looking at exports and a market outside India. Two factors forced Kalyani to do this. First, competition, which made him realize how old and outdated Bharat Forge's technology was. He knew he had to look at ways of importing and bringing in modern machinery and not depend on old ordnance factory rejects. Second, the foreign exchange required to shop abroad could come only from exports.

The Rajiv Gandhi government had given a series of sops to exporters, whetting their appetite for new markets, but, sadly, tight money reserves meant that the government asked companies to fend for themselves and earn the 'forex' they needed through exports. With this avenue in hand and hungry to move ahead, Kalyani formulated a watertight plan of using his and his company's experience and tapping opportunities abroad. But his confidence was short-lived and he was in for a shock when he went to make a pitch to his first prospective buyer, one in Europe.

He still shudders at the memory of what followed. 'Bharat Forge was completely unsuccessful in breaking into the European market. The perception of European original equipment manufacturers about Indian manufacturers was quite dismal. Every attempt to break through was met with a thick wall of resistance. Short of throwing us out of the office, they did everything. It was terrible.'

With avenues to the West closed, Kalyani looked towards Eastern Europe, to the erstwhile Soviet Union and the Communist Bloc it had influence over. Bharat Forge was able to get its first export order from auto companies in Poland and erstwhile Czechoslovakia. Everyone was relieved the day they got their first order for crankshafts from one of the Leyland Engine plants in Poland. An order from Russia followed.

Getting out of the insular mindset, which years of control had instilled in companies in India, was a big achievement in itself. 'Back then, when we started exporting, we were still running a company with the old mindset. It was labour intensive and low on technology. Bharat Forge just had a lot of people.' Kalyani realized that this was not the way to gain an entry into the world markets. But before he could act, another problem necessitated quick action. By the late 1980s, the Soviet Union was hurtling towards a financial collapse, following the crippling effects of a long war in Afghanistan. In the years before the collapse of the Soviet Union, orders to Indian companies like Bharat Forge stopped. This could hinder Kalyani's plans and choke Bharat Forge, both in terms of money and technology. So he decided to strengthen himself even if it meant betting his last buck on it.

THE BUILD-UP

The high-tech forging plants at Bharat Forge today are a far cry from the dark, dimly lit shed from where the company rolled out the first forged metal part in 1966. The new plants are airy, sunny, spread-out and busy, with very few people inside. Robots, straight out of a science-fiction film, man the presses and computer-generated diagrams define just how much pressure at what angle needs to be applied to forge raw metal into an ancillary with the right density and specifications. It is a testimony to the company's success that in a business where you have to compete in markets where precision is measured in .001 mm, Bharat Forge is as good as the best. A lot has gone into this transformation. There was a time when Kalyani was at a crossroads and had to choose between concentrating on India without expanding and spreading his wings into new markets even if it meant transforming the way his company and factory worked.

Kalyani chose to follow his heart. 'We realized that we had to strengthen our core. Tough action was needed. We had to improve. Be the best in the world!' Decision taken, there was no time to lose. 'We got down to work and launched a massive reorganization and refocussing exercise. We dubbed it the "Modernization Programme" internally.' At the heart of this plan was his belief that knowledge and high-end innovation were the keys for the transformation he had in mind. Already exposed to the best at MIT and at the plants he had visited, Kalyani could easily lay out a strategy that would inject the much-needed dose of adrenaline across the shop floor. 'If you create excitement and provide leadership, people will run with the challenges you throw at them.'

Baba N. Kalyani; he believes that quality is always the result of high intentions, sincere effort, intelligent direction and skilful execution

But to succeed, the plan needed more than just vision and passion. 'The first step in the programme was to create a forge modernization division. We got together a bunch of young, aggressive and ambitious engineers who were asked to draw up a plan to change the shop floor with the latest cutting-edge technology. We didn't want a linear growth in technology; marginal improvements weren't going to be enough. We wanted to leap into the highest league and be as good, if not better, than the best in the world.'

The forge modernization exercise was big and costly and the reason it worked was the young engineers. 'I didn't want any old guys. We started putting new ideas in place and that's how we came up with our first forge plant, fully automated with robotics and high-tech machines. At that time, no one had even heard of robotics and we had to develop all the processes necessary to run this fully automated facility,' he says. In 1989, at the height of the export crisis, Kalyani and his team shocked everyone, not just within the plant but also across the automotive industry and the financial community, by coming out with details of a business upgradation plan which would cost a whopping Rs 150 crore. This sum was much larger than the entire sales figure of Bharat Forge at that time.

'After a lot of arguments and counter-arguments, the bankers agreed. We had to make numerous presentations to them. The financial community was quick to write me off. They said, "Baba Kalyani is creating a white elephant which will take the company down"!' He agrees that there may have been some justification for the scepticism. 'We were taking quite a major leap in technology, and no one really believed we could do it on our own. Everyone thought one would have to tie up with someone for any venture to be a success. There was little faith in our own capabilities.'

'Having a young, confident and ambitious team of freshers not dulled by cynicism and self-doubt was the biggest help.' No wonder then that more than two decades after being formed, the modernization department remains the core of the company. The technology and innovation leap was just one part of the plan. Kalyani knew he would have to change the entire character of the workforce at Bharat Forge.

But there was one serious problem. Like most manufacturing units of the time, Bharat Forge depended on a large number of unskilled labour to run the shop. For example, at the time Kalyani was looking at changing the dynamics of the company, in 1989, 2,000 labourers comprised 85 per cent of the company's workforce. With the new high-tech machines and revamp at the plant, over the next few years he would have to focus on reversing this ratio, ensuring that the bulk of the workforce was highly trained engineers. 'If we had to take the high-technology route, we would have to change the balance on the shop floor from muscle to brain power.'

So, over the next few years, the company 'retooled' the entire organization through a combination of VRS packages for nearly 1,800 workers and a freeze on hiring. Also, consciously, the company upped the hiring of young engineering graduates who could run the new machines being ordered.

Kalyani had to take some tough decisions and this resulted in friction, essentially between his father and him, about the road to be followed. But in hindsight, it seems that the two-pronged strategy—to go up the technology chain and ensure that the company had the bench strength or the engineers to do so—worked.

By 1990, Bharat Forge's brand new plant was up and running.

Interestingly, alongside this plant-building exercise, another plan was assiduously being worked upon—getting into the US market for exports.

Probably because of his earlier experience in Europe and the fact that US automobile companies or original equipment companies (OEMs) were the first to start global outsourcing (Europe, the Mecca of automobiles, began outsourcing only seven or eight years later), Kalyani turned his attention to North America. For two years, 1989 to '91, Kalyani and his team embarked on a massive roadshow across the US, zeroing in on a single product, front axles for trucks. 'We used to make this product for the domestic truck companies. We knew the product well and, of course, had added the most modern technology to it, so we were confident.'

The first breakthrough came after months when US conglomerate Rockwell International, a company that makes everything from aircraft to auto parts, came to the market to find a supplier for its automobile parts. When he came across Rockwell's global tender, Kalyani told them that Bharat Forge had the best forging facility. Kalyani's confidence probably stemmed from the fact that Bharat Forge had a successful, albeit very small, joint venture with Rockwell to make front axles in Mysore. But Kalyani clarified that they had never sold forgings to the company. What finally swung the deal for him was having a team of Rockwell's engineers visit the new facilities that he had built to check out the lofty claims this engineer from India was making.

Bharat Forge hit two birds with one stone. He says, 'They gave us an order for the front axle beam and they were so happy with what we did that they gave us a large part of their business. That was our big breakthrough and it was a crucial one, given that the company was investing such a lot in changing its entire production paradigm. We never looked back after this. We just grew and grew and grew. Today, Bharat Forge is still a leading player in the US for the products it began exporting then.'

Even as Kalyani was wooing prospective partners and engineering the changes in his plant, a year before the Rockwell deal, the business landscape in India had changed forever.

In 1989–90, he probably hadn't realized just how much was at stake because barely a year later, a balance of payments crisis would force the government to open up the economy. 'The good thing is, we did all this in 1990, not knowing that the economy would open up and get liberalized. That came as a shock and a surprise.' With a brand new facility and a big order from the US, Kalyani was ready to march ahead. The timing of Bharat Forge's modernization exercise couldn't have been better.

The rules of the game changed for manufacturers like Bharat Forge. More and more competitors started coming to India to set up shop. 'We were lucky to drive the kind of technology innovations that we did ourselves and at the time we did it. If we hadn't, the company would have gone down.' He adds, 'Look at where it has taken the company. In business there is no reward without risk.'

ANOTHER CRISIS, ANOTHER OPPORTUNITY

In 2006, Baba Kalyani shocked everyone by saying that he was going to broad-base the company he had built, beyond the automobile components' segment in which it had become a world leader. Bharat Forge had spent a decade coming out of the worst kind of crisis possible.

It may have been two decades since the opening up of the Indian economy, but for the major part of it, Indian companies did not seem to know how to cope with what hit them, with the opportunities the new India offered. If the first flush of liberalization brought with it a wide array of global companies that felt they could swoop in and capture a chunk of the new market, it also had technology-starved Indian companies going ahead and forming collaborations with global partners. But sadly, for both sides, the best-laid plans came to naught. Foreign multinationals, more often than not, got the Indian market wrong and those who stayed on and flourished learnt it the hard way.

From the Indian companies' perspective too, there was a fair bit of bleed. The crux of the problem was that everyone had overestimated the size and potential of the Indian market when the process of liberalization started in 1991. No one probably understood that it would take time for wealth to be created, old mindsets to change and aspirations to create the strong domestic demand that would transform India into one of the fastest-growing economies in the world.

The first lot to drive straight into a problem in the mid-1990s was the Indian automobile segment. The slowdown it faced was so protracted that it didn't come out of it till 2001. 'After liberalization, everyone was so gung-ho about the market opening up that they were just pushing more and more products into the market without realizing that it didn't have the buying power to take all this.' Companies, in the first rush of excitement, made the classical and cardinal mistake of not understanding their market or what it needed.

The automobile crisis had a devastating impact across the many ancillary companies that were supplying to it. Things were worse for Bharat Forge because it had spent a lot of money expanding capacity and 85 per cent of its business came from these Indian companies. The company had declared a sharp fall in profits in 1996. Kalyani recounts, 'The crisis hurt us a lot. We had built up capacities, spent a whole lot of money, and India was still our biggest market.' After 1989, and the big transformation that was engineered within Bharat Forge, 1996 was the next big inflection point for the company. Once again, it was back to survival mode.

More than two-thirds of the business came from the domestic market. During the crisis, sales halved and the company had to cut down plant operations to just three days a week. After spending all that money to modernize and upgrade, Bharat Forge was forced to start a massive cost-cutting exercise. Kalyani had to work out a new strategy of finding an alternative market and hedge against the ebbs and tides of the Indian marketplace. The first thing the problem reiterated for him was the need to look at new markets. There was no point waiting for the recovery in India and the crumbs that would be thrown his company's way. He decided that he would rather re-focus on taking his company to the next level as he had done the last time. 'The first thing we decided to do was increase our exports to 40 per cent of our sales.' This was an ambitious target for a company that had just two overseas clients. Moreover, the company would have to go far beyond North America, into the heart of Europe, which was seen as a bastion of technology and the toughest market to penetrate.

Business came in slow, from big engine makers like Cummins and Lister Petter in Europe. But Kalyani was clear he wanted more than just small orders. 'Somewhere we realized that there was not one reason why we couldn't work towards getting a leadership position on the international stage. Also, why not be among the top three or four in the forging business worldwide?'

This might have been construed as far-fetched at that time. After all, Bharat Forge was still a small company, barely worth $100m. The market leader, German multinational ThyssenKrupp, which also had forging as part of its portfolio, was fifteen times its size. The market leader set the benchmark for Kalyani and, as the company crystallized its goal, it also realized the easiest way to access big global markets was to have a local presence there. As Kalyani puts it, 'Our strategy was simple. To be in the reckoning in the global market, we would have to have a footprint there, and the advantage was that we could access the market faster, especially local clients, since they would have some level of trust. It not only improves the relationship between an international client and supplier, it adds a lot of depth to it.'

Another factor that added to the need for an acquisition was that Bharat Forge had limitations in expanding in Pune and it wanted a far more foolproof array of markets that could steer it out of the periodic cyclical downturns the auto industry seemed to be getting in and out of. With all this in mind, in January 2002, Bharat Forge bought its first company in the UK. It so happened that one of its many US customers, an Ohio-based Fortune 500 company, the $14bn automotive parts major Dana Corporation, had a forging plant in Kirkstall, a suburb of Leeds, which it wanted to shut down. 'It was a very small plant with sales of just £10m to 12m and continuing with the operations was making no sense to them,' Kalyani says.

But, for Bharat Forge, it was an obvious fit. The company was supplying to many of the big automobile companies in the region like Daimler and Volvo, apart from clients in Europe and the US.

So Kalyani went out and pitched a structured deal that would be a complete winner for Bharat Forge. 'We said we'll buy out the business and you have to give us a seven-year contract for supplying components to all your clients. This single deal of less than £3m (about Rs 21 crore then) got us guaranteed business of Rs 70 crore of exports every year and ten more customers in Europe.'

The deal made Kalyani realize the power of an acquisition and how it could help a company leapfrog ahead. 'This small company had allowed us to do, in a matter of months, what it would have taken us six years to achieve!' The acquisition and its success whetted Kalyani's appetite for more. There was also growing pressure from his big European customers to put more on the table and have a larger presence in Europe. 'They were telling us, you can't have it one way. If you want more orders and a longer relationship, you will have to invest money in Europe.' An acquisition was the best way out, because building a new plant or factory in Europe would have been difficult, in fact, next to impossible. The first acquisition and the easy success Kalyani made of it also infused in him the confidence to run companies in Europe. The big breakthrough came with the acquisition of a sizeable German forging company, Carl Dan Peddinghaus, which was filing for bankruptcy. The company was a high-end, niche supplier of high-technology-driven forgings to the best auto companies in Europe. 'A company with a great history and even better set of clients,' Kalyani remarks.

It was supplying to some of the largest German automobile companies, but, like many companies run by pure technocrats, it had run into trouble and filed for bankruptcy. The problem was a classic one. 'Technologists sometimes get so carried away with a new fad, a new R&D breakthrough that they have been pushing, they quite literally bet their last buck on it, jeopardizing the entire business. As it often happens, they don't keep an eye on the balance sheet.'

Bankruptcy rules are stringent in Germany and are triggered by a single payment default. CDP had been handed over to a local court-appointed administrator who was put in charge of ensuring that the company was sold to the right party. The moment Kalyani heard about CDP, he was sure that this acquisition would be the best bet for Bharat Forge's global plans. So, in 2002, he decided to bid for the company. 'We made a detailed presentation and our approach was that we wanted to make the business profitable and grow it. We weren't looking at layoffs and production cuts that the other bidders had come with.' In fact, far from it. Not only did he put a 29m Euro bid on the table for the company, he also presented a detailed restructuring plan. The administrator and the management were impressed by the passion with which Kalyani made his case. In Germany, if a company has to be taken over, the unions, employees, managements, bankers and customers have to agree. In this case, the bankers were the easiest. They bought into the plan the moment they realized that they wouldn't have to take the hit. The management, too, was easy, because it connected with the big plans Kalyani had laid out. The real clincher was the company's biggest client, Daimler Chrysler, buying into the plan. But there was another hurdle Kalyani would have to cross to make CDP a success.

He still remembers the tension in the air that cold winter morning as he addressed the workers, despite being advised that it would be a foolhardy thing to do. There were about two hundred of them on the shop floor and they didn't seem too accommodating. But Kalyani walked in and addressed their concerns with the help of an interpreter. As he started explaining his plan, he began to see the first signs of a thaw. 'Within minutes, I realized I had touched a chord. That I had gone there in person and they were actually able to put a face to who was going to do the takeover clinched the deal for us.' Tough questions were asked. 'Almost 40 per cent of the workers thought I was there to take away their jobs and technology.' It didn't help at all that Kalyani's bid to acquire the company had created a lot of attention in the local media, none of it flattering. But, as he fielded each question and the workers realized that their jobs were secure, they too came around.

In six months, Kalyani turned the company around. This was done not by laying off workers but by actually pumping cash and new technology into the firm. 'In the first two or three months, we pumped in a couple of million dollars for capital expenditure to get new production facilities in place because there was a lot of demand. This convinced even the sceptics who had been worried about the takeover and the big moment came soon after. When CDP turned around and made a cash profit, every big OEM sat up and took notice of us.' Kalyani lets slip an interesting fact. 'I was naïve those days. I used to do all these takeover negotiations myself, we didn't have any investment bankers advising us.' But that didn't make too much of a difference, if CDP's acquisition and subsequent turnaround are anything to go by. It is not surprising then that Kalyani has such a reputation amongst the top investment bankers. 'He has a nose for buying cheap and driving a hard bargain,' they say.

The CDP success proved to be a turning point in Kalyani's fortunes in Europe. It gave Bharat Forge the scale and client base it needed, expertise in the passenger-car segment, which was CDP's forte (over 60 per cent of Bharat Forge's revenues came from commercial vehicles then) and modern technology. It went on to become the world's second-largest forging company over the next four years.

On a broader level, the success wiped out any apprehension anyone might have had about an audacious Indian company looking at acquisitions of high-technology firms. In three years, Bharat Forge bought five companies—in Sweden, Scotland, the US, and even a stake in a Chinese firm, FAW, in Changchun. Each of these acquisitions provided access to new markets and clients, the last adding an important dimension to Kalyani's plans of getting a toehold in the world's fastest-growing market.

But buying is just one part of it. Analysts who have watched the company for years say Kalyani's greatest success has been that he has quickly amalgamated the new companies he bought and used each one of them to consolidate his position in the market. The strategy was simple: get closer to the key clients through these acquisitions and then combine the high-technology expertise of the acquired companies with cost efficiencies of the core operations in India.

Over time, this has proved a lethal combination and Bharat Forge can now service almost every part of the globe through its various arms, in the shortest time. But scale and spread also require nimbleness and Kalyani's success comes from a simple mantra he follows. He even has a term for it, 'Commonsense Manufacturing', which is essentially focussed, organized work and quick decision making.

Kalyani's biggest trump card was the speed of decision making. He thinks people take a lot of time to arrive at any decision. If one knows one's business well, the decisions should be quick. In a few years, Bharat Forge became the largest forging manufacturer in Europe. Before the global downturn of 2008, Bharat Forge and its companies in Europe were doing 400m Euros sales out of Europe. Those were heady days and, for Kalyani, they must have been more than gratifying. He narrates a small incident that underlines his journey. 'We have a little factory in a small village near Frankfurt. Once, when we sent some of our young engineers to train there, they met an Indian who had been living there for thirty years. The old man saw them and began weeping. He said, "I have never felt so proud in my life, to see the Indian flag flying here."'

By 2007, 75 per cent of the company's business came from overseas. But it is perhaps the same quality of astuteness that Kalyani showed way back in 1989 that made him look at his business very closely, and take an important decision: to reduce his dependence on the automotive business he knew so well and diversify further afield by 2012.

It has been providence, perhaps, because Kalyani had no clue then that after the years of heady growth, he and his company were going straight into another problem that would see them incur a loss, the first one since he walked into Bharat Forge in 1972.

LOOKING BEYOND

The US subprime crisis in 2007–08, which dovetailed into a global slowdown, hit Bharat Forge's key markets across the US and Europe, from where the company was deriving 75 per cent of its total revenue of $1.2bn by now. This triggered a protracted crisis, with the company making a loss for the first time since Kalyani took over. It had to rationalize its subsidiaries and look at shutting down some, including those in Scotland and the US. But Kalyani had a plan this time too, one that had been worked out much in advance, in 2006.

He probably had a premonition of sorts, which made him look beyond the automobile industry that Bharat Forge knew so well. The idea was to broaden his base. Kalyani says the decision made a lot of sense. 'By 2005, after we had completed all our acquisitions outside, we had a fairly stable position in terms of market share and products in the automotive industry. It was also clear that even though we would keep increasing our market share here, it wasn't as though we could ever have 100 per cent of the market in the automotive space. Growth seemed capped somewhere, because Bharat Forge had already supplied products to the biggest automobile companies across the world, and though emerging markets like India and China had started seeing the big consumption and market push, in the developed world, growth was stagnating.'

The new high-speed and higher-precision, computer-generated manufacturing technology, which was driving all the work Bharat Forge did, allowed the company to look at much larger forging products in the non-automotive space. The best bet was to create growth in new areas. 'Look at the big

Japanese players like Mitsubishi. All of them started small and expanded into new areas of growth on a much larger scale, and that's how they made a mark in the global sphere.'

It is obvious that these companies had scaled up because of innovation and diversification and Kalyani had the technical capabilities for both. 'The idea was to look at the opportunity which the company's strengths provided. After years of work in the forging space, the company understood the metal production cycle and we decided we would focus on engineering skills and not commodity-type production.' So, in 2005, Kalyani, well before time once again, put out another two-pronged strategy for the company—first, diversify, and second, look at the emerging markets. The first step was to identify the new areas. 'We decided to move into manufacturing of larger components. After our experience in automotives, we took three or four verticals. Energy was the core because this was an area of huge potential in the Indian market and we decided to go with thermal, nuclear, as well as renewable energy.'

With this in mind, in 2007, the company started building a large components manufacturing base and a new facility for large manufacturing in Baramati, close to Pune. This was followed by a series of strategic partnerships. First, with French equipment manufacturer, Alstom, then a venture with the public sector National Thermal Power Corporation (NTPC).

The vision was clear for Bharat Forge: to capture one of the fastest-growing segments in the Indian market—power. But just as Kalyani was laying out these ambitious plans, the Americans pulled the rug from under all of them. The sudden turn of tide had a devastating impact on the order books of OEMs around the world. Sales dropped 40 to 70 per cent in just a year. Car sales in the US plunged as the Detroit giants—General Motors, Ford and Chrysler—hit a wall and the global slowdown expanded. Although the signs had been clear, no one had noticed because of the heady growth they were witnessing. But when things came crumbling down, everyone was hit across industries (in manufacturing) and geographies. Bharat Forge's expansion and diversification drive, which had just about started before the crisis, couldn't have come at a worse time.

The facilities in Scotland had to be shut down and a major restructuring drive had to be initiated. Rapid growth in India and a quick recovery in the automobile sector in the US meant that the company could come out of the bump pretty fast, but the crisis had served its purpose. Though the diversification drive had seemed ill thought out at the height of the problem, it began to make sense now.

Bharat Forge had been a company looking only at growth. It had never considered the flip side but suddenly, in 2009, it posted an 80 per cent fall in profits.

Today, the company has big plans outside the automotive sector, particularly in power, which is the single largest bet the company is making. With its new plants and joint ventures, Bharat Forge is now capable of supplying all the equipment required to run a power plant.

There aren't many companies in India, save big ones like BHEL and Larsen & Toubro (L&T), which can actually do this. So, in a bid to capture this space, Kalyani has gone beyond his company's traditional work of forgings and machinery and set up an entire engineering, procurement and construction (EPC) unit because he believes his clients are looking not just at equipment suppliers but also people who can set it in place. Apart from axles and crankshafts, Bharat Forge will soon start rolling out turbines and generators and, in time, boilers. The diversification drive at Bharat Forge seemed timely, but it hasn't been easy. The past two years have seen a major setback and the power sector, at the heart of Kalyani's big plans, has borne the brunt of it.

There is undoubtedly a dire need for the build-up of this sector in India (one-third of the country still doesn't have access to power) and investments here are going to be massive. Estimates are that over the next few years, India will see investments of over $500bn in the power sector.

At the same time, thousands of crores of rupees of investments have been stuck and most power companies are trying not to go under. Nuclear power has been a non-starter. Under the circumstances, one wonders who will invest in buying Bharat Forge's ready-to-be-shipped equipment. But the company is still getting parts of the business right. A growing 27 per cent of its revenues come from the non-automotive side. Despite the setbacks, which Kalyani calls momentary, he believes this was the only option for the company he has so painstakingly built. The 'core' of the diversifications is that he and his engineers know the basics so well. From a small hammer shop, Bharat Forge has moved quickly to becoming a specialist, a state-of-the-art manufacturer, a complete solutions provider, a company that can use the same manufacturing capabilities and technologies to diversify into a slew of new areas like energy, transportation and even defence manufacturing.

Despite the obvious sense this diversification makes, some sceptics say that Kalyani is attempting the impossible. He may have made a mark in the auto space, but that was largely because it was based outside India and so not bound down by the politicking and delays so common here. There are others who say that the new ventures have several complexities, and Kalyani has bitten off far more than he and Bharat Forge can chew.

In response, he says, 'How can you not bet on the India infrastructure story? More importantly, who knows the forging space as well as we do?' While some of Kalyani's ventures—nuclear power is a case in point—have been delayed, the numbers reiterate the soundness of his strategy.

Kalyani has already achieved the ambitious and seemingly impossible target that he had set in 2006: in six years, 40 per cent of the company's profits were to come from the non-automotive side of the business. But even this hasn't silenced critics as they watch Kalyani's newest and perhaps most aggressive and risky bet play out. The next big challenge will be in 2015, when the company is hoping that the bulk of its business will come from the non-automotive side, even as the core grows rapidly. Managing the hurdles and living up to his reputation are not the only challenges in his life now.

DOING IT THE KALYANI WAY

Baba Kalyani's success has come from his focus and the many firsts to his credit. He was one of the first to go down the innovation and high-technology path in Indian manufacturing and compete in the most evolved marketplaces in the world. At the core of his success has been his immense confidence in himself, his clarity of vision, and the nimbleness with which he has reoriented strategies to meet the challenges of the times.

What also makes him stand out by a mile from many others

has been his decision to go for the most modern manufacturing. When most Indian companies were trying to ward off global competitors during the first flush of liberalization in 1991, he had already decided to plunge into the global marketplace. A decade later, when the Indian automotive sector was recovering from a protracted slump, Kalyani was aggressively acquiring companies and, with it, high-technology and blue-chip clients.

The difficult years following 2008 have seen him take a new bet on India and its infrastructure. Kalyani and his company have been able to navigate so effortlessly through complex and volatile markets because he knows his business and keeps himself updated on any information out there. Information helps him to chalk out a clear strategy, be it the need to acquire or diversify, and this, in turn, makes decision making quick. The other thing he has always made clear is that he would rather harness the intelligence of a handful of educated and skilled employees and engineers than the brawn of thousands of unskilled workers.

While Kalyani's son, Amit, is being groomed to take over the company, the HR head of Bharat Forge emphasizes how Kalyani has driven change in mindset by insisting that everyone in the team constantly upgrades skills and keeps pace with the needs of a rapidly growing company and group. This is not just a nice HR tool to keep the employees engaged; it is essential for Bharat Forge's survival. And it is at the core of its success. Over the years, at every meeting with Kalyani, he has always lamented the paucity of young skilled engineers, a view mirrored across corporate India. But in a bid to keep the best talent loyal and ensure there is access to a skilled workforce, he has developed a strategy that is smart and should be replicated. Here is how it works:

Bharat Forge has tied up with a few polytechnics—the Industrial Training Institutes (ITI)—to train school dropouts in basic skills so that they can work on the company's shop floors. The company has also collaborated with engineering colleges and schools in rural Maharashtra to rework academic programmes to make them more practical. Young students are hired from these vernacular colleges in the third year to develop a talent pool.

For the hundreds of science graduates it employs for regular work, the company has devised a programme in collaboration with BITS Pilani, the engineering college where Kalyani studied. It is structured in such a way that many of these graduates get access to the BITS faculty and on-the-shop-floor experience in the company itself. Engineering classes are held here every weekend and in the last seven years, over 1,500 students have availed of this facility; nearly all of them have rapidly moved up the corporate ladder. At a more advanced level, there is a tie-up with IIT Powai in Mumbai for high-end PhD and research work. Apart from entry-level workers, mid-management-level staff are also being trained in specialized courses, like an MSc in manufacturing management, in collaboration with Warwick University, UK. A structured course in manufacturing is also in the pipeline and the company is in talks with a German university.

This multi-pronged attempt to develop the workforce as manufacturing facilities get more high-tech has not just helped the company get access to talent but has also helped it retain good-quality workers. Also, the multiple manufacturing facilities across Europe and even China help give managers the international exposure they need. In a bid to ensure quality, the company has standardized all its research and development facilities and clearly laid out its processes.

THE ROAD AHEAD

Almost every big company from Bosch to Mitsubishi started like Bharat Forge did, as small firms nibbling one small end of the manufacturing pie. Today, they have scale and size and conduct business seamlessly across segments the world over.

The one company Kalyani truly admires is Bosch, the technology conglomerate, which is one of the biggest players in the automotive space. 'Bosch has an amazing ability to look into the future, is extremely technology oriented, and this gives it immense power, which it can channelize in any direction it wants. It is also quick to go after opportunity when it sees it.' And it is even more commendable because of its size. It has twenty subsidiaries, a global footprint and over 100,000 employees worldwide.

'About two to three years ago, Bosch decided that renewable energy was going to be a big thing. While everyone was talking about it, Bosch focussed specifically on solar energy. After this, it turned to the hybrid vehicles space. It created a new division out of nothing and I am sure it will be the biggest player in this business too. Bosch, of course, had the money to do this,' he adds, as an afterthought. Interestingly, Kalyani is on the global advisory board of the company he so admires.

Kalyani is eyeing big things. Today he wants to replicate in other areas what he had done in the automotive space because he believes he has the right skills and technology. After what he has achieved, it's hard not to believe the man or be swept away by the spectacular journey he has scripted. A journey that is not just about business and a company but the vision of the man at the helm.

A little framed quote hanging on one of the walls at the Bharat Forge R&D centre in Mundhwa says: 'Quality is never an accident. It's always the result of high intentions, sincere effort, intelligent direction and skilful execution. It represents a wise choice from many alternatives.' This would have definitely come straight from the chairman's desk. It has the practical, sincere and measured quality of the man who has driven Bharat Forge out of Pune, on to the global expressway.

AJAY PIRAMAL

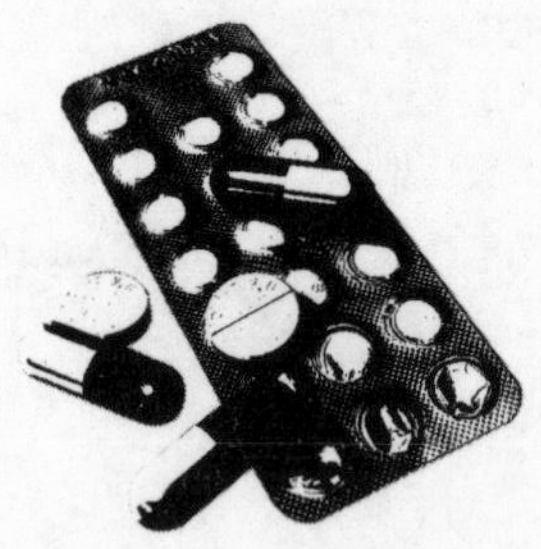

It is a windy morning in June as Ajay Piramal waits to meet the chairman of one of the world's biggest pharmaceutical companies, Illinois-based Abbott. The venue: the Four Seasons Hotel in Chicago.

A lot has gone into scheduling this breakfast meeting and Ajay is more than a little curious, maybe even nervous. He is keen to meet the former McKinsey consultant, Miles D. White, one of the longest-serving and most successful CEOs in the global pharmaceuticals industry. Miles has brought an aggressive, almost feverish urgency to Abbott with a string of acquisitions and a new focus on research that have been the talk of company boardrooms across the world. By now, in 2009, a lot of this aggression has begun to pay off.

Ajay's company, Nicholas Piramal, was a well-known name in India but a very small player in the global landscape. Lately, the big pharma companies had become even bigger. There had been unimaginable alliances and buyouts across the sector. Pfizer had bought the New Jersey-headquartered Wyeth for $68bn, and another New Jersey-based company, Merck, had bought Schering Plough for $41bn.

Ajay knew how insignificant he, his company and the entire Indian pharmaceutical industry seemed amid these giants. The sales of the ten big global pharma companies ran into over $300bn. The entire industry in India was not even one-tenth of that. But he hadn't done badly either.

Who would have thought that someone who grew up around the old, broke, creaking textile mills of Mumbai would be waiting to talk business and discuss the new frontiers of medical research with an old hand like Miles White?

Ajay had worked hard, learning the ropes of the pharmaceutical business. He had known little about it when he started out two decades ago. Then his only connection with it had been his wife, Swati, who is a doctor. She helped him understand pharmaceuticals, what went into medicines, their marketing and manufacturing, and how new drugs were discovered. He hadn't done badly for himself and had indeed managed to create a good portfolio over the years.

Who knew, by the end of the day, he would be able to convince the Abbott chief to send more customized medicine manufacturing work to Nicholas Piramal. This outsourcing of manufacturing by MNCs to companies like his, since it was cheaper, had helped his team keep abreast of the latest, most high-end work that the world's best brains were doing. This was crucial given that the Indian economy had been so closed for so long.

Custom manufacturing was steady and growing within Nicholas Piramal, and Abbott had been an old partner. The chairman of the world's eighth-largest pharmaceutical company had gone out of his way to schedule the meeting. One that would at first throw Ajay completely off-track and then, over the year, set the stage for the biggest, most transformational deal of his career, catapulting him into the league of India's richest fifty and one of the most closely watched and talked-about men in Indian business.

After a year of relentless meetings and discussions, on 21 May 2010, Abbott announced that it was buying one part of Nicholas Piramal's business, the domestic formulations arm, for \$3.72bn (Rs 17,000 crore) in two tranches—a \$2.12bn upfront payment followed by an annual payout of \$400m till 2015.

This wasn't the first time that the promoters of an Indian pharmaceutical company had sold out. In 2008, the Ranbaxy owners, brothers Malvinder and Shivinder Singh, had sold their stake in the company to Japanese firm Daiichi Sankyo. But what made everyone sit up and take notice was the price the sale got. As a pharmaceutical sector analyst from a global consultancy put it: 'If there is one thing I would want to know from Ajay, it is how he swung the deal. What did he say to Miles White that made him pay more than Rs 17,000 crore for a business that barely got revenues of Rs 1,800 crore?'

It was the mother of all deals. He had managed to sell part of his business for more value than what the Ranbaxy brothers had got for their entire share. But had he really wanted to sell off something he had built so painstakingly, piece by piece, over the years? As things panned out, experts said a sale to a global giant was what he had been planning all along. He might deny it but, looking back, it was undeniable that there was always a method in the way he built his pharmaceutical business, all the way from the time he bid for Nicholas, in 1988, to 2010, when he sold most of it.

But even before this deal, Ajay's story was a compelling one. He has faced what would seem like insurmountable personal and professional setbacks to chart the road to success and he had done all this with an acumen and vision that would stand him in good stead in future. With Ajay, one is never sure if he has played his final hand or if there is more to come.

THE FIRST WEAVE

At over six feet, two inches and close to 100 kilos, Ajay is a big man. Looking at him, few would believe that he was once a deft polo player who, as he says, 'made up in strength what he lost out in flexibility'. Ajay had a near-fatal fall when he was fourteen but love for the sport egged him on to get back in the saddle very soon after the accident. He suffered a concussion that made him lose his memory for one whole day. 'Everyone thought I wouldn't make it. But I did, and I was back in the saddle within days.'

The Mumbai of Ajay's childhood, in the 1960s, was a different city. Worli in central Mumbai, where the Piramals still live, was the centre of their lives. Close by, in Parel, were the textile mills the family owned. To the south were the stables at the Mahalaxmi Racecourse, where Ajay spent his evenings.

The textile mills, surrounded by the one-room tenements (chawls) where the workers lived, defined the city's character. Central Mumbai teemed with thousands of blue-collar workers who had come from the villages of Vidarbha and Marathwada in Maharashtra, UP and Bihar and made the city their home. And while they worked hard at the power looms, working shifts in the mills, they kept up their noisy clatter through the night.

Like all the big and powerful textile families of the period, the Piramal story also started from the cotton trade. Ajay's grandfather, Seth Piramal Chaturbhuj, was a cotton trader working in the famous wholesale markets and cotton exchanges of Mumbai in pre-Independence India. His own origins were humble. In 1934, unable to afford a camel ride, he walked all the way from his village in Bagar, Rajasthan, where the family's traditional-style house is now a small boutique hotel, to Mumbai.

Very soon, he became a successful trader dealing in a cross section of commodities, including cotton. In the 1920s, he bought one of Mumbai's oldest textile mills, Morarjee Goculdas Spinning and Weaving Mills, set up by Narottam Morarjee, who had, interestingly, also joined hands with Seth Walchand Hirachand to finance and start the Scindia Steam Navigation Company. The mill was established as early as 1871 and was one of the first five companies to be listed on the Indian stock exchange.

Ajay's childhood revolved around the mill and the people in it and some of his earliest memories are of pottering around the noisy and dimly lit mill floors among the workers. 'Mills then looked nothing like the organized assembly lines of later years. They were crowded, chaotic and noisy places one could get lost in.' But Ajay and his brothers knew the mills well, given the time they spent on the factory floor, amid the maze of teeming workers, inhaling the cotton fluff which often triggered off a bad cough.

'There used to be hordes of migrant labourers in the mills and I remember we would celebrate Dussehra with them. It was a big thing, and all of us used to be at the mill.' If he hasn't forgotten these celebrations with the workers, there was another meeting that he remembers vividly. 'All the bonhomie would disappear when my father and the millworkers' representatives would sit across the table for heated discussions over salaries and annual bonuses each year. Sometimes the discussions would get vicious. It was like living in this tinderbox of sorts.' The mills and their workers were a fertile ground for powerful labour unions backed by political parties and labour-management relations were often tense.

What Ajay grew to appreciate later was how his father Gopikisan Piramal managed these tense situations and how he ensured that his sons learnt some important lessons of life by being present during the negotiations.

Gopikisan led the discussions himself. 'He was always calm and quiet amid the shouting, humble and soft spoken. I don't remember him ever losing his temper. Later, when the storm had passed, he would tell us, "Always keep things simple. Nothing is complicated." What stood out was that he connected to the workers directly at all times, always laying the facts on the table.'

This was just one of the many business lessons Gopikisan imparted to Ajay. What Ajay and his brothers, Ashok and Dilip, didn't realize then was that their father, through all those years, seemed to have been in a hurry to carve out a future for each of his sons.

'It was almost as though he had a premonition that he wouldn't live long.' And it was probably this that made Ajay's father do three things that would help the Piramal brothers in the years to come. First, he ensured that he diversified the family business beyond textiles. It had become clear to him that a combination of high labour costs and crippling taxes would make the textile mills loss-making units by the time the boys were grown up and it was important to diversify.

Second, he made some significant acquisitions. All through the 1970s, Gopikisan did his own version of an acquisition drive, picking up a host of companies—from luggage-maker VIP to Kemps Pharma, after which Mumbai's Kemps Corner is named (this was actually the Piramal family's entry into the pharmaceutical business). Apart from having a few brands of medicines, Kemps Pharma also ran a chain of pharmacy shops, including the one in Mumbai's Taj Mahal Hotel.

The third thing Gopikisan did was put each of the three Piramal brothers in charge of a company, no matter how young they were. He ensured that each of his sons managed entire businesses on their own, early in life. Ajay had his first go as a managing director straight out of management school, when his father acquired a small company, Miranda Tools, in 1978. The company made cutting tools for engineering firms and the acquisition was made in a style that almost defined the way Gopikisan conducted business.

'At first, I didn't even know why I was sitting in on the negotiations, but it was fascinating to see what my father did. He took one look at the balance sheet and the decision was made. It was as simple as that.' Years later, those who sat across Ajay to thrash out deals with him said almost the same thing about him. 'It doesn't take very long for Ajay Piramal to decide on a deal. He comes completely prepared. He always leads the negotiations and he never touches anything he is not sure of, be it even the smallest detail.' This was precisely why

Gopikisan ensured that Ajay and his brothers sat through every deal he made and every union he negotiated with. He was preparing his sons for the road ahead.

Miranda Tools, which still makes drills and metal-cutting blades for manufacturers, belonged to two at-war brothers who wanted a clear separation of their inheritance. Ajay's father quickly saw that this was the only reason they wanted to sell.

'The fundamentals were strong and business potential decent.' Decision taken, the deal was done within days and Ajay was in for a surprise when his father handed him the charge of the company. 'I don't think my father even visited the company once after he bought it!'

Taking over a company must have been quite an experience for a twenty-three-year-old. Ajay made mistakes along the way. But his business was strong and it helped make him stronger as a manager. 'You should get into a business which is already doing well. A profitable business that helps you build confidence in yourself.'

A TOUGH ROAD AHEAD

Within three years of the patriarch's death, Ajay's house was rocked by a series of events that could have marked the end of the family in business.

The first was a split between the Piramal brothers. By 1979, when his father died, Ashok, the eldest brother, was in charge of Morarjee Goculdas Spinning and Weaving Mills, his brother Dilip had VIP Industries and twenty-four-year-old Ajay was earning his stripes as head of Miranda Tools.

Three years later, the script changed. After a lot of discussion and dialogue, which began in 1981 and went on till early 1982, the brothers decided to split their father's business. Dilip wanted to go it alone, and it was easy, because he was already running the luggage company. He was given VIP and a few other small investments, while Ashok and Ajay pooled their lot to venture out with the rest of the businesses.

The division seemed fair then. It was only natural that in a traditional Marwari family, the biggest business, in this case the textile mill, went to the eldest son. No one insisted otherwise. But the division was the easier part. Within days, everything changed. 'Actually, it was just sixteen days after our settlement, on 18 January 1982, when the entire textile industry in Mumbai, its heart and its lifeblood, came to a standstill.' That was when one of the biggest, longest and most far-reaching labour strikes in modern India's history began. The strike, involving hundreds of thousands of millworkers, was led by the union leader Dr Datta Samant. The strike was never actually called off. The end of Mumbai's textile mills was slow and painful.

As tensions mounted, both sides dug in their heels, the stand-off dragged on, and workers fled or starved. Even after it was all over, the industry never quite managed to get back on its feet. By the end of 1982, most of what Ashok and Ajay had acquired as part of their inheritance had become worthless. 'Simply put, we got the short end of the stick,' Ajay says.

The odds were stacked against them. Samant was one of the most feared names in industrial circles. A socialist trade union leader, he had started off as a doctor, treating injured stone quarry workers who came in from the mines in Ghatkopar to his clinic. Their heart-wrenching stories and the callousness with which the mine owners treated them made Samant take up the cause of worker rights and fair wages. His first big success came in 1972, when he led a strike at Godrej's Vikhroli plant in Mumbai. In the clashes with the police that followed, several workers were killed and Samant went to jail, only to return as more of a hero to workers. Next, he brought Premier Automobiles Limited (PAL) to its knees in what was his finest hour. Once one of the country's biggest automobile companies, PAL never recovered from the strike.

But in 1982, when Samant turned his attention to the textile mills of Mumbai, he made one of the biggest mistakes of his life. At the industry's peak, the central areas of Mumbai were identified with the mills they housed. Spread across Parel, Lower Parel, Prabhadevi, Dadar and Worli were mills whose names had resonated across the country for decades—Elphinstone, Century, Mafatlal and Morarjee, to name a few. Samant didn't quite realize what he was getting into—a prolonged textile strike that would hurt the mill workers as much as it would the owners. As weeks turned into months, and then a year and more, the tired mill owners lost their capacity to meet the demands and the workers their ability to wait it out.

Many historians who studied this strike were critical of Samant. 'Samant's biggest failing was that he was most often unreasonable, with little concern for the finances of the companies he was trying to arm twist. The result: the already under-stress companies could never recover after giving in to his demand of higher wages for their employees and would slide into oblivion with an even more crippling impact on the workers.' But that was when the companies didn't fight back. What Samant didn't realize was that in the case of the textile strike, the mill owners would simply dig their heels in because they didn't have an option.

Within months of the strike, it became clear that Samant had failed because he had misjudged the reality of the textile industry. Carried away by the outward opulence and power the mill owners enjoyed, his big mistake was that he saw their refusal to come to an agreement over wages as posturing and not a necessity. What he didn't realize was the deep decay within.

As Dutch economist H. Van Wersch, who spent a year researching the strike—even living in the chawls where the workers lived—pointed out in his doctoral dissertation to the University of Amsterdam in 1989:

> The textile industry [in Mumbai] with its 200,000 workers was in deep decay. Around 25–40 per cent of its machinery was more than forty years old. With such equipment it was no wonder that value addition per worker was just 15 per cent of what other industries in Mumbai could achieve.

As the fight became extended, the study points out, nearly half the workers were forced to return to their villages. With Samant's support almost gone, the strike just fizzled out.

'Even at the height of their success, the fortunes of the textile mills were volatile. The margins were always thin because labour costs were high and policies didn't favour the industry. It didn't help that the old textile families had built a reputation for themselves. Over the years, they had invested very little in developing or updating the mills,' Ajay says. Instead, they spent even the little money they made on their lavish lifestyles.

Since the business was not doing well at all, it was impossible for the mill owners to concede to the demands of Samant and his unions. The strike was the last straw that led to the collapse of an entire industry.

A PROBLEM AT HOME

Through 1982–84, while Morarjee mills was facing the heat, Ajay had begun to face another problem, one that was far more crippling for the Piramal family.

At the height of the mill strike and face-off, Ashok, the head of the joint family and business, was diagnosed with cancer. Ajay's wife and business partner, Dr Swati Piramal, says, 'It was as though everything was going wrong. Ashok's cancer was spreading rapidly; at work, losses were mounting and the long strike had frayed everyone's nerves. On the family front, Ashok had three boys, all under eleven, who required care.'

Within months, Ashok's condition deteriorated and everything fell apart. Ajay had to take care of his brother's three boys and secure their future. Thankfully, his father had not only been foresighted when it came to planning his sons' futures, he had also made sure that his textile mill would be able to weather any kind of storm.

Even in the toughest of times, Gopikisan Piramal had ensured modernization of the mill and focussed on keeping it as technologically upgraded as possible. What also helped the family to bounce back was his early decision to diversify. Ajay had realized the logic behind the diversification strategy. In 1984, he acquired a company called Gujarat Glass (now Piramal Glass), which made vials and tubes used by pharmaceutical companies. But the real game changer for him came four years later, after a conversation he overheard over lunch at a friend's house in the neighbourhood.

THE BID FOR NICHOLAS

It was for Sunday lunch that Ajay and Swati had gone to a friend's house. Things were looking up for Morarjee mills, which was gradually spinning back to normal. But no one had any inkling that by the end of the day, Ajay would be looking far beyond textiles. He remembers the entire conversation to this day.

Ajay Piramal with co-workers of Morarjee Spinning and Weaving Mills; Ajay helped the mill make a comeback after the strike led by Dr Datta Samant paralysed it

A lawyer friend was telling another that the owners of a small pharmaceutical company, Nicholas, were looking for potential buyers. The news wasn't one to cause a flutter. Pretty much all the multinational pharmaceutical companies were marching out of India at the time in the face of tough market regulations. Initially, Ajay hardly paid attention to the discussion, but as the conversation became more detailed, his interest was piqued. The company was a marquee name with familiar products, and there was really no reason for it to be sold off.

PricewaterhouseCooper's Sujay Shetty, one of the most sought-after experts in the pharmaceutical sector, narrates what really happened that afternoon. The genesis of the story lay in 1971, when Prime Minister Indira Gandhi's government rewrote the Indian Patents Act to do away with 'product' patents—an accepted norm worldwide—and move to 'process' patents. Since the Indian government didn't recognize the regular intellectual property (IP) that any company enjoyed over a product, in this case the drug, it meant that any Indian company could get to the same product through a different route or manufacturing process.

The decision to change the Patents Act was aimed at giving domestic companies a boost and doing away with the monopoly MNCs had. 'Patents, and the fact that no one can copy their drug, is at the heart of the whole business of big multinational pharma companies, and when they realized their patents were not secure, they were quick to exit India or scale back operations,' Shetty explains. There were exceptions, however. Companies like GlaxoSmithKline continued to invest, which is why it is still amongst the top players in the country today. Domestic pharma companies were quick to cash in. First, by trying to fill the gap left by the exiting pharma companies by recreating the product through a different process; and second, as they got better at it, meeting the stringent regulatory requirements in developed markets such as the US and Europe to sell cheaper generic versions of drugs that had gone off patent.

Listening in on the discussion on Nicholas, Ajay had hardly

any inkling of what was brewing in the pharmaceutical world. But less than twenty-four hours after that fateful Sunday lunch, he wanted to acquire the company. Ajay did some research about Nicholas and found that it was an Australian drug company owned by US firm Sara Lee. The company was ranked forty-eighth among companies in the Indian pharma sector. The more he read about the company and the industry, the more ideas he had. 'It didn't take me long to pick up the phone and call Barker, the man who was in charge of the sale from Nicholas's side.' Barker agreed to meet readily. But he was in for a shock.

The first meeting between Barker and Ajay took place at the old Oberoi coffee shop, overlooking the Arabian Sea. Anyone watching the two would have seen that they had little in common. Ajay was a tall lanky young man in his early thirties, Barker, an old, typically British gentleman close to retirement. But as they sat and sipped their coffee, sudden whoops of laughter could be heard from their table at regular intervals. At one point, Barker laughed so much that he almost fell off his chair. 'Barker was shocked when I told him that I wanted to buy Nicholas. He looked at me sceptically and asked, "What do you know of the business?" To which I responded in all earnestness, "Nothing." So he asked me, "Why should I give it to you?" My response nearly shocked Barker. I don't know what got into me, but I told him that I would make Nicholas one of the five largest pharmaceutical companies in the country.'

There was no rationale behind what Ajay said. He had no clue about the workings of the company, the business or the sector. By the end of the second cup of coffee, however, he had won a friend and supporter. 'I think he liked my frankness and earnestness. I was just a young man making what seemed an impossible claim, but he probably saw the hunger in me. And I finally got the company, even though I was competing with the biggest in the business. You know, Swati and I went to meet him in Kenya, where he moved after his retirement. We showed him Nicholas Piramal's annual report and how we had achieved our target. In 1998, we were the fifth-largest pharmaceutical company in India.'

Over the next decade, Ajay built on his success. In 1988, he had bought Nicholas for Rs 6 crore. Twenty-two years later, he sold a part of the company for over Rs 17,000 crore.

THE TURNAROUND FORMULA

In 1988, when Nicholas became Nicholas Piramal, the pharmaceutical business was a tough place to be in in India. Years of pricing control by the government and the insecurity about patents had forced the biggest pharma companies in the world to gradually cut down their presence or even withdraw from India. A few Indian companies—from Dr Reddy's in Hyderabad to Parminder Singh's Ranbaxy in Delhi—were quickly learning the ropes, producing cheaper generic versions of big drugs and eyeing global markets.

In the year between actually bidding for the company and getting it, Ajay had studied the pharmaceutical sector and the company fairly well and he knew what he wanted to do.

Nicholas was one of the many small multinational pharmaceutical companies situated in Mumbai. And though it was one of the few MNCs that stayed back in India, it was a company that hadn't grown. Very little money had been put into it and there seemed to be no real strategy or plan. For instance, the company's main plant was in Chembur, a Mumbai suburb. Very little effort had gone into modernizing it and, even if money was available to increase and improve production, there was no way it could be done, since the factory was in a residential area and acquiring new land would have been expensive. The plant had to go, Ajay decided, but it wasn't going to be easy. It would take at least two years and a big investment to redeploy the work. Given the odds and the promise he had made to himself and the man he had bought the company from, he decided to take it one step at a time.

The first one was to commission a new high-tech pharma manufacturing facility in Pithampur, near Indore in Madhya Pradesh. The best consultants were brought in to put in place the new plant with modern manufacturing processes, something quite unheard of in pre-liberalization India. Nicholas's Chembur plant was to be phased out as the new facility became operational.

If the medium-term plan was to reduce costs, unlock value in terms of the sale of the Chembur land and set up the stage for expansion, for the short term, the field force was tripled. 'The decisions we took meant a lot of expenditure. For instance, we spent Rs 18 crore on the new factory at a time when the sales of the company were around that much. It required guts, but in a way I think it helped because it showed our commitment towards wanting to make a mark.'

But while all this did improve the situation in Nicholas, it was a larger plan that became the bedrock of Piramal's success in the pharma industry. Ajay's big idea was to play the contrarian.

While most Indian pharmaceutical companies were either trying to crack the ingredients of top-selling drugs to replicate them, or selling these drugs at a cheaper price abroad, Ajay bet on being an ally of the fast-fleeing MNCs and staying clear of a fight. 'I have always taken the road less travelled and somehow, I couldn't picture myself fighting long court cases. As a group, we are not comfortable with any sort of litigation.' Over time, this became the philosophy behind a lot of his acquisitions.

Also, while other Indian pharma companies like Ranbaxy and Dr Reddy's looked at exports, Ajay decided to look at the domestic Indian market, in the hope that over the years, the trend would change and the Indian market would explode. Even this bet paid off over time.

Within two years of acquiring Nicholas, as the new plant in Pithampur became functional, profits were growing at 55 per cent and, more importantly, Ajay was getting noticed. 'Every pharmaceutical company in India that was looking at an exit approached us. They realized that we were not here just to squeeze out profits.' Investing in Nicholas and backing the acquisition with a clear strategy was a bet that paid off many times over. It also established Ajay as a businessman who often had far deeper plans and bigger ambitions for his enterprises than one might expect.

WEAVING IN SUCCESS

Morarjee Goculdas Spinning and Weaving Mills continued to be in the news as Ajay gradually helped it make a comeback after the debilitating strike led by Dr Samant. A lot of the steps that he took to get things back on track were fundamental. And nearly all of it was learnt from his father.

First on Ajay's agenda was modernization. Soon after the strike, contrary to what the other mill owners were doing, he put in money to overhaul his textile mill and improve and expand capacity. 'All the money we had was put into upgrading the mill, and it began showing results. Our next focus was the overseas market and exports.' Sops that the government gave for exporters, both in terms of tax-free income and the ability to use foreign exchange to import machinery, proved to be a boon for Ajay and, if old press clippings of the time are anything to go by, Morarjee mills started making significant inroads into international markets. Exposure to evolved markets also made Ajay realize that he would have to improve the quality of the textiles the mill produced. This created a cycle of fresh investment, orders and demand. In the next few years, profits at Morarjee mills went up seven-fold. In fact, seeing the quick turnaround, press reports of the time heralded its second coming.

It was also busy getting a face-lift, roping in fashion designers, tying up with Italian design houses for joint ventures in home furnishings and aggressively marketing itself. This was a success, though it was only a decade later that the retail boom really hit India. Alongside modernization and new markets, Ajay was assiduously working at removing the other big problem that had hurt the textile companies: the expensive location, Mumbai. So a new mill was set up in a far more inexpensive area: Butibori, near Nagpur. These developments probably also sowed the seed of a new idea in Ajay's mind: 'Why not relocate the mills and free up land in central Mumbai?' An idea that he put down on paper, rallied support around and fought for.

It is a little-known fact that Ajay was part architect of the one-third formula in mill land redevelopment, which involved freeing up large tracts of mill land and developing it for commercial purposes. This resulted in the transformation of Parel and Lower Parel into the new business district of Mumbai.

To garner support for the plan, he and the other owners worked out a formula that promised to take care of all the stakeholders. It meant developing a third of the land, landscaping a third, and providing low-cost housing to take care of the displaced workers on the remaining. Despite the initial controversies around this, and the fact that many of the mill land developers were accused of not living up to the promise of providing low-cost housing to the displaced workers, it did work well for Morarjee mills. What won it support eventually was that it was a practical plan that not only bailed out the mill owners, who were by now under stress, it also provided the battle-weary workers an exit plan. In the case of Morarjee mills, for instance, a large part of the money raised through the land sale was given to the workers in the form of a lump sum for their VRS packages. And the entire mill was relocated.

It is hard to believe that just two decades ago, the swanky office complex, Peninsula Towers, and the building that houses the Piramal corporate headquarters in Lower Parel, was a sleepy mothballed mill, part of Sayaji Mills Limited that Ashok and Ajay had acquired a year after their father's death and was, soon after, worth just a pittance. Similar developments across the adjoining areas have opened up land for large commercial and housing high-rises and helped in the development of an otherwise land-starved city.

In 2005, there was another split in the Piramal group. Ajay passed on a sizeable part of what he had built to the sons of his brother Ashok. Ashok's sons had grown up by now; he had trained them himself. The eldest, Harsh, had worked closely as Ajay's executive assistant. The three—Harsh, Rajeev and Nandan—got Morarjee Goculdas Spinning and Weaving Mills;

the retail forays including Crossroads, one of Mumbai's first malls; Miranda Tools, with which Ajay had begun his career; and the substantial real estate meticulously acquired over the years as part of the many acquisitions, and some other companies. Ajay retained Nicholas Piramal and Piramal Glass, though he was quick to announce his own foray into real estate subsequently.

Today, Morarjee mills is one of the few textile mills to have survived the face-off in the industry. It supplies high-end fabrics to the biggest fashion brands in the world—the likes of Hugo Boss and Zara. Morarjee is also enjoying the boom in Indian retail, supplying fabric to the most popular brands here. Miranda Tools is still small but very profitable and Peninsula Land Ltd, owned by Ajay's nephews, develops some of the priciest real estate in the city.

Ajay says, 'The other mill owners always saw me as an outsider in textiles. There was speculation that I was there only to make money and sell out.' And this tag remains because that is exactly how the pharmaceutical industry has viewed Ajay Piramal and, to be fair, he has not proved them wrong.

NICHOLAS AND PHARMACEUTICALS

Between 1985 and '91, Ajay went into overdrive getting his businesses going, be it Morarjee mills, or later, Nicholas Piramal. But had he left things there, he would have been just a successful businessman who managed to get a handful of companies back on track. Not the deal maker he came to be known as over the years. The deal-maker tag got reinforced between 1993 and '98 as Nicholas Piramal went on an acquisition spree, buying the Indian operations of some of the leading multinational pharmaceutical companies in the country. In the beginning, the deals were small, but over time, the true worth of what Ajay was doing became apparent.

Within three years of the turnaround of Nicholas, Piramal got an opportunity to acquire pharma giant Roche's India operations. Roche had bought the suite of Nicholas's products worldwide and they were wary of what was happening in India. 'The fact that we didn't do exports of any branded generic drugs also gave them a lot of confidence. They felt much more comfortable with us.' This helped because all the big Indian pharma companies of the time were eyeing this acquisition.

One of the criticisms about Ajay's subsequent acquisition strategy (after Nicholas) has been that he was often more interested in the real estate he got from old MNC pharma offshoots that were looking to move out of India. When he acquired Roche Products, the company had a massive production facility in Tardeo, close to Mumbai's Haji Ali station. Again, like Nicholas's Chembur factory, this was right in the middle of the many residential complexes situated there. 'Not only did this increase the cost of production a lot [labour costs were much higher], it also meant that with no place to grow, the company could not expand operations.' So, one of the first things Ajay did when he took over the company was to close down the plant and move the production set-up to a new and upgraded one that the Piramals had built soon after taking over Nicholas in Madhya Pradesh.

Ajay says, 'Within a year of acquiring Roche, I managed to script a turnaround there too. You know, opportunities in acquisitions come when there are some basic flaws in the business. If everything is perfect, why would anyone want to sell out?' To his credit, he seems to have always been quick to identify the flaws.

Apart from the Tardeo facility, the Roche acquisition also brought with it its own field force, product basket and manufacturing facilities—the three things Nicholas Piramal was looking for. For Roche, too, the deal was a godsend. Not only did it get a buyer, it also got a partner because the company was quick to get into marketing and manufacturing tie-ups with Piramal that allowed it to bring new drugs into India. For sixteen years before the deal, Roche had not brought a single new drug into India. But in three years after signing with Piramal, it brought in six. Between 1993 and 2003, Ajay was back in fifth gear, buying a company every two years. Each acquisition had a logic, a new area of focus and pass-through benefits, but this would become obvious only after a few years. The acquisitions were smart, timely, with far more hidden value than the price suggested, and they gave rise to Ajay's formidable reputation as a deal maker with guts. For example, the acquisition of the Indian arm of the German pharmaceutical company Boehringer Mannheim, in 1996, surprising many. The company was in the news because three cataract patients had died after being administered one of its drugs, Comsat Forte. It was found later that the medicine had been contaminated. Things got worse when the company's managing director decided to flee the country. The Food and Drug Administration (FDA) had cancelled the licence of the company's Thane plant, stopping all production. The stock price of the pharma giant crashed on the Bombay Stock Exchange. The situation was such that no one was ready to touch it.

Ajay's announcement at the height of this problem that he was acquiring the company shocked everyone. In his defence, he said he had been in talks with the company long before the trouble started and the turn of events had only expedited the acquisition process. What he was really interested in then was the diagnostic business of the company—Boehringer Mannheim was the largest diagnostics company in the world and the second largest in India.

Between 2000 and 2003, Piramal acquired three more companies. ICI India gave it a range of critical care products while Rhone Poulenc's India arm gave it a cache of products in the respiratory space. In 2003, Nicholas Piramal picked up the partner's stake in Sarabhai Nicholas Pharmaceuticals, which brought in new drugs in the pain management and anti-infective space. The company also entered a host of joint ventures with international companies for manufacture and marketing of their drugs, for example, Boots Piramal, which produces and sells Clearasil, Lacto Calamine and Strepsils in India.

It is not surprising then that Ajay came to be known as the 'Takeover Tycoon' in the pharmaceuticals industry. There was a lot of conjecture about what he was actually up to, but he had a much larger plan in his mind. All these acquisitions were pieces of a jigsaw he was putting together to fulfil that plan. Also, he was getting ready for the second round of regulatory changes that was coming India's way starting 2005, when India would accept the product patent regime once again and change the rules of the pharmaceutical game.

This also coincided with the emergence of India as the most promising new market and Ajay was the best placed to cash in on this since he had the largest number of global pharmaceutical products and a domestic sales force that was far more potent than any other. Then, just when everything seemed to be going well for him, he decided to sell out most of his business.

THE ABBOTT DEAL

India's acceptance of the product patent regime that recognized the intellectual property rights of the international pharma companies over new drugs discovered by them brought about a major change in the Indian medicinal drugs industry.

Sceptics said this regime would render the Indian model of reverse engineering drugs (the process of developing versions of existing drugs) and marketing the generic version internationally when global patents came off obsolete, thus sounding the death knell for Indian pharma companies. Especially so, because under the new regime, MNC pharma companies would be only too willing to return to India and sell drugs. The pharma industry and the companies that had grown into multinationals supplying cheaper generic versions of drugs, on the other hand, said they should focus on the larger picture. With drugs worth $60bn going off patent in 2010 alone and most developed countries including the US adopting legislations mandating a fall in drug prices, and hence encouraging cheaper generic versions from India, Indian companies would witness a doubling of sales.

Between 2005 and now, both theories have held good and the sector has undergone a lot of changes. In fact, today India is recognized as the pharmacy of the world. Exports of generics have boomed and it is estimated that one in four tablets sold across the world is produced by an Indian company. In critical illnesses like Acquired Immuno Deficiency Syndrome (AIDS) and tuberculosis (TB), where the stress is on lowering costs, 90 per cent of the medicines are made by Indian firms. While Indian generic manufacturers have benefitted, the promise of patent protection has brought back the big multinational pharma companies to India and their refocus has been just in time, when emerging markets are proving to be the fastest growing in the world.

Ajay was one of the first businessmen to understand the ramifications of what was about to happen and a lot of what he did since 1998 was really with this in mind. Despite a population of over a billion people, India's healthcare industry is a small fraction of that of the US, the world's biggest medicine market, with over $300bn in sales; second is Japan, followed by Germany. India and China are far behind, but growth has been so fast that many believe the sector will leapfrog in size and scale over the next few years. The first signs that the tide had changed came in 2008, when just months before the economic slowdown, Ranbaxy founder Parvinder Singh's sons Malvinder and Shivinder shocked their father's elderly peers by selling out their share in the company to Daiichi Sankyo. The deal was concluded at a spectacular $4.6bn. The Indian pharmaceutical industry was shaken to the core and there was speculation on who would sell out next.

Two years later, Ajay decided to sell the domestic formulations arm of his business in Nicholas Piramal, which accounted for about 55 per cent of sales, to Abbott, for $3.72bn, a whopping Rs 17,000 crore. When the deal was announced, the papers were quick to say 'we told you so' and experts pointed out how the takeover man had always had intentions of selling out. Ajay, when asked about this says, 'No, it was never part of the plan. I would never have made such long-term investments if I wanted to sell out. Look at our field force, our R&D centre, these were not put together for short-term gains. There has always been a much larger vision in mind.' A vision that the Indian market would become one of the fastest-growing in the world and that one day an Indian company would be able to discover the next big blockbuster.

The decision to sell out was taken over a full year, after a series of meetings and a lot of persuasion by the Abbott chairman and his team, who visited India and Ajay's company numerous times. 'Miles knew a lot about India and each of the big players in the pharma business here. He was convinced about the deal from the start and he had come prepared.' At first, Ajay said no, and even suggested other Indian businesses that Abbott could look at to buy. But after a year of what seemed like persistent pursuit on the part of Miles, Ajay seems to have come to the conclusion that it wasn't a bad idea after all. 'I think they were very keen to not only launch their products in a market like India and build scale, but to also use this to catapult them into the big league across emerging markets. In the light of all this, they could obviously give us more value than we could create!' Moreover, his bets were now on another area.

Ajay credits his company's track record for the staggering price the sale fetched. Before the deal, for eight quarters in a row, Nicholas Piramal had outgrown the industry with a 20 per cent sales growth. 'We had a clean history; there was no hint of any litigation and after Glaxo SmithKline Pharmaceuticals, we had the biggest number of branded drugs in India.' The field force was also very efficient and Nicholas had the best manufacturing facilities.

Ajay lets on another interesting fact about the Abbott deal.

'Everyone talks about the value we got from Abbott. But it took a lot of guts on our side to put down what we would sell for on paper. It's not easy to ask for that kind of money.' He had wanted more. The deal was finally closed at a valuation that was 5 per cent lower than what he had first asked for.

THE NEXT BIG BET

Following the Abbott deal, Ajay sold his diagnostics business to Super Religare Laboratories for Rs 600 crore (also at a massive profit). Ever since, there has been speculation about what he is going to do with all the money he has made.

Ajay's first bet is R&D. An old Nirlon tyrecord factory building in Mumbai's suburb of Goregaon, set up in the 1970s, is the new epicentre of his ambitious plans. The massive Piramal Life Sciences Centre, the group's R&D facility set up in November 2004, is one of the most ambitious projects that the Piramals have invested in. Dr Somesh Sharma, a scientist who has worked in the most high-end R&D centres in the world, is the man in charge. His aim is to put together all the pieces in the puzzle that go into making a new drug. It is the lure and excitement of the big new drug discovery that has brought Sharma and the 370-odd scientists who work there together. Many of them, like Sharma, have worked in the laboratories of the biggest pharma companies across the world. Sharma, who constantly shuttles between the US and India, says the centre is developing thirteen new molecules and they are at different stages of clinical trial.

The only other company that is banking in such a committed manner on discovering the next big blockbuster is Glenn Saldanha's Glenmark Pharma. The reason why very few people are betting on R&D is because this is a difficult business that needs patience, time and a lot of money. Also, one can spend years chasing the wrong molecule and hit a wall. But as any scientist, doctor or businessman in this field will tell you, an actual drug discovery is well worth the wait. The money aside, the fact that no Indian company has been successful in this over the last sixty-three years is reason enough to try. Sharma says, 'I have taken up the challenge because everyone in the world believes that we in India are not capable of drug discovery; I want to prove them wrong.'

Over the last decade, there has hardly been any big drug discovery anywhere in the world. This is largely due to escalating costs, which have made the whole process of discovering a drug prohibitively expensive. Already under pressure because of falling sales, many pharmaceutical majors have cut back on spending in this area, which means that whole teams of scientists have been laid off.

In the light of all this, Ajay's focus on the R&D centre was a smart move. R&D costs in India are one-third that of the Western world, and given the excess scientific labour floating around, things have never looked better for the R&D business. Ajay also realized that considering the costs of drug discovery and the value of doing it here, he could, over time, partner with the biggest names in the business to jointly develop drugs, and, if lucky, share the spoils.

Drug discovery is slowly and gradually gaining ground because apart from the fact that despite years of research, medical science has still not been able to find a cure for most of the life-threatening diseases, especially cancer, in money terms too, there is a lot at stake. Take, for example, Lipitor, the cholesterol-reducing drug from Pfizer, which is also the world's most widely selling drug. Estimates are that Pfizer had been earning an estimated $12bn in sales each year on this drug for over a decade, while the actual cost of producing it must have been barely $500m, Ajay opines.

Seeing the passion in the team of young scientists at the Piramal R&D centre, it is hard not to hope that we will get there eventually. The R&D centre has another interesting thing going for it. It has meticulous documentation of research carried out on plants from across the Indian subcontinent. Scientists believe this could be a storehouse of information on new breakthroughs and open up opportunities in converting old Indian traditional wisdom, like ayurveda, to modern science. Who knows, the next big drug could be more homegrown than anyone can think?

Alongside R&D, Ajay is also gunning for custom manufacturing and critical care. With high-tech manufacturing facilities and its track record of launching drugs in the Indian market, custom manufacturing is a safe, steady bet Piramal Healthcare is counting on. It earned Piramal Healthcare one-third of its revenue, roughly $218m, in 2008–09. All the work Ajay's company has done with pharma MNCs for distribution and marketing of their prized products has been a big help and he is hoping that Piramal Healthcare will be their first choice as partner when they re-enter the Indian market.

Critical care is another steady warhorse. Today, this arm of the company, which finds little mention in press articles, is one of the biggest suppliers of anaesthetic products to hospitals across the world.

The other exciting business Ajay is betting on is that of the so-called over-the-counter (OTC) non-prescription drugs. This includes a cache of familiar names: Strepsils, Clearasil, Saridon, I-Pill (acquired in 2010) and a number of others.

Ajay is obviously playing the domestic consumption game and with what remains of Piramal's field force and the kind of deep pockets he has, few would be able to take him on.

LOOKING AHEAD

Ajay speaks very little. Even while a deal is being concluded or in the middle of any acquisition, though the excitement is palpable, his office exudes an almost indescribable calm. The long silent corridors are dimly lit, with very expensive art—a substantial collection of M.F. Husains and an assortment of Japanese artists—all over, and not a single person walking about anywhere.

At the heart of Ajay's endeavour is an attempt to hit the big league internationally by discovering the next big multibillion-dollar drug and taking Piramal Enterprises Limited onto the global stage. 'Going ahead, drug discovery is going to be crucial. That's how you make a fortune in this business. The bet I am making is that the next big drug discovery will come from India, from us.'

While he is waiting to do this, Ajay is also positioning his company as one of the biggest players in the fast-moving OTC drug space by creating a consumer connect in one of the fastest-growing markets in the world: India. He also bought an 11 per cent stake in Vodafone India at a time when the company was going through a rough patch in India. By staying with it as an investor who put in even more money at the height of the company's tax woes with the Indian government, Ajay has probably endeared himself to the company's global board.

He also bought several small strategic companies—the string

of pearls, as he calls them—with the aim of capturing the next big opportunity in the pharma business. In May 2012, he bought the Massachusetts-based company Decision Resource, Inc. for $635m (Rs 3,400 crore). The acquisition of this group, which has worked in the healthcare information space, came close on the heels of the purchase of Bayer Pharma's global molecular imaging research and development portfolio, which would help the company in its R&D and diagnostics business.

Through 2011, Ajay was the only Indian businessman buying anything overseas and, as Swati Piramal says, every small step he took generated headlines in the global press. There were approximately 190 articles on him and his acquisitions between November 2011 and April 2012. The headlines didn't stop there. Back home, when Ajay was not buying companies overseas, he seemed to be indulging in an old obsession that has been part of all the acquisitions he made—buying property. At a time when every big real estate company was in a financial mess, thanks to a credit squeeze, high interest rates and even higher debt and hence leverages, he was the only one with ready cash to buy prominent pieces of real estate that came up for grabs in Mumbai.

Rarely does one get to see a new business empire being scripted, but that is exactly what Ajay is doing today as he bides his time and watches for the next big opportunity from his office on the tenth floor of Piramal House in Lower Parel. The world around him has changed, but he has been able to stay one step ahead of it all till now.

Ajay is not scared to take risks. 'I have done that all through my business career,' he says. Luck has always been on his side, but he lists out traits that have helped him through the years. To succeed, one has to have the courage to take some tough decisions, one has to look for an opportunity in adversity, one has to be a die-hard optimist and be clear and fast in decision making. 'Often, that's the biggest failing in people.'

He also believes there are other traits that have helped him. For instance, he always keeps the company of those who he can learn from. Two of Ajay's closest and oldest friends are HDFC chairman Deepak Parekh and Reliance chairman Mukesh Ambani. Parekh, who was a close friend of Ashok Piramal, helped Ajay with some sound advice through the tough early years and Mukesh is like a brother. Their association goes back to the time when Reliance supplied rayon fibre to Morarjee mills.

Even the people on the board of his company are a diverse lot and include the likes of N. Vaghul, former ICICI chairman, S. Ramadorai, TCS vice chairman, Dr R.A. Mashelkar, member of the prime minister's Scientific Advisory Council, Deepak Satwalekar, former head of HDFC Standard Life and Keki Dadiseth, former chairman of Hindustan Lever Ltd.

Apart from this, there are other basic principles that have held Ajay in good stead. He has always been straightforward in his dealings and this has not only won his company respect, it has often been the reason why he has clinched his deals. He wants to be a global pharmaceutical player and he has been carefully building up his credentials. The only hurdle he has to cross is that of a big drug discovery in his R&D centre.

Everything else is in place: his team of world-class scientists, his advisors, and his active engagement with alma mater Harvard University, where Ajay and his wife are on the Board of Dean's Advisors at Harvard Business School. Apart from this connection with the world's most famous business school, he also has easy access and rapport with the heads of global majors from Abbott to Vodafone. Backing all this are, of course, his fairly deep pockets, strategic acquisitions across the world and his rising cache of products.

With so much in hand, Ajay Piramal is ready to play the patience game and walk down a whole new road, or another one less travelled. Because that is what he enjoys doing the most.

PART III

THE OUTSIDERS

G.M. RAO

A hot and humid July day in New Delhi. A posse of vehicles makes its way through the quiet military cantonment area towards the international airport. Earlier, in the morning, a convoy of police buses had brought security men who had spent hours combing the area around the airport. Now, as the cars approach the new terminal, the passengers pause to read the detailed directions on the signposts along the road and match them with the equally detailed instructions on their invites.

All roads this sultry July morning seem to lead to the new terminal three (T3) of Delhi's Indira Gandhi International Airport. Over 6,000 people, among them an assortment of government officials, CEOs, heads of the country's top airlines and construction companies and journalists sit in silence. There is a sudden shuffle of feet and shutterbugs begin a frenzied beeline to the front, cameras ready. Prime Minister Manmohan Singh walks in first, followed by Delhi Chief Minister Sheila Dikshit and then United Progressive Alliance (UPA) chairperson Sonia Gandhi. Behind her is India's Civil Aviation Minister Praful Patel and then a slightly portly, balding and smiling man whom few people in the crowd have seen before.

The opening of a new terminal at New Delhi's Indira Gandhi International Airport, dubbed by then as 'India's runway to the future', was a big deal for the country and for each one of those standing centre stage. Preparations had been going on for months. Heads of the biggest event management companies had been flown in from London and Paris for the spectacular opening ceremony.

For the prime minister and the Congress president, the inauguration was a much-needed statement that the government was capable of facilitating large infrastructure projects. For Dikshit, it was an important feather in the cap ahead of the much-awaited Commonwealth Games, which Delhi was playing host to. For the weary civil aviation minister, warding off crisis after crisis, thanks to the woes of the national carrier, Air India, it was a face-saver. And for the man who was smiling the broadest, G.M. Rao, whose company, GMR Group, had led the consortium that built the airport, it was a moment he had been working towards forever.

In a country known for its bad roads, collapsing infrastructure, policy bottlenecks and project delays, the T3 was an important reiteration that India could do it too. It was possible not only to build one of the world's biggest airports in India, it was also possible to do so in a record time of thirty-seven months, half of what it had taken to create the new Terminal 5 at London's Heathrow Airport, which had cost an enormous amount of money and had faced innumerable glitches after its opening in March 2008. So amazing was this achievement in the Indian context that Praful Patel was overheard joking, 'It is rare for the same minister to preside over the "bhoomi poojan" and the inauguration of an infrastructure project in India.'

What made the timely completion of the T3 even more significant was that there were enough reasons for it to be delayed.

The terminal had to be constructed without any flights getting disrupted in the adjoining, and overlapping, old airport. This also meant that before building the terminal covering an area of over 5m sq. ft, GMR had to create a new departure terminal, relocate sixty buildings around the old airport, and win over and rehabilitate the thousands who had lived for years on the land where the new terminal was to come up. Everyone present at the inauguration would have been impressed by the last feat. After all, acquiring land to build new factories or even expand older ones had become impossible because of the social and political unrest around land acquisition in recent years.

But Grandhi Mallikarjuna Rao, the man who stood beaming on stage, had managed it despite all the attention the project had attracted and the frequent headlines that predicted he would never be able to finish its construction on time. Rao had also ensured that all the negative press the project had invited was countered by a build-up worthy of this moment.

In the run-up to this day, newspapers had been full of big 'Believe it or not' facts around T3; how the floor area of the terminal was equivalent to nearly 90 acres, 42 acres of which were carpeted, and how the cement used to build this spectacular structure could fill enough gunny bags to go half way across the globe!

Looking at Rao explaining a point to Dr Manmohan Singh, or giving a guided tour to Sonia Gandhi in an airport buggy with Patel in the driver's seat, few would have realized just how far he had come and how improbable his success would have seemed till just a few years ago.

The road to success also prepared him for the biggest challenge of his career: to ensure that the billions he had put in to build the massive airport did not turn out to be the biggest mistake of his life—which is how it seemed a year after the inauguration.

Rao met with heavy losses. Additionally, he had to face critics who slammed his company's stock price, and disgruntled investors who had lost half the money they had invested in GMR Infrastructure shares on the National Stock Exchange, as their price crashed by 45 per cent within just one year of the launch of T3.

By then Delhi's swanky new airport, heralded as the symbol of a new India, stood for all the problems within the country—policy confusion, the risk to investment, and a question mark on growth.

THE ROAD FROM RAJAM

G.M. Rao has a down-to-earth quality that is evident in interactions with him. Those who sit across the table and talk business with him are struck by two things. First, even though he has proved himself to be a shrewd and successful businessman, he comes across as an affable guy one could bump into in the neighbourhood. He addresses everyone sitting across the table as 'Sir', irrespective of age. Rao can put anyone at ease. 'He is not the kind of man who overawes you,' the head of a big consultancy who has worked closely with the group recalls.

The second thing is his insatiable curiosity and his willingness to learn. A senior manager at GMR Infrastructure once said, 'Rao is almost obsessive about roping in consultants and experts every time he starts a big project. He can spend hours at strategy meetings. Often you will see him sitting with all of us, taking down notes and asking the simplest, most basic questions. You will see him write down an idea, an observation or a question, and at the end of the day, he will forward it to one of us, asking us to find out more.'

Business rivals are wary of this image Rao has created for himself and say his 'humility' is a well-cultivated 'tool' to ensure that he is 'everyone's friend'. In any case, it pays to be humble in dealing with the government or with politicians, and Rao's business depends on both. Which may be a rather uncharitable way of looking at him, because it is probably where he comes from that shapes the kind of person he is.

Any conversation with Rao is peppered with references to the town where he was born—Rajam—and lived till he was well into his forties. The story of how he came out of the nondescript town and went on to become India's 'Airport man' is fascinating. Rajam is a small town in Srikakulam, one of the poorest districts of Andhra Pradesh, bordering Odisha. The only time this area makes it to mainstream news is when there is a discussion on poverty or the Naxalite-led insurgency. But the drive along the side road that goes into the town leads one to an oasis bustling with enterprise.

Rao's father was a small trader in Rajam who traded in everything from gold to grams and pulses, and Rao, the fifth of seven children, was expected to eventually join the small family enterprise. And he had no other plans or ambitions.

But ordinary lives can take unexpected turns and the first such turn in Rao's life came when he failed the secondary school-leaving certificate (SSLC) exam. He pleaded with his father to be given a second chance. Though it would mean the family having to stretch themselves monetarily, they gave in. Rao acquired a new drive and confidence that helped him go far beyond books—significantly, his academic ambitions made him push himself harder.

Gradually ambition triggered aspirations and these took him far beyond Rajam. He made it to the coveted Andhra University College of Engineering in Visakhapatnam. Here there was another round of lessons in store for Rao, the small-town boy, on how to be independent, win friends and participate in campus life. The otherwise reticent Rao dabbled in student politics, rubbing shoulders with other students, some of whom went on to become powerful politicians.

In his final year of engineering, Rao heard that Andhra Pradesh Scooters Ltd, a state-owned company, was looking for a local dealer in Visakhapatnam. He jumped at the opportunity of acquiring the dealership and moving out of his town. But, no matter how hard he lobbied with local officials, bankers and businessmen, he couldn't get the dealership. He says, 'I really wanted it, but thank god I didn't get it. Otherwise I would have been a small two-wheeler or car dealer in Visakhapatnam today.'

Rao, who was already married by then, went back to Rajam, depressed, only to become even more frustrated by his next few attempts to make it on his own. First came a job as a shift engineer at a paper mill in Rajahmundry, 200 kilometres from Rajam, for a princely salary of Rs 500 per month. But that didn't last long.

G.M. Rao (*extreme right*) when he was a student of the Andhra University College of Engineering in Visakhapatnam

Rao's second job was with the district public works department as executive assistant to the executive engineer heading the Vamsadhara project. The project involved building a small dam on the Vamsadhara river, near Rajam. Fresh out of college, with a mechanical engineering degree, Rao was asked to help design a sluice to control the dam's water flow. The project was a simple one and crucial to the farming-dependent villages in the catchment area, but it was evident that it was a complete non-starter. He would go to work each day and have nothing to do. 'There were no funds, no plans, and no one was really interested. All the funds that came in went into salaries,' he says. 'It took thirty years for the project to come through.'

The Vamsadhara project finally got completed only around 2002–03. No less than two chief ministers had to intervene to make it happen. In the same period, he managed to get out of Rajam and create an empire, doing projects several times bigger.

But in 1974, even Rao didn't know where life would take him or what he would make of it. It seemed he was destined to remain in his home town and do what his father and others before him had done.

Within a year of Rao leaving college, his father passed away. Without a steady job or a way to fend for himself, he had to put aside his engineering degree and join his brothers to make something of the family business. Here, his education helped. Soon he managed to do what his fathers and forefathers hadn't—scale up the small business.

Rao began to examine how it was being run.

'It was evident that a large amount of the money that was made was going into the pockets of the middlemen. First, we used to sell to the middlemen, who would sell to the small traders. These small traders would then sell to the shops. We gradually began to sell directly to the markets and the big traders.' This improved margins dramatically and Rao also brought in organization and processes. Within a few months, the brothers began to sell what they picked up from the farmers in Rajam and the adjoining villages directly, to markets as far as Chennai, Nagpur and even Delhi in a good year!

But it wasn't easy. Rao remembers spending days cycling

A young Ajit Gulabchand (*in tie*) with his parents inside a tunnel built by Hindustan Construction Company (HCC); HCC has also built the Bandra–Worli Sea Link in Mumbai and a stretch of the Mumbai–Pune Expressway

HCC founder Seth Walchand Hirachand Doshi; his larger-than-life bust can be seen at the entrance to Gulabchand's office

Union Minister for Agriculture Sharad Pawar (*right*) with Gulabchand at the latter's daughter's wedding; the two have been close friends for over thirty years

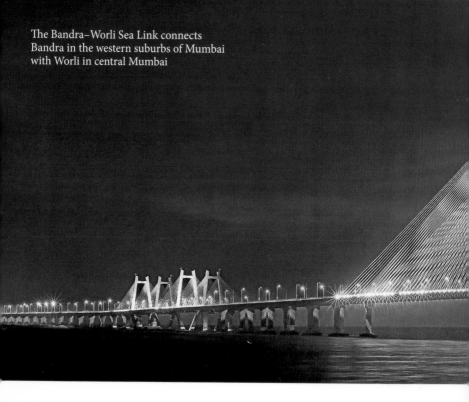

The Bandra–Worli Sea Link connects Bandra in the western suburbs of Mumbai with Worli in central Mumbai

HCC's Lavasa township; HCC entered into an agreement with the Government of Maharashtra to build the hill station in 1999–2000

Gautam Thapar, founder and chairman of the Avantha Group

The Bhigwan facility near Pune was acquired from Sinar Mas in 2001; the acquisition gave BILT a high-end technology

GT with his uncle Lalit Mohan Thapar, who was the chairman of Ballarpur Industries Limited (BILT)

BILT acquired Sabah Forest Industries (SFI), Malaysia, in 2007; Sabah allowed BILT to access raw material and lucrative markets in South East Asia

Baba N. Kalyani, CMD of Bharat Forge; the company supplies parts to some of the top automobile firms across the world

Kalyani with his son Amit Kalyani

From left to right: Baba Kalyani, late Dr Neelkanth Kalyani, Kalyani's grandson and Amit Kalyani

Baba Kalyani and his pet Great Dane

Ajay Piramal at the Mahalaxmi Racecourse near Worli, Mumbai

Ajay and Dr Swati Piramal with daughter Nandini, son Anand and their pets

Former president A.P.J. Abdul Kalam at the inauguration of the state-of-the-art Piramal Life Sciences Centre in Mumbai in 2004

Ajay and US President Barack Obama on the latter's first visit to India in 2010

The first jute mill set up in G.M. Rao's village Rajam, Andhra Pradesh, in 1978

G.M. Rao, chairman of the GMR Group

Rao's house in Rajam

The swanky T3 at New Delhi's Indira Gandhi International Airport; construction of the terminal was completed by the team led by the GMR Group in 2010

E
G
J
L

Ronnie Screwvala with posters of one of his international productions, Mira Nair's *The Namesake*, and the 2006 hit film *Rang De Basanti*

Screwvala on the cover of *Newsweek;* the magazine called him the frontrunner in the race to become Bollywood's Jack Warner

Screwvala in his study with his pet labrador

Rajeev with his children Ved and Devika in front of the Bombardier 300 jet

Rajeev Chandrasekhar, Rajya Sabha MP and venture capitalist

Rajeev with Prime Minister Dr Manmohan Singh during a meeting organized by FICCI; in 2008, Rajeev was elected its president

through the streets of Chennai, in the sweltering heat, calling on buyers who had picked up material on credit and owed the brothers money. 'Sometimes I travelled 25 kilometres a day by cycle to collect dues.' But the daily struggle to get the money back made him realize its value and how difficult it was to make it.

He attributes a lot of what he is today and the way he functions to his trading days. 'The fundamentals of my business sense and success came from my trading days. Negotiating with farmers, small to mid-sized businessmen and banks required a totally different set of skills.' He quickly realized that he was quite good at striking a deal, building relationships and winning loyalties. A learning that helped him when he roped in over fifty partners from across the world to build the T3 in Delhi in record time.

Everything, including the Rao family's trading enterprise in Rajam, seemed to be doing quite well when Rao spotted an opportunity that would mark his first step towards something far bigger—becoming a businessman.

AN OPPORTUNITY WELL SPOTTED

It was a hot summer day in Chennai and the twenty-five-year-old Rao had been on his cycle since morning, making calls and meeting traders. The crop had been good, the brothers had done well, and he had collected a lot of money as payment from the wholesalers. Yet, he couldn't help thinking how he was throwing away an engineering degree he had worked so hard for. He had done so well. Had his friends got a job? What would his teachers say when they saw him?

As he waited to meet a local trader, he overheard a small

businessman wanting to sell the licence he had got for a jute factory he had set up in Chennai. He had shut down the factory because it had been incurring huge losses. As the conversation continued, Rao realized that the businessman was facing a fundamental issue—while he had a licence to run the jute mill in Chennai, his business would never make money because there was no jute anywhere near the city. The closest source of raw material for his mill was hundreds of kilometres away and the transportation costs were huge. One of the things Rao and his brothers transported and traded in was jute, the low-quality variety that grew around Rajam and was sent up north to Kolkata, the hub of India's jute industry.

After mulling over the jute mill for the rest of the day, he surprised everyone when he announced to his brothers the next day that he would try and buy the licence and the mill. Normally the brothers would have brushed aside such a bizarre idea, but they gave him permission since they trusted his judgement. Thus Rao took the first step towards what would make him stand out as the gutsy entrepreneur he was to become one day. He put down all that he had inherited, his life's savings, a princely sum of Rs 2.1 lakh, to buy the mill and move it to Rajam, even though he didn't have the licence to run it. All this was done purely on the basis of his gut feel.

In early 1975, a year after joining and expanding his father's trading business, Rao decided to go to Kolkata. He knew how crucial it was to make a mark in his home town if he wanted a future in the jute business. One memory from the time he spent in Kolkata is the loneliness he felt, living in a dingy little room in a small south Indian hotel in Chittaranjan Avenue. Every morning, Rao would make the trip to the Office of the Jute Commissioner, where he would be pushed from one clerk's desk to another's. Every afternoon, he would sit on a bench or the pavement, waiting for the clerks to finish their leisurely lunch and nap. His patience was finally rewarded after a four-month-long wait. By the time he got his licence, Rao knew every person in the Jute Commissioner's headquarters.

Over the next year, back in Rajam, Rao had to get his other licences in place. Steel and cement licences were needed to build the factory and it was only a year later, in 1976, backed by a loan of Rs 45 lakh from Andhra Bank, that Rao began constructing the mill in Rajam. Three long years after acquiring the jute licence, production started here in 1978.

Rao set up his office in a small double-storeyed block next to the mill, which today houses the support staff that manages his affairs in Rajam. Part of their job is to open up and air the office that he first sat in. Ostentatious in a 1970s kind of way and lined with wall-to-wall panelling and carpets, the office is a far cry from the elegantly understated marble-lined high-rise Rao sits in now. The only embellishments, apart from the dark wood panels, are a massive upholstered swivel chair, a large idol of Lord Tirupati Venkateswara, and a wall lined with small, rusty trophies.

After setting up the jute mill in Rajam, Rao spent years making it work. According to his brother-in-law, a full-time director in the now leased-out mill, one of the first things Rao did after setting it up was to modernize the machines. Every morning and evening, he would personally oversee the activities inside the factory. 'Those days, I used to buy the jute and sell it. I put it on trucks, negotiated with the brokers and the transporters and sent the jute twine across markets,' says Rao. The hard work and personal supervision paid off. Within nine months, Rao recovered the entire investment he had made and, in a year, the full cost of the project—a sum of around Rs 45 lakh—was paid up. Rao had not only changed his family fortunes, he had also learnt some important lessons in setting up a business and turning it around.

This was only the beginning. For years in a row, Rao's factory was judged one of the best and most efficiently run small-scale enterprises in Andhra Pradesh. N.T. Rama Rao, the state's chief minister through most of the 1980s, gave him an award for this each year. Over the next few years, Rao went on to apply for and procure as many licences as he could lay his hands on. Between 1978 and '91, he set up a series of other businesses, twenty-eight in all, mostly around Rajam.

This period also saw him venture out of the country to scout for new investment opportunities. The further he went, the more he realized that the opportunities were limitless. On one of his visits to South Korea, he was fascinated by the proliferation of small businesses like his. Each visit opened up a new vista. 'I went wherever there was a business opportunity,' he says. There was indeed no big design template, no game plan, and he could have been any of the millions of small businessmen who had managed to do well, working the complex system of licences in the 1980s. But his script changed, allowing him to take off within less than a decade. The first step came by default.

LESSONS IN BANKING

For Jagannadham Thunuguntla, the research head of the Delhi-based equity broking firm SMC Global Securities, and many others growing up in Andhra Pradesh, Rao is a hero. 'We would read all about him and follow every move he made in Vijayawada. Often we would discuss his successes. Anyone who had any interest in business knew Rao. Our first introduction to him came when he hit the headlines after taking over Vysya Bank. He actually saved the bank, and by the time he sold it to ING, he had become a poster boy for enterprise in the state.' Thunuguntla, however, believes Rao has never been given his due outside Andhra Pradesh. 'He has been such an audacious businessman, he should have been a national business icon for having changed the face of Indira Gandhi International Airport. Instead, he is getting pushed around needlessly.' This is an opinion shared by many, but Rao himself would probably shrug it off, saying that in the line of business he is in, only three things work: a clear plan, patience and perseverance, lessons he learnt during his crash course in banking over a decade ago.

It was really a quirk of fate and the changing dynamics on the policy front that set the stage for this transformational phase in Rao's career. During this time, the RBI asked several small private banks to shape up. They were told to bring in new independent board members, change them at regular intervals, and also bring in fresh equity capital to ensure they were able to manage their businesses.

Like many businessmen across India, Rao is part of the Vysya community that controls trade, business and commerce. The community had set up a small bank called Vysya Bank, headquartered in Bengaluru, in 1930. The bank had a capital base of a mere Rs 60 lakh, but the deposits were sizeable at Rs 200 crore, making it one of the biggest private-sector banks of the time. Though Rao had little to do with the bank—he had never even banked with it—the new RBI norms required a periodical change of directors to ensure that the banks weren't reduced to enterprises controlled by family networks. Also, the bank's attempts to expand its customer base and move to the increasingly lucrative coastal Andhra and Tamil Nadu belt led its board to zero in on him as a potential candidate. Rao did not really know what he was getting into. 'It was very respectable and I saw it as social recognition for what I had achieved,' he says.

So, in 1984, Rao put his money into another business, banking, though the intention was never to get actively involved in it. For nearly a decade, he was content, until a series of events created a near run on the bank.

In the early 1980s, when he joined Vysya Bank, the banking landscape was very different. The government-owned public sector banks controlled the banking space. The process had started in 1969, when Prime Minister Indira Gandhi had nationalized fourteen of the biggest commercial banks in India. Her government claimed this was done to keep banking and finance outside the purview of private-sector owners who were 'misusing' their banks. By 1980, when half a dozen more banks were brought under the public sector ambit, the government controlled 91 per cent of the banking sector. What remained outside, the 9 per cent, were local banks rather than regional.

Concerns regarding the management of these emerged. Many like the Catholic Syrian Bank in Kerala, Dhanalakshmi Bank, Karur Vysya Bank and Federal Bank were small but had a loyal community following. There were fears that these small banks were at risk of succumbing to political influence and biased lending and the RBI was worried that they were so small, they could even go under. As a result, it decided to tighten the norms for these private players. They were asked to shore up their liquidity, to have more stable cash in the form of fresh equity and ensure they had an independent board that would take unbiased lending decisions. Added to this was a gentle nudge to broaden their horizons and look at growing rather than 'serving a few'. It was with this purpose that Vysya Bank approached Rao to join its board. And soon after, in 1987, the bank offered its board members, including Rao, a 1:1 rights issue to raise money. This meant that for each share they held, they were offered a second at a cheaper price.

No sooner was the plan announced than Ramesh Gelli, the bank's CEO, who had been brought in to give the bank a corporate makeover in 1980, realized there were very few board members at Vysya who were willing to take up the offer. Gelli was worried that if the money wasn't raised, he and the bank would be in trouble with India's central bank. Rao, who had by now become a close friend, agreed to support him. Since he felt a moral responsibility towards the bank, he asked his family to chip in. 'I invested Rs 5–6 lakh and also requested all my friends and family members to invest a little. Seeing this, other board members also put in Rs 1 lakh each and the issue was subscribed fully, but with great difficulty.'

Vysya Bank got its money. Just when it seemed that Rao had bailed the bank out and everything was fine, it faced another problem. The script was the same this time, but the stakes were much higher. A year later, the bank came out with another rights issue. Once again, Rao came to the rescue. By now he had put in almost all the money he had into the bank, but the others were more wary this time. So he had to put in a lot more than expected. This also meant that by the end of round two, he was not only left with no money, he had become the biggest shareholder of Vysya Bank. Alongside businesses ranging from jute to ear buds, he had become the owner of a small bank.

In 1994 came a major crisis. The RBI started offering new banking licences and Ramesh Gelli decided to move out with the bank's entire top brass and set up his own outfit—the Global Trust Bank. His exit left Vysya Bank in the lurch.

The little bank in which Rao had a major stake was now on the verge of collapse. 'Some of the long-standing shareholders and the bank's former directors wanted to sell out and there were a lot of others wanting to buy a bank,' Rao recounts. With so many people leaving, depositors who had banked with Vysya for years began to get jittery.

Rao realized that he couldn't allow the problem to fester. He had little time to decide. After all, what was at stake was the savings of thousands, including Rao himself. Though Rao could have very easily sold out at this stage, he did not do so. Instead, he decided to take charge of the situation, even if it meant shifting base with his entire family to Bengaluru.

The forty-five-year-old small-time businessman from Rajam was clueless about running a bank. He had never lived outside Rajam and he knew no one in the RBI or in banking circles. He felt out of place in Bengaluru, his family was miserable, and it seemed as though he would lose all the money he had put into the bank. The odds were stacked against him on all counts.

The RBI's decision to issue new banking licences to private players meant a sea change for the sector. Some of the big guns in the Indian financial space threw their hats into the ring. India's largest project finance company, ICICI, started ICICI Bank, the biggest house mortgage firm HDFC started HDFC Bank, the largest asset management company started UTI Bank (now Axis Bank) and even the country's biggest media house, Times Group, came up with Times Bank. There was an aggressiveness in the Indian banking sector not hitherto witnessed. The stakes were high and each of these players was jostling for talent, know-how and market share. Under the circumstances, it must have been tough for a small bank like Vysya and a novice like Rao to hold the fort.

As the single biggest shareholder, Rao had a lot at stake. He was also responsible to the many investors who had put their money in the bank as he had, and there was no one else he could turn to. As he went through the bank accounts, he realized that the bank had spread itself across various segments. It had acquired a number of associated subsidiaries that handled everything from leasing to housing and portfolio management. But most of these businesses had not even started making money.

The expansion had been too extensive, the investment in Vysya Bank seemed too little, the balance sheet was stretched, but the bank had not put money back into strengthening its core banking business. It had no experienced hands, no technology, and it needed a fresh infusion of ideas. Undaunted, Rao got down to work. His experience in turning around the jute mill helped, even though banking was a new segment. This was perhaps the biggest challenge of his career so far. 'It was a big learning experience for me. Overnight, I had to recruit two hundred people, and this was done largely from public sector banks. It would take me days to even get an appointment with RBI officials. I didn't know anyone in Bengaluru, leave alone Mumbai. I had come straight from a small town,' he recalls.

Most people had written him off by now. He was an outsider in the banking world and few had even heard of him. They were sure that the bank would collapse.

Those who worked with him at that time say it was nothing but stubborn grit that pushed him on. The first challenge for Rao was to prove that the bank could survive the exit of its CEO. 'At that time, the bank was known because of its CEO and when he left, there was a big vacuum,' he says. In a business where trust is critical, people didn't want to put money in a headless bank that seemed to be going nowhere.

Rao began by getting the right man at the helm—the former chairman of the state-owned Corporation Bank, K. Ramamurthy, who brought the much-needed experience and credibility the bank required at that time. People were hired from across the public sector banks and the latest technology, which came at a heavy price and with a long payback, was introduced.

'I brought some high-end core banking software technology from the US and implemented it in Vysya Bank. We were among the first banks in India to do so,' says Rao. He also decided that Vysya would focus only on core banking. The bank exited its leasing and home-loans business to focus on what it did best, plain vanilla lending.

To take the bank to the next level, Rao went scouting for solid partners. Once the basics were taken care of, he was convinced that this would be essential to ensure that Vysya Bank could stand up to the big aggressive private sector banks. As luck would have it, here too an interesting opportunity came his way when Belgian bank Banque Brussels Lambert (BBL) expressed interest in getting a foothold in the Indian market. The fit seemed right and Rao sold a 5 per cent stake in Vysya to BBL. But it didn't end with just a stake sale. He also ensured that BBL brought far more to the table than its name and money. 'I not only gave them a place on the board, but also a representation on every board committee set up to revive the bank. That helped us learn a lot!' Within a year of this deal, BBL raised its stake in Vysya Bank to 10 per cent as the insurance business in India opened up, and soon after, BBL was bought by the Dutch financial giant ING. Rao now found himself with an even stronger partner.

It was at this time that the Indian economy slipped into a long slowdown. It was actually confined to a few sectors, but it hit most Indian manufacturers and the banks that lent to them quite hard. As the initial flush of pent-up demand in the domestic market waned and exports took a hit because of the emerging Asian crisis, signs of impending disaster became obvious. Industrial output in India fell from 12.5 per cent in 1995–96 to just half in 1997–98. For big and small companies, it was a hard knock and many businessmen who had borrowed money (at high interest rates) from big and small banks got into serious trouble.

Rao recalls, 'As the economy went into a slump, our non-performing assets touched a high of 15.6 per cent. I created a separate team that was focussed only on the recovery of loans. We did nothing but recovery for the next two years.' This would not just save the bank, it would also prove to be a training ground for Rao.

LEARNING WHAT NOT TO DO

A man was explaining something to a group of stern-looking men with their shirt sleeves rolled up, sitting on the other side of a rough wooden table in a dingy room in a hotel in Coimbatore. The discussion had been going on for long. It was evident from the expressions on the faces of everyone present in the room that what was being said wasn't new. There was very little sympathy.

The businessman was a familiar face. Till a year ago, the local bank manager from even the biggest public sector bank in Coimbatore would have spent hours in the anteroom of the businessman's office, waiting for an audience with him. But he was on the other side of the table today.

Instead of focussing on his business and working on expanding it, the businessman had squandered his company's profits, which should have been used to fund expansions or at least put in a safe fixed deposit, by venturing into other areas, such as loans to stock-market brokers. These loans attracted huge rates of interest and were easy money. In good times, when stock markets in Mumbai soared, everyone made a neat packet. But that was a temporary phase. When the tide turned, so did the fortunes.

He sat across the table, trying to convince the panel how much he regretted his decisions. The bets, the debt he had taken to fund some of his passions, and the fact that he hadn't put a paisa into his own business—textiles—had made him almost bankrupt. He confessed that the one thing that he hadn't accounted for was an economic slowdown.

Rao was at the centre of the group of bank officials trying to get the businessman's textile mill back on track. He remembers many such cases. 'It was all the same. This businessman was from such a big family and yet, he had come to this state. The more I listened to him, I realized that the formula for disaster and bankruptcy was common across businesses.' Instead of investing in technology and people, these businesses used their surpluses to invest in stock markets and films.

Another important lesson he learnt was about balancing the family's ambitions and business interests. The biggest eye-opener for him was the fact that 80 per cent of all business defaults stemmed from family disputes. 'The best-laid business plans come to naught if your family members fight over it.' And finally, the biggest lesson of all: a banker would give money to a businessman only if he ran a clean shop that was strong and sustainable.

In the case of Vysya, financial records proved that it was one of the quickest to rebound after the crisis and, within two years, its non-performing assets or bad loans came down from a worrisome 15.6 per cent to just 4.5 per cent.

By 1999, barely five years after coming to Bengaluru, Rao had been through a crash course in high finance and had successfully turned around a bank. During this time, the Dutch partner expressed a desire to buy out Vysya's stake. ING made an offer and Rao agreed to let go. He pocketed a good profit, well worth the money and the time he had invested in building up Vysya Bank. It wasn't easy for him to get out of the bank, but he was a practical man. 'I realized that banking was a difficult business. To grow, you have to put in capital. Where would I have got it from?' No big bank the world over was actually owned by a family, and it was a telling sign.

Today, Rao is proud of ING Vysya's success. But he also knows that if he hadn't sold then, he wouldn't have been able to do what he did next. The sale gave him over Rs 700 crore and the experience to make his foray into India's big infrastructure sector through power, roads and airports.

POWERING AHEAD

A lot of people remember a small yellow notepad Rao carries with him to jot down any idea that comes to his mind or a question that crops up. Sometime in the mid-1990s, Rao made two significant entries in the notepad: first, he would dream bigger and focus on two things—agriculture and related industries, which he knew well; and second, infrastructure, which he knew intuitively would be crucial for India during its growth.

He also realized that to fund these ambitions, he would have to move out of non-core businesses and raise cash. This decision came at an opportune moment when India was not just changing, but also because Rao's sons were ready to join him. But having made the plan, his actual entry into the first of the three big infrastructure projects that he would focus on—power—came purely by accident.

In 1992, Rao got the licence to build a brewery and sugar mill in Rajam. To fund the mills, he tapped the Indian stock markets. The issue went through, but just as it did, he faced an unforeseen setback. N.T. Rama Rao, who came back as chief minister of Andhra Pradesh in 1994, put a spanner in the works and declared prohibition across the state. Under these circumstances, it made little sense to produce alcohol.

He went ahead and built the sugar mill, which he later sold to the Chennai-based Murugappa Group, but the brewery took a back seat.

When economic liberalization began, one of the first sectors the P.V. Narasimha Rao government looked at to bring in reforms was power. Acute shortages and increasing corruption had made reforms in the power sector crucial and, in a hurry to build up capacity, the government sought private participation by opening up power generation and distribution, in some pockets, to the private sector.

The Central government set the tariffs and for many players, mostly large international ones like Enron, the terms were attractive—a steady 16 per cent return on equity and full repatriation of profits out of India. But the initial strategy soon fell through. Without the necessary reforms at the state electricity board level, where a lot of the problem lay, and the constantly shifting terms of the contract, especially over the cost of power and the delays in commissioning plants, most big independent power projects seemed to fail.

Rao entered the power sector at this juncture. If the Centre's early attempts to attract investments in the sector had yielded mixed results, by the end of the 1990s, various state governments had decided to liberalize the power sector as well. Almost bankrupt, they invited private players to set up power generation units. While Rao had missed the first leg (when the power sector had opened up) of these independent power projects or IPPs, he was quick to bid for this one. The first opportunity came from Tamil Nadu. The state invited tenders to set up a privately owned and run power plant in Chennai. Rao had built his business by pitching for every possible licence he could lay his hands on, and he did the same here. He had no clue how to run a plant, let alone build one, but that was pretty much the case in every licence-based business he had ventured into till now.

He roped in experienced and strategic partners in crucial areas. Two years after bagging the rights to build and run the power plant, he got it going. As part of the agreement to woo private enterprise into power generation, the Tamil Nadu government had also promised to provide a steady supply of water, essential for running any power plant, free of cost. Instead of seeing it as a sop, the astute businessman in Rao had mixed feelings. He was quick to realize that this clause would put his project at risk. Chennai was short of water and there was no way the government could live up to its promise of supplying water to his plant when the city was running out of it.

Rao said no to the free water and decided instead to spend money and put up a massive sewage water treatment plant to recycle water and use it to generate power. His logic was simple: Chennai would never run out of sewage water. The idea worked and the project was a success from the word go. Today, the plant recycles about 7,200 cubic metres of the city's sewage water and uses it for its operations. The exercise was costly to set up but it was worth it. 'The plant would have shut down within months if we had gone with the government's promise of water.'

If the Chennai power plant, in the heart of the city, was novel in its scope and scale, the next power venture was even more ambitious.

FLOATING ON WATER

In 1998, the year the Chennai power plant became operational, Rao got the go ahead for another power venture. The Karnataka government, faced with an acute shortage of power, wanted private players to build a plant quickly. Very few companies expressed interest in the beginning. Most said it was impossible to build a plant at such short notice. The American-Malaysian joint venture company which finally won the bid ran into trouble when one of the partners faced a financial problem. They were forced to sell their licence and Rao was ready to buy it. But the project seemed difficult. No matter how hard the team tried, it appeared impossible to meet the demands of the state government and build as well as run a plant within the timeline it had set.

Caught in a bind, Rao remembered something he had seen on his frequent visits to South East Asia, when he was a small businessman in Rajam. Not only were these countries rapidly scaling up their infrastructure, building super highways, airports and ports, small businessmen like him were redefining the rules of global trade. Rao had been a keen observer of the rapid changes happening there and he wanted to do more. In fact, on one of his visits he had seen several barge-mounted power-generating plants like those littered around the island of Macau and Malaysia. These floating plants anchored in the sea were powered by propellers similar to the ones used in aircraft and they were extremely efficient, mobile and easy to maintain.

The question was how to get this done in Mangalore. He decided to simply ship one in. A barge-mounted plant (formerly known as the Tannir Bhavi Power Project) was custom-built in South Korea. At 220 MW, it was to be the biggest of its kind in the world. It travelled all the way to Mangalore, where it was to be fed with naphtha, which was easily available from the government-owned refineries in Mangalore and Cochin. Despite facing a lot of delays because of differences over pricing and displacement, it survived and prospered. This was the only project that had a government-backed escrow cover, which assures timely payment for the power supplied, funding it. The guarantee was the product of a protracted court battle in the High Court after Rao sued the state government for reneging on its promise of paying GMR for the power that it was supplying.

In August 2010, villagers along the east coast, a couple of kilometres beyond the port of Kakinada, were surprised to see a massive vessel, the colour of the midnight sky, with the name *Hawk* painted on the side in bold white lettering. Though it was the size of the vessel that caught everyone's attention, the structure it was carrying and the three, much smaller, boats that were leading the colossus also held everyone spellbound. On board the small boats were engineers from the GMR Group, while a helicopter buzzed around the vessel. The movement of the 14,000 tonne barge-mounted power plant was an amazing feat.

The long journey had been ambitious and precarious, over 2,400 kilometres, double the distance between Mangalore and Kakinada by road. To record this journey, Rao had even commissioned a documentary film. The engineers explained how months of planning had gone into the shift and how delicate it had been. A single mistake could have jeopardized the whole process.

But this journey comes much later in the G.M. Rao story. In 1999, an opportunity opened up a new avenue that eventually turned out to be a big launch pad for GMR—airports.

INDIA'S 'AIRPORT MAN'

The date was 24 March 2000 and Hyderabad was spruced up for a visit that would catapult the city and Chief Minister Chandrababu Naidu on to the international stage.

US President Bill Clinton was in town to endorse the

transformation of this old Nizam's capital into an alternative global IT hub dubbed Cyberabad. Hundreds of thousands of people watched the live telecast of the ceremony as Clinton sat on stage, flanked by Naidu and Ramalinga Raju, the head of Hyderabad's biggest IT firm, Satyam, on either side. Even for those watching the proceedings on television, the excitement and nervousness were clearly palpable.

Though this was Hyderabad's moment, one man who was conspicuously absent on stage was G.M. Rao. Rao, however, was to play a pivotal role in the future. After all, he would go on to build Hyderabad's new international airport, which was integral to Naidu's vision for the transformation of Hyderabad into Cyberabad. Two years earlier, consultancy firm McKinsey & Company had been roped in to create a new 'Vision 2020' for Hyderabad and the state. The aims were lofty: create a 9–10 per cent sustainable growth in the state over the next twenty-five years; work towards a thirteen-fold increase in industry; create 20 million jobs and script the transition of the state from an agriculture-led economy to a new-age, services-oriented one.

Naidu wanted to harness the capabilities of the many young techies who left Hyderabad each year to power IT start-ups across the US's Silicon Valley. And the McKinsey plan fitted in well. Andhra Pradesh was at an interesting stage of growth in those days. Successive governments had embarked on projects across the large tracts of barren land in the state's hinterland that would see the emergence of a lot of construction companies. The big turning point had been the construction of the massive Rs 1,300 crore Nagarjuna Sagar dam, work on which had begun in the 1950s. It took twenty years to construct and employed more than 70,000 people. The project gave birth to a network of canals, dams and irrigation projects, spawning more construction work and a lot of mid-sized infrastructure companies. These companies, like IVRCL, Nagarjuna Construction, GVK and a host of others, have come to be known as the 'Andhra Club' within the infrastructure sector.

Naidu's plan was to combine the intrinsic strengths of the state's construction entrepreneurs and new-age techies to create a new economic hub.

Integral to the airport plans was a study by McKinsey which said over the next two decades Hyderabad would see a huge influx of visitors. The study projected that by 2020, 2.5 million international and 70 million domestic tourists would visit the state as opposed to a mere 60,000 international and 33 million domestic tourists who had bought tickets to the state in 1996. For this, the state needed two big international airports and five or six domestic ones.

Building an airport is not as easy as laying a road. And to make matters worse, the state government had acquired land in Shamshabad, 22 kilometres from Hyderabad, to house this structure. Naidu invited bids for India's first greenfield airport project under a public–private partnership format, but the bidders were sceptical.

Twenty-six players showed interest, but as they received more and more details, they fell out of the race. Finally, it came down to three players, one of them being GMR, which was in partnership with another developer—Malaysia Airports Holding Berhad.

Rao made headlines by offering the highest bid (and seeking the lowest government grant) to build the Hyderabad international airport. Nearly everyone said it was impossible to build an airport of this size at that price and with that kind of revenue in place. But Rao was plain lucky. 'I don't think I knew the full worth of what we could do here when we won the bid. It was made on a hunch. There was no doubt in my mind that the figure of 0.7 million people who used the Hyderabad airport each year would go up to 7 million in a matter of years. The connection between a growing economy and the air traffic hubs it created were only too clear to me when I visited Changi airport in Singapore or Dubai's international airport.' But that was a long haul. As he delved deeper into the project he had bid for, he realized the upside could be far more immediate.

For over three months, after getting the Hyderabad airport contract, Rao and his top team travelled across the world in small groups to study airports. The teams went to Singapore's Changi, Amsterdam's Schiphol and European hubs like Zurich and Munich. The mandate was clear: learn how the best do the best. Each visit opened up a new idea, a new opportunity and a new expert to partner with.

How difficult was it to build India's first big greenfield airport? Rao says, 'I had the confidence after setting up the power plants. They are very complex and once you are able to do that, you can do anything.'

As he learnt his way around the airports business, Rao also realized he could do a lot with the land around the airport. The Hyderabad airport came with over 5,000 acres of land. Without developing the ecosystem and hubs around it, the airport would be nothing but a lonely outpost. Developed fully, it would be an architectural marvel in the city of the Nizams.

On 30 March 2008, nearly three years after the project's initiation, the Rajiv Gandhi International Airport was inaugurated. Its passenger terminals occupy six floors and are expected to handle an estimated 50 million passengers every year. As one drives through the vast expanse of mostly barren landscape towards the airport, flowering trees and shrubs, remarkably well maintained, can be seen flanking the road on both sides. The airport's glass and metal structure looms large up ahead, and the towering building seems as if it is almost touching the sky.

Despite the big build-up, Rao's very first airport seems to be jinxed. Its opening coincided with the global financial crisis and slowdown. Next came a raging political debate. At the heart of the controversy was the spectre of the bifurcation of Andhra Pradesh and the creation of the new state of Telangana. As the debate raged and anger spilled over, there were questions about what would happen next. How it would impact GMR's Hyderabad airport and interfere with the big plans around it. But after years of confusion, there has been some respite for GMR. On 30 July 2013, under immense political pressure ahead of the elections, the UPA government at the Centre gave its clearance for the creation of Telangana, India's twenty-ninth state. Hyderabad will be the joint capital of Andhra Pradesh and Telangana for a period of ten years. With this, some of the uncertainty regarding the future of the capital city ends.

But Rao had always been confident through the years. 'If Telangana happens, it's even better! How many cities do you see like Hyderabad? I think Hyderabad has the best infrastructure in the country. Bengaluru seems to be crumbling as infrastructure is not keeping pace with growth. Land costs are also not high in Hyderabad and, over the years, it has been the only state without an energy shortage.' Rao was not worried. 'The issue [separate statehood] will have an impact for one or two months. After that, there will be no looking back!'

While all this was happening, Rao came up with the idea of bidding for international airports since geography was never a constraint for him. In 2008, he won the bid to develop the Sabiha Gokcen International Airport in Turkey. This was followed by a project in Male, but that's currently in limbo.

THE T3

In 2003, Delhi won the bid to host the Commonwealth Games to be held in 2011 and the new government that came to power a year later, the United Progressive Alliance (UPA) led by Dr Manmohan Singh, decided that a new airport would make a wonderful statement at the games.

The issue of privatization of the Delhi and Mumbai airports had been floating around for nearly a decade. It was first mooted in 1996, but virulent opposition from the powerful airport worker's unions, who were backed by the left parties, had ensured that the idea remained buried. In 2003, the National Democratic Alliance (NDA) government, led by Atal Bihari Vajpayee, resurrected it in a 'Build India' rush, but it was left to the UPA government to implement it.

When the bid was finally opened in May 2004, there was a great deal of excitement. So much so that a wide range of Indian businessmen, from telecom giant Bharti's Sunil Mittal to Anil Dhirubhai Ambani Group's Anil Ambani and Videocon's Venugopal Dhoot made a pitch for it. Each came with a partner who knew the ropes of airport construction well. Bharti had a tie-up with Singapore's Changi Airport Company, L&T tied up with the Piramals, and Anil Ambani came in with Mexico's ASA. Rao felt small and insignificant in that group even though his partner was Frankfurt's airport company, Fraport.

By the time bidding for the Mumbai and Delhi airports closed on 14 September 2005, only five of the ten consortia who had set their sights on Delhi remained in the fray. In Mumbai's case, the final tally was six.

Bharti and Changi and L&T-Piramal-Hochtief pulled out, citing stiff performance criteria in the transaction documents. The partnership between DLF and its partner, Malaysia's MANSB, a wholly-owned subsidiary of Malaysia Airports Holdings Berhad, dissolved.

Those left standing with bids in hand had layers of committees to go through before the winner would be announced. It took four months of nail-biting suspense, drama and a big fight in the courts before the victor's name was announced.

Winning the bid wasn't about the tangible or calculable lowest price bid. According to the terms and conditions, the evaluation process was to be in four stages: first, assessment of the basic mandatory requirements; second, assessment of the financial commitments of the bidders; third, assessment of the technical pre-qualification criteria including management and development capabilities; and finally, assessment of the financial consideration, whether the bidder is offering the highest financial bid. The bidder qualifying on all these counts was to be declared the winner.

Crucial to the evaluation was the stipulation that bidders who scored at least 80 per cent marks in the third stage would move to the final one. By the time the process reached this stage, only two bidders qualified for both the airports—Reliance ASA and GMR Fraport.

In the end, GMR Fraport emerged the winner and Rao was asked to choose between the two airports. He chose Delhi. Mumbai went to another Hyderabad-based company, GVK.

While Rao had won the war for the bid, there was one battle still left to be fought. This time, it was in Delhi High Court, as Reliance ADAG took him to court saying that the selection process for the Delhi airport had flouted every rule in the book. Rao won this round too, as the court ruled that the subjectivity of the final decision was justified given the enormity of the task at hand.

The challenges that Rao faced while constructing T3 would have undone a lesser man. 'When we got into the project, I was not fully aware of what I was in for. Within months, it was clear that the project wasn't as simple as had been envisaged.' To make it viable, Rao would need to build a second low-cost terminal and an underpass leading to the new one to ensure that there weren't any traffic snarls on the road. Each of these decisions needed permissions from over forty departments, apart from additional funds. It seemed the project would cost more money than anticipated.

To prove his point that a new underpass was critical, Rao drove K.M. Chandrasekhar, who was the cabinet secretary at that time, through the traffic on the highway to show just how bad things could get at peak time.

Rao divided the project into 200 packages or contracts and outsourced them to a host of contractors. Twenty-four companies and people from across the world worked together to make the project happen in a record thirty-seven months. GMR's airport division oversaw the entire effort, set out the tasks and ensured that they were done in the most efficient manner.

The GMR Group team had pulled off the impossible. It had worked closely with fifty-eight government departments and got the work done on time. The result was a magnificent state-of-the-art, integrated terminal. There is an advanced five-level-in-line baggage handling system with explosive detection technology for greater efficiency and security. There are more than 168 check-in counters and eighteen aerobridges. The two-tier terminal building houses the departure complex on the upper level and the arrivals on the lower level. Access to the terminal is via a six-lane approach road.

But despite the accolades and the attention Rao got in the run-up to T3, less than a year on, it seemed he was facing the toughest challenge of his life. The making of the new terminal had cost a lot of money, upwards of Rs 14,000 crore, more than the entire net worth of the company. GMR had taken on a lot of debt to pay for the building. By 2011, the net debt on GMR Infrastructure's books was Rs 22,000 crore, a lot of it thanks to Delhi's international airport, and based on some guarantees that the government had made at the time of bidding. Guarantees that ensured that the project was financially viable.

According to the initial agreement, the developer was allowed to charge passengers a certain amount of money as 'development charges' till revenue from the broader project, such as the facilities around it, like the restaurants and hotels nearby, started to come in. But no sooner did the new airport regulator, the Airports Economic Regulatory Authority of India (AERA), come in place than it reneged on the promise. Its logic was that passengers couldn't be burdened with the cost overruns of a project.

For Rao, the logic of his entire investment and his financial projections had gone for a toss. Today, as the GMR Group fights for the new airport and its viability, Rao seems friendless. The stock market hasn't been very kind either. Not just because of the uncertainty but because of the overall slowdown across Rao's businesses.

No wonder then that between Friday, 2 July 2010, a day before the inauguration of T3, to Friday, 1 July 2011, two days before the first anniversary celebrations, the stock price of GMR Infrastructure had come down 45 per cent. And by March 2013, the stock was down 68 per cent from its 2010 high. Not to mention the flak the airport received when a spell of torrential rain in July 2013 flooded the terminals, severely denting its world-class aspirations and leaving its engineers red-faced.

Weeks before the first anniversary of the inauguration of T3, the 17 June issue of *Forbes India* magazine had Rao on the cover with a forlorn expression on his face and the headline 'One Step Up, Two Steps Down'. The story proclaimed that the story of GMR and G.M. Rao was symbolic and representative of the crisis the Indian infrastructure sector faced. Across industries, hundreds and thousands of crores of investment were stuck due to project delays and policy changes by the government.

And amidst all this, each of the businesses Rao had his fingers in seemed to have been hit.

In March 2012, it was reported that GMR Infrastructure had put the development of its Rs 7,000 crore power project in Shahdol, Madhya Pradesh, on hold because of acute coal shortage faced by the company and the power sector.

This was despite the fact that months earlier, given the fuel crisis in the power sector, Prime Minister Manmohan Singh had personally intervened to ensure additional power. Rao had accompanied the biggest businessmen, including Tata Group Chairman Cyrus Mistry and Anil Ambani of the Anil

Dhirubhai Ambani Group (ADAG), to a meeting with Singh to discuss power sector woes. But even a year later, nothing seemed to have moved.

Instead, as time went by, there were reports of more projects being shelved.

In Kakinada too, the GMR Group's ambitious plans to have a 'power zone' at its 11,000-acre special economic zone (SEZ) came to naught. Along the coast in Kakinada, the shortage of gas left a series of plants, including its barge-mounted one, idle or barely working.

There were hints of trouble in the roads venture too. High costs of funds as interest rates zoomed, land acquisition issues, painful bureaucratic delays and the need for multiple clearances brought India's ambitious road project to a crawl through 2011–12. In January 2013, GMR Infrastructure once again hit the headlines when it pulled out of the Rs 7,700 crore Kishangarh–Udaipur–Ahmedabad project. Other developers like GVK followed suit.

Between June and August 2012, Delhi International Airport Limited (DIAL), T3 and GMR were in the eye of another storm, this one scripted by the powerful comptroller and auditor general of India (CAG) and its head, Vinod Rai. The questions Rai's office raised on DIAL and the bid GMR won for the Delhi airport were basic. It slammed the government, claiming that the land that was handed over to DIAL had a potential earning capacity of an astounding Rs 163,557 crore. And it had been given away to the GMR-run consortium for a song: Rs 2,450 crore! The calculation was based on the potential of the land and its appreciation over the next sixty years. It also questioned the development fee that the civil aviation ministry had allowed DIAL to levy as part of the contract.

DIAL quickly issued a statement: 'The bid process and conditions were reviewed and upheld by the Supreme Court in 2006.' This was in reference to the case it had won against ADAG in 2006.

It also claimed that the figure of Rs 163,557 crore was misleading. It was the absolute value of projected revenues over fifty-eight years. It didn't represent the time value of money and that the present value of land was just Rs 4,547 crore.

As this debate raged, another crisis came GMR's way. This time from a cluster of 1,190 coral islands in the Arabian Sea, the Republic of Maldives. Here, GMR was caught in the eye of a political storm after a coup. On the night of 7 December 2012, the state-owned Maldives Airport Company took over the operations of the Ibrahim Nassir International Airport. A few days earlier, on 27 November, the new government had cancelled the existing contract with GMR. Two years earlier, GMR and its partner Malaysia Airport Holdings had been awarded the contract by President Mohamed Nasheed. Nasheed, who had led the first democratically elected government in the country in thirty years, had been ousted in February 2012.

At the time of the cancellation, the Male airport accounted for 20 per cent of GMR's revenues from the airport division, and this was a major setback for the already-in-trouble company. After losing out in a Singapore court, arbitration proceedings are on in the case. GMR and its partner are demanding a compensation of $700m.

For a man who has worked so hard to reach where he has to say 'There is always confusion when something new happens' is ironic. Rao's take on business, infrastructure in particular is a basic one. 'For me, PPP is about patience, perseverance and passion, not just public–private partnership, and you need large quantities of all three to do business here.' He remains as bullish on the Indian growth story today as he was two years ago. The noise and problems in infrastructure are largly teething issues, he believes, as policies try and keep up with the hectic pace of growth.

Manish Agarwal, a partner at PricewaterhouseCoopers, says Rao has been successful because he understands the system. Agarwal points out that this marks out a whole new breed of infrastructure and business barons across the developing world where there is continuous economic activity, and that too at a very fast pace. Agarwal is right. That's how it has been with Rao as well, from his beginnings as a trader, through the transition to a small businessman, a banker and, finally, an infrastructure developer.

GROUP CSR

Like most small rural hamlets and cluster of villages spilling into market towns across India, Rajam too has a local deity—Navadurga Mata—one of the many reincarnations of the fiery demon slayer, goddess Durga. Locals believe that their goddess has nine manifestations: creativity, energy, sacrifice, ambition, charm, radiance, nurturance, aggression and tenacity. Rao has exhibited all these qualities in different ways through his journey from Rajam. A journey that definitely hasn't been a bed of roses.

One of his delayed projects has been in Odisha at the group's 1,050 MW coal-based Kamalanga Power Project. GMR bagged the project in 2004 but actual work began only in 2010 and the project was finally commissioned two years later.

In 2005, Odisha made national headlines when the Biju Janata Dal-government, led by Naveen Patnaik, announced that the Pohang Steel Company, POSCO, the fourth largest steel company in the world, had decided to make its single largest investment outside its country by setting up a $12bn plant in the mineral-rich state. The site for the project was to be Jagatsinghpur in Paradip district. This triggered a virtual rush to Odisha.

India's top industrialists landed in Bhubaneswar. ADAG announced Rs 60,000 crore of investments; India's biggest industrial group, the Tatas, promised to set up a steel plant. London-based Vedanta group chairman Anil Agarwal announced that he would not only set up factories but also schools and colleges.

Each plan was bigger and grander than the last.

But as the excitement built up, there were also concerns on the impact of all this development on the environment, as well as the villagers, especially if it was to cause their displacement. All this became a potent platform for political strife. At the core of the problem was the future and livelihood of the thousands of poor tribals who had lived in and off the forests for generations.

The problems festered, the crisis continued and none of the massive investment plans fructified. When the stand-off around the POSCO's plans first grabbed the nation's attention, Rao realized it would be impossible to build his power plant or risk the massive investments required for it without winning the support of the locals of Kamalanga.

So, in 2007, a group of employees from the GMR Varalakshmi Foundation, the corporate social responsibility (CSR) wing of the company that Rao had set up, decided to go to Kamalanga and start working with the communities.

The strategy was to provide the villagers around the project site with all that they did not have. Schools, hospitals, training schools and skill-development centres were established to convince them that they wouldn't be displaced just because a big project was being planned. Instead, they would actually get better jobs.

Rao knew that antagonizing the locals, who were the backbone of any such big investment, would be counterproductive. He took a cue for this strategy from the international partners he was working with. Relief and rehabilitation plans were indispensable. Rao had learnt this early in Rajam at his jute factory where local political goons rarely stirred up a strike, otherwise a common occurrence in the area, because he was always liberal in sharing the profits through bonuses.

More than just a CSR activity, the training classes had become an important storehouse of talent for Rao's projects.

For example, outside the Shamshabad airport, adjoining the landscaped greens and the Chinmaya Mission School, is a single-storey complex that houses a cross section of student groups. The students are from the airport catchment area and they are trying to master skills that can earn them money. Today they earn a living from within the same airport that they once saw being built, manning the many retail outlets there.

There is a small double-storeyed building that acts as a residential school for young school dropouts who learn various skills at the GMR-run engineering college in Rajam, sponsored by the Andhra Bank and the GMR Varalakshmi Foundation. A group of mechanics, electricians and engineers teach batches of students how to earn a living. Most of the boys here are locals, largely from the villages on the Andhra-Odisha border.

The school runs an exchange programme too and some of the boys come all the way from Kamalanga.

In March 2011, Rao became one of the first Indian businessmen to pledge over Rs 1,540 crore to create an endowment for his family's GMR Varalakshmi Foundation, headed by former IIMA professor and author V. Raghunathan. The endowment comprised almost all the money he had as a personal share in his business and, while the announcement was low key, one thing that stood out was the thought behind it. Rao says, 'It has been a long journey and it has been satisfying to create and leave something behind!' So much so that over the next few years, he wants to spend a lot more time and energy on the foundation he has put in place.

THE ROAD AHEAD

The outlays for infrastructure in India are mind-boggling and understandably so. A decade of rapid growth has meant that infrastructure is woefully lacking and anyone even on a short pit stop to India will realize that every city needs more roads, better power connections, bridges, houses and airports.

With the need, the opportunity and the build-up so far, infrastructure companies like GMR have grown exponentially. Even though major projects have been postponed as the Indian government battled issues from soaring prices to corruption, experts believe this is just a passing phase. Delhi-based infrastructure advisory firm Feedback's chairman Vinayak Chatterjee says that GMR is only facing the first pangs of growth. Chatterjee first met Rao when he was a small-time Andhra-based businessman trying to have a go at the new national highway building project the government had invited bids for. Chatterjee had advised Rao then and has watched him through the years. He thinks Rao was very clear that he wanted to be a serious player in the infrastructure sector and he realized early that to do so, he would have to run a clean shop. He was one of the first entrepreneurs in this sector to talk of and practise corporate governance, bringing in professionals and experts and creating the kind of company that would attract investors. 'GMR is like a boa constrictor that has consumed a big animal. It needs time to digest what it has swallowed. The Delhi and Hyderabad airports are big investments,' he says.

As Rao waits for this, he has been smart enough to make sure that he is ready to run by the time his company does digest the big projects it has on its plate.

Core to his plan is the wish to ensure that what he has built lives on after him.

From his experience in Vysya Bank, when he sat across the table and negotiated with an almost bankrupt businessman, Rao learnt an important lesson: the best-laid plans and strategies of an entrepreneur can come to nothing, if your children and grandchildren destroy value.

The 'Rao family constitution' runs into many pages. It dictates what each member can do and not do in terms of business. This is one of the reasons why not a single family member, except Rao, makes a public statement. It dictates that family fights, even petty domestic ones, be discussed openly and sorted out, no matter how many tears are shed or egos are hurt. It even goes to the extent of dictating what cars each family member can own or drive.

For now, Rao has a lot of plans up his sleeve.

First, he has a one-, three- and five-year plan he is working on. At the end of the plan period, he wants to become a significant—and the most efficient—player in every segment he is in, and he is gearing up for phase two of the development.

Take roads, for example. While the company has been one of the first developers of the national highways project, the big bet ahead is on phase two, in which many highways will morph into fast traffic expressways. These projects will be much bigger and will require far more than just construction skills, and work is already under way here. This could really be the next big kicker for the sector and the companies in the space.

In the power sector, the group is hoping to wait it out till the sector gets back on track and become an important player. Over the next few years, it is estimated that India will spend over $500bn in power. The group will be ready to cash in on that.

The most high-profile and visible business in the GMR portfolio and the only one that is really interfacing with users directly has to be the airports business. The prominent GMR logo in Hyderabad airport and New Delhi's T3 has been the biggest advertisement the company could have asked for. The extra effort has put the company in the reckoning as a credible airports builder that could bid for work anywhere in the world. The thousand of travellers who pass through each day would corroborate that.

GMR clearly has the next three to five years well charted out. Rao doesn't want to build the biggest infrastructure company in India but the most efficient one, because 'in business, one should not run after size, but ensure that one is the best'.

Today, despite the problems he faces, Rao is sitting at the helm of a promising empire and he is a name to reckon with across the country. But it is to Rajam that Rao will go back one day. As he has done, every year, since the time he left his home town over fifteen years ago.

His annual homecoming has grown in scale and size. Each year, he and his family visit this little town for a yearly pilgrimage around the time of Pongal and hand out ubiquitous parcels with saris, dhotis and food packets. Through the year, the entire GMR Varalakshmi Foundation team works hard to make this event happen. Over 2,500 volunteers are roped in for the meticulously planned mission. It gets more expensive each year. Last year, the Rao family paid Rs 1 crore for it. Not surprising given there were 30,000 people who thronged from all over Andhra Pradesh and Odisha. And it's not the numbers that stand out, but the manner in which the whole Herculean exercise is conducted. It gets done with precision and is wrapped up within just forty-five minutes! That says a lot about the legacy of the man. It also underlines that no matter how successful he gets, or how far he goes, for Grandhi Mallikarjuna Rao, home is where his heart is—in Rajam.

RONNIE SCREWVALA

It was a film no one in Bollywood would have touched with the proverbial bargepole. In an industry which usually churned out feel-good romantic musicals and family dramas at regular intervals, the 2006 box-office hit *Rang De Basanti* stood out by a mile.

Everyone in the Indian movie business had rejected it, saying it wouldn't work. The story wasn't like anything anyone had seen. Why would anyone watch a film that chronicled the journey of a bunch of carefree college kids stumbling upon an almost-forgotten chapter of Indian history and being inspired by it to take on a corrupt system and almost fail? Most of the film was shot in sepia-toned black and white. There was no romance, no glamour, and the best-known actor cast in the film looked old and puffy-eyed. *Rang De Basanti* did extremely well and few remember its arduous journey to the can and the years it took to come alive. In the Indian box-office, driven more by passion than science at the best of times, it clicked and became a sensation.

Years later, a national daily listed the film amongst the ten most influential films ever made in India. The movie made nationalism cool and brought youngsters from college canteens out on the streets. The paper referred to a series of citizen-led movements, fanned to a great extent by the media and inspired by the film for a couple of years after its release. Justice for Jessica; justice for Nitish Katara; justice for Priyadarshini Mattoo; and crusades against government apathy: in each case, the story was the same—long-pending cases, corruption and delayed justice. The film inspired candle-light vigils and street marches.

But there was more to it than the sentiments it aroused and the marches it inspired. As days rolled into weeks and box-office revenues poured in from all over the country, there was frenzy. Veterans of the industry tried to fathom the magnitude of the success. Others cringed at how mundane their productions looked in comparison. Everyone wanted to know who could have had the gumption to greenlight a project like this one.

Rohinton 'Ronnie' Screwvala remembers how he backed the film's director, Rakeysh Om Prakash Mehra, a relatively unknown ad film-maker then, to co-produce the film. The one thing that strikes you about Ronnie is his frank manner. And he makes no bones about the fact that *Rang De Basanti* became his calling card in the Indian movie business, not because it became a sensation but because it opened up channels for him in the most unlikely way.

A few weeks after the film's release, Screwvala's company, UTV Motion Pictures, took out a full-page ad in the *Bombay Times* and across national dailies, declaring that *Rang De Basanti* had become the third biggest grosser in the Indian film business. The film had raked in box-office revenues of over Rs 90 crore.

The morning the spread appeared, Screwvala got a series of terse messages from the offices of the biggest movie producers of the time. 'When they saw the ad they must have thought, "*who* is this guy, *where* has he come from?" But when I met them and explained that I had put out the ad only because I needed to establish my credentials, something they didn't need to, they saw reason.'

But it wasn't so simple. Charm and flattery were just a small part of Screwvala's defence. 'When I met Karan [Johar] and Adi [Chopra], I simply pointed out that we have to make the pie bigger. Despite the number of films the industry churned out each year, the total revenue for the movie business was less than what was made annually by the biggest Hollywood studio! And it wasn't because there wasn't a market. It was because most of it was slipping out.'

By the end of the evening, Screwvala turned the young 'old' guard into compatriots who were quick to grasp what he was alluding to: the huge untapped potential of the Indian movie business and how they could build it and gain from it, if only they worked together. And they did just that, as co-producers or for marketing and distribution of movies: Ronnie's UTV joined hands with Karan's Dharma Productions several times; and Adi's Yash Raj Films and UTV also fought the case for film producers against multiplex owners on revenue sharing in 2011.

In a sense, this episode reflects the kind of businessman Screwvala has been and how he has made a mark in India's movie business.

Often compared to Warner Brothers' founder, Jack Warner, the man credited with making parochial American movies global, Screwvala has done in India what Warner did so many decades ago. This is interesting indeed because he only stumbled upon the virtues of the movie-making business rather late in life.

Between 1998 and 2011, Screwvala went from being an underdog, a nobody, to one of the most successful and powerful movie barons in the country. He wasn't part of the group of film-making families and stars who had been running the Indian film-making business like a closed club for decades. Yet he managed to change not just the kind of movies made in India but also how they were made, distributed and sold.

SETTING THE STAGE

Nearly everyone remembers Screwvala, some for the movies he has made, and old-timers for his appearance in an ad on TV—the only one he has done, that of the Vicks Inhaler—or on stage and TV as a host, a long time ago. An exasperated Screwvala says he still meets people who remind him about that 'sniffs' ad.

It began with theatre. Though the stage was small in its scope and reach in Mumbai, it's on stage that he spent his formative years, all the way from school and beyond college, acting, directing and producing plays. It was also the place where he found most of his friends, his first business partners and his wife.

But though this would seem to be just the right platform for someone who would eventually make it big in the movie business in India, English-language theatre was as far removed from the lights, sounds, songs and action of Hindi cinema as was possible in those days. Everything, from the language, the cast, their sensibilities and the audience was different.

Theatre was just a hobby for Screwvala and he realized that except for the thrill of being on stage, there was nothing in it for him. 'I was far too ambitious. I always wanted to do something of my own. And I was very clear about what it should be.' It was not necessary that he had to be in a line related to the theatre as an entrepreneur. 'For me it was like playing squash or tennis. I would have made a success of any kind of business.' But his connection with theatre cannot be denied.

Heavily built and now in his early fifties, Screwvala is a casual dresser. If the expected actor's vanity is missing, so is the natural ease with people which comes with the job. When you meet him for the first time, he is curt and to the point. At work, he will not stop and chat just for the sake of it. He always seems in a hurry, peering over a sheaf of papers with his reading glasses perched on the edge of his nose, or striding through the office gate, too impatient to wait for his car to drive in.

A younger Ronnie Screwvala

Sitting in his high-ceilinged old apartment, a stone's throw from Ronnie's own penthouse in one of the most expensive sea-facing neighbourhoods of south Mumbai, eighty-year-old ad guru and theatre veteran Alyque Padamsee speaks about the young man he first met over thirty years ago. Padamsee directed the last play Screwvala did, in 1990, and also, perhaps, the first major one he was in, straight out of school.

He remembers Screwvala as a strikingly good-looking young man who wanted to be an actor. 'He was a good actor, not great, but possessed excellent comic timing. He fit well into any funny role he was given because he was exactly like that in real life. He was the life of every party, the joker of the little band and a happy-go-lucky charmer who always had women clustering around him as he entertained them with a fair dose of jokes and mimicry.' It's hard to imagine Screwvala like that and Padamsee's take on this is simple.

'Ronnie has become so serious. It's probably because of the money he deals in. As you grow older and start dabbling in so much money, such big deals, you become more serious and cautious and that becomes your nature in real life too. The only time I see him let his hair down and shake a leg is when the old theatre gang gets together. Then he is back to being the old Ronnie we knew.'

It's not difficult to imagine Screwvala on stage. It is amazing how he can transform himself when he wants to. When he makes a point, be it while addressing his employees, talking to investors or engaging business partners, he does it with a heady mix of charm, conversational skills, showmanship and brilliance, each aspect well calibrated.

As Padamsee says, 'That's the theatre training, you know. It allows you to mould yourself into any person the other side wants.' But that's not all that Screwvala learnt from theatre, he believes.

A close, albeit critical watcher of the movie business, Padamsee points out that it has to be theatre that gave Screwvala this creative grounding. The same training that went on to form the basis of what he would do in media. 'Live theatre teaches you to gauge the reactions of the audience,' Padamsee continues. 'It also helps to customize the content according to what the audience wants because their reactions and feedback are instant. That apart, if you are a producer you have to understand how the finances work, all of which were important lessons for Ronnie as he geared up for what he would do later.'

Screwvala's stint in plays also opened up many avenues for him. In the late 1970s and '80s, the English theatre circle in Mumbai was a small club of like-minded enthusiasts who came together every evening to talk Shakespeare and the latest Broadway hit, or rehearse and stage productions. Though the club was small, it was influential. People like Padamsee and Gerson Da Cunha were not only the leading lights on stage, they also headed creative ad agencies and were good at business and marketing. Screwvala thrived in this charmed set-up, not just because he came from the same background, but also because he was good at what he did and comfortable with this group of people.

It was during this time that he chanced upon an interesting proposition that would play a pivotal role in the future, though it might not have seemed so then.

'BRUSH' WITH BUSINESS

Once, when Screwvala was accompanying his dad, who was a general manager at the British firm J.L. Morrison (the company that had the licence for marketing Nivea), to London, he chanced upon an opportunity that seemed like a no-brainer to him. 'I don't even remember why I went with my father to the London offices of Wisdom, a company that manufactured hairbrushes and toothbrushes, in the first place. The company was discarding four toothbrush-making machines for £1,000 each and by the end of the meeting, we decided to purchase them. I said, fine, give me four weeks and let me see if I can raise that money.'

Screwvala did a quick ground check back home. His hunch that the demand for brushes from domestic companies like Colgate or Forhans would only go up in the next couple of years was right. It didn't take him long to plan his next move. But saying 'I will' wasn't as simple. In an era when imports were restricted, heavy duties were to be paid and there were a thousand other hurdles, it took about three months to acquire the licences for the import of the machines. By then, he got a bank loan and an advance to raise the capital from one of the companies they would supply the brushes to.

While he doesn't remember which of the big FMCG companies gave him the advance for his business, he has the numbers right. 'The advance covered even my contribution of 25 per cent. I had to put that upfront to get the rest of the money as a loan from the bank. I don't remember putting a rupee of my money into the enterprise.' This was step one. Screwvala had managed to spot an opportunity, see the potential and raise money for it, without putting in any money himself.

Within the next year, he realized the full scope of the business and put together a team of managers to run and expand it effectively. Then he let go. 'I figured that except for three hours a week, I had nothing much to do there because it was all being handled by a factory manager. I used to just glance through the production report each evening and visit the plant once a week.' 'Lazer Brushes', as it was then called, expanded, brought in more machines as the economy opened up, and became one of the biggest suppliers to multinationals making brushes in India.

By 2005, when Screwvala finally decided to sell the business, his first attempt at entrepreneurship had paid off well. His company was making 6 million brushes a month. 'The business was raking in Rs 75 crore as revenue. We had factories across India, which is not bad for a small contract manufacturer.'

Today, the only remnant of Screwvala's first brush with success can be found in the name of his holding company that owned UTV before it was sold to Disney: Unilazer Exports and Management Consultants Ltd. Not only did the venture play an important role in many ways, it gave him a crash course in business and how to make a success of it. It also gave the young man a steady income and lots of time to do other things.

For instance, as Screwvala began work at his factory, he couldn't just act in plays any more, he had to do more. 'Initially, I had to spend my time at the factory and often I couldn't make it for rehearsals. The way out was to actually start producing plays myself so that I could work out a timetable for the rehearsals according to my schedule.'

As things got hectic at work, he veered more and more towards being a producer. 'As a producer, I had to manage the ship. I approached all the spirits companies like the UB Group, and met the likes of Vijay Mallya for sponsorship. The producer had to make sure tickets were sold and the play made money.'

It was during this time that he met the two people who would play an important role in his life and business plans—

Deven Khote and Zarina Mehta. It so happened that when Screwvala turned 'producer', he was keen to stage the Broadway rage *Children of a Lesser God* on the Mumbai stage. He roped in theatre doyen Pearl Padamsee as director, and the cast included two young students, Deven Khote and Zarina Mehta. The play was about a teacher who falls in love with his deaf and dumb student and how he connects with her.

Speaking about what she considers her husband Ronnie Screwvala's best stage performance, Zarina, sitting in her colourful office overlooking the beautiful Mumbai skyline, says, '*Children of a Lesser God* required the entire cast of the play to learn sign language in a matter of weeks. After many delays, and months of rehearsals, when the play was finally in the last leg, just a few weeks before its opening, its lead actor backed off and the producer, desperate to ensure that "the already sold show must go on", decided to step in. The rest, as they say, was magic.'

Screwvala did not just take a crash course in sign language, which was integral to the story, he also gave a stunning performance, made more spectacular because he had to do the talking for both the lead actors! And as he was learning these important lessons, Screwvala was doing other things as well. Theatre was followed by advertisements though he did only one ad in his whole life, the one for the Vicks Inhaler.

Then there was television, which really opened up a new realm, even though it didn't quite seem that way so long ago. In 1980, several years before India's national broadcaster, Doordarshan (DD), began to allow privately made programmes, he anchored a prime-time show on the channel every Wednesday at 9 p.m. It was a show in the vein of *The Tonight Show* with Jay Leno and was called *Young World Live*. It was a breeze. 'It was just a question of an hour a week, during which I interviewed prominent people and got a cheque for Rs 65 in hand.' There was little else to watch on TV at that time, and the show was a massive hit.

More than the cheque, it was about the instant recognition. 'Between my surname, my theatre and *Young World Live*, I could break the ice anywhere and at any time.' This definitely helped in anything he did afterwards, even his next business venture of setting up a cable TV service.

In 1981, a decade before private or satellite television came to India, he took his first big leap of faith in this segment. He decided to test-market a new concept: give an alternative form of entertainment on TV to a small group of people in an area he was familiar with—south Mumbai.

The idea was novel and the demand was obvious. But the task of putting it all together was far from easy. Not only did Screwvala have to put in place the physical infrastructure of wiring and cabling, he would also need to source content from the US or UK, where most of these shows were made.

But the hard work paid off. Within months of getting the content and format in order, his big idea clicked and he was on to business venture number two. All through 1981 and '82, between 7 and 11 p.m., households across south Mumbai got a taste of a new world of entertainment they otherwise had little access to. The programmes were largely reruns of old British and American soaps and shows but for an audience starved for content and bored stiff with what was being dished out to them, it was a delight. Demand for the new service grew rapidly.

Now Screwvala faced a frustrating predicament—the need to scale up the business and the inability to do so. 'It was probably much too early for the times because while I thought that this second alternative to the national broadcaster, Doordarshan, could create a momentum of sorts, legislation took a long time to come through.' In fact, it was still ten years away.

While his dream of running the first alternative to DD didn't quite work out, the next couple of ventures did prepare him for the time when there would finally be one. And the stage for that was set with India's first privately produced show, *Mashoor Mahal*, conjured up by his old mentor, Alyque Padamsee, and sponsored by Hindustan Unilever. The show was simple and combined a fun game with a celebrity thrown in. Padamsee is proud to have set the ball rolling to create the 'celeb' culture in India. Screwvala directed it with help from two of his buddies from theatre—Deven Khote and Zarina Mehta. The show was an instant hit and the team clicked so well that it created UTV. The start of UTV after *Mashoor Mahal* was slow but like many others who had made the transition from theatre to advertising, ad agencies and companies that the team had worked with provided enough business to keep the firm going.

Khote says, 'We quickly divided the work between ourselves. Zarina would do documentaries and corporate films, I would do ads and Ronnie would make sure that business kept coming in. It was a practical arrangement. Ronnie could have done either of what both of us did, but he was so much better with money and getting business—he just managed that aspect.'

Suddenly, in 1989, the floodgates opened. Doordarshan decided to start outsourcing programmes to private producers. Screwvala was obviously a good bet for anyone in the channel headquarters because not only had he presented a very successful show, he had also directed the first privately made show on the channel.

Khote and Zarina remember with a lot of fondness what they did all those years ago. 'We did some of our best work like *Lifeline* and *Contact* then.'

While UTV could have remained a prolific production house making TV content, ambition and the changing Indian television landscape gave it a platform to do much more.

What stands out through Screwvala's journey in business is his insatiable appetite to get more business and become bigger. So, by 1990, as UTV was making a series of shows, documentary films and ads, he had also figured out multiple sources of revenue: selling ad space for other TV producers, making shows for Doordarshan; providing in-flight entertainment for airlines like Singapore Airlines. There is an interesting story behind how the Singapore Airlines deal came about as well.

Always on the lookout for new business, Screwvala would often attend exhibitions across world capitals and try to get contracts by setting up stalls and talking about his company. On one such trip, he 'overheard' somebody say that the head of the Singapore Airlines division looking after in-flight entertainment had been invited to the Atlanta office of CNN because the channel was trying to sell him content for his airline. He figured out which flight the airline chief was on, booked himself into the seat next to him, and by the end of the flight, the contract was his!

But that was nothing compared to what he pulled off months later when a little-known businessman, Subhash Chandra Goel, decided to change the contours of Indian TV by starting India's first private channel—Zee TV. This 24/7 Hindi language channel would telecast general entertainment. It would also herald a new era and a boom in Indian television.

THE BIG PITCH

It was more than an ambitious pitch; it was an impossible one. But the thirty-four-year-old was adamant that UTV should get it. Nearly a decade after Screwvala's small but grand plan of creating an alternative to the monopolistic Doordarshan, here was a businessman who was taking it a step forward. And he was not going to miss this opportunity. News was that a rice trader whom no one had heard of was trying to put in place a Hindi-language entertainment channel as an alternative to not just the national broadcaster but also the slew of new global English-language channels that were beaming their way into the hearts of the Indian audience.

So, one morning, with a clear plan and agenda in mind, Screwvala marched into Subhash Chandra's office, demanding an audience. For the next hour, as Screwvala laid down his plans, Subhash Chandra's face gradually took on a look of disbelief. It was impossible that this young man would be able to pull it off, he thought. The young man's pitch to Zee had been simple. 'I told Subhash Chandra, "What if UTV were to provide 40 per cent of the content on Zee? You can focus on the channel while we give you the bulk of the content you need, as long as you pay us a lump sum."'

Screwvala's proposal would mean hours of daily programming seven days a week, a form of factory production of content no one had tried their hand at in India till then. Subhash Chandra was sceptical at first, but he saw the possible benefits of what Screwvala was selling him. It made sense for them both. For Zee, it took away the headache of ensuring good-quality programmes, for UTV, it would add scale and steady business.

Convincing Subhash Chandra was easy. What was tough was selling the story in office. Apart from the regular shows UTV produced for DD, the small production house would have to more than triple its output and size. Khote says, 'I can't forget that day. It was a rather busy morning when Ronnie called the team. Everyone was called in that day. UTV was then based out of a decrepit basement in Worli and all the producers were working on different shows, editing in different time zones as most TV programme editing is done overnight. The general feeling was that it was probably one of those regular townhouse meetings that happened sometimes. Instead, it turned out to be a turning point of sorts.'

There was first a shocked silence and then a resounding 'no' the moment Screwvala mentioned what he had decided to do. The very idea of producing four daily programmes for fifty-two weeks in a row while also doing a series of other shows, ads and corporate films was unthinkable. But a calm and matter-of-fact Screwvala convinced everyone. He was well prepared for the reactions and had obviously done his homework. Nobody could argue with his logic.

His argument was well thought out. 'Let's just look at it like a production where you do all the technicals and lighting a day before, and you have the cameras set to roll. So even if you give two hours to each half-hour show, you can do four in an eight-hour shift, which means sixteen in four days.' The team did exactly that.

Overnight, UTV went from being a small production house to a 250-member strong 'factory' churning out a daily supply of content. This included everything from what Screwvala refers to as 'cheap and cheery studio-based shows' to popular game shows like *Saanp Seedi*, soaps, documentaries and ads.

Once again, it could well have stayed there, content to be the most prolific TV content company, but one small decision taken in New York changed the dynamics of UTV.

COMING INTO MONEY

The early 1990s were an interesting period in Indian television. The first flash of satellite TV and CNN's blow-by-blow account of the Gulf War in 1991 changed the way people viewed TV across the world. In India, just when viewers were getting used to the first taste of real-time international programmes, Subhash Chandra decided to bring in Zee TV. Meanwhile, in the south, in Chennai, another businessman and a member of a powerful political family, Kalanidhi Maran, did the same with Sun Network, starting a Tamil-language entertainment channel, a first of its kind.

The period saw Rupert Murdoch, already possessing a stake in Star TV, which he had bought from Richard Li (the son of Li Ka Shing, the promoter of telecom giant Hutchison Whampoa), look more closely at India and make two significant investments here. The first was in the Zee Group and the second in UTV, the biggest programme supplier to Zee and Sun.

'I got a call from the BSkyB [Murdoch's UK arm] head in London,' Screwvala remarks. 'I flew there and the agreement and deal were done in a single day. Murdoch decided to invest $5m to pick up a 49 per cent stake in UTV. This was a very significant amount of money for us, but it also had serious repercussions.'

Ernst & Young partner Farokh Balsara, who has covered the Indian media and entertainment industry for a long time, gives an insight into how the deal came together. Balsara has had a close association with Screwvala. After all, he was the man who audited the UTV balance sheet for Star when it was deciding to put money in the company and in Screwvala. 'What really worked from Star's perspective, apart from the fact that it was obvious that Ronnie could run a scaled-up business, was that he seemed so open to a partnership and involvement from Star. Ronnie realized early that to grow, he would need the capital and stability of long-term investment and money.'

And, for this, he was only too willing to open up, bring in a far more corporate culture and think even bigger.

The plan worked. Screwvala and the UTV team connected with the top brass at News Corp so well that soon he was producing a show on Indian business for Star in London. With this track record, within months, UTV got a second tranche of private equity money, this time from Warburg Pincus. Interestingly, UTV was Warburg's first investment in India, much before it famously bet on another young Indian entrepreneur, Sunil Bharti Mittal, and Bharti Airtel.

But while these investments gave Screwvala and UTV money and a fresh shot of adrenaline, they also posed a challenge that threatened the very core of UTV. 'For some inane reason, Subhash Chandra took away ten shows from us!' Subhash Chandra was perhaps uncomfortable about the fact that his biggest content producer had a direct line to his partners overseas. The fact that UTV began doing programming for

Murdoch's London arm didn't help matters.

Over time, Screwvala inadvertently got caught in the war between Rupert Murdoch and Subhash Chandra, as Star decided to take on its partner Zee and go Hindi. As differences became obvious, rumours were rampant that Star was talking to UTV to set up a Hindi news channel. They eventually did this in partnership with the Ananda Bazar Patrika (ABP) Group and, in March 2012, Star decided to exit news in India completely.

All this only worsened relations between Zee and UTV and was reflected in the company's balance sheet. Zee pulled out ten UTV-produced shows from its channel overnight. Screwvala and his team were forced to go back to the drawing board. But the fix was also quick. Between 1998 and 2001, Star emerged as the biggest client of UTV, accounting for 93 per cent of UTV's revenues by 2001. But that wasn't the end of Screwvala's woes.

His acerbic response says it all: 'There was a sharp disconnect with the Indian office of Star, more so because they knew that we had a direct line with the head office in Hong Kong or London.' Screwvala says the relationship soured over the years because Star was so bureaucratic. 'It didn't help that we felt we knew more about the content that would work in India than they did, and it became tough for us to deal with them,' he adds.

Screwvala has some very senior ex-functionaries at the channel to thank for what became the biggest decision within UTV—the decision to move away from being a content creator for broadcasters, a business-to-business kind of player, to dealing directly with the viewers. 'This required a full overhaul of our thought process and strategy.'

Screwvala had two other strong reasons to change. First, the investors had not only given the much-needed cash to run the ship, they provided a stability that was enviable in a market still recovering from a slowdown. Investor money also meant that you were answerable to them and it was imperative that one kept a foot on the accelerator. And no one wanted this more than Screwvala.

But there were other issues to sort out before UTV could change course drastically. Star still owned 30 per cent of the company (after the dilution that followed the Warburg Pincus investment) and the two had a 50–50 joint venture with Vijay Mallya's local TV channel, Vijay TV—which was turning out to be a bit of a headache.

So how did Vijay TV come into the picture? 'Soon after Warburg picked up a stake in UTV and saw how we had made inroads into the content play in the south through our programmes on Sun TV, they were keen for us to expand there.' As luck would have it, just around that time, Mallya was looking at selling Vijay TV. Screwvala got it for a steal at just Rs 9 crore.

Vijay TV turned out to be worth every penny. Enthused by the channel's success in the south, and with hopes to expand its own regional fare, Star picked up a stake in the company, forming a joint venture with UTV.

But then the problems started. Screwvala is very critical of Star's functioning in India and says that two of Star's business development officers sat together and made the most bizarre revenue projections for Vijay TV. They said they would run it and give his company their due share of the revenue. 'I was sure the figure would never work. In fact, for the next two years, they were cutting a big cheque to us and Star was bleeding dry. Things got so out of hand that James Murdoch had to intervene.' He said, 'I know we have bungled this up, but how can we get out of it?' Screwvala responded by selling back his stake in Vijay to Star in return of a promise that he would get a chance to buy back Star's stake in UTV. This happened over the next few years, and, as always, Screwvala got out of the deal with a clean profit. He says the Murdochs bet on the wrong people. 'They lost a billion dollars before they began to get things right in India. It was a very expensive mistake.'

After two tough partnerships, Screwvala realized that private equity investments are a double-edged sword because easy access to money means being under constant pressure to make your company grow and expand your business. This period also saw Screwvala and UTV take a big decision: to reevaluate all that the company had done so far and change strategy completely.

MOVIES, MONEY AND MORE

Was there a turning point in Screwvala's journey as an entrepreneur? 'I don't think there is anything like a turning point. Success is many small steps taken,' is his response.

He concedes that three things helped UTV and him. First, the decision to keep growing and expanding; second, the coming in of private equity money—both in a way linked to each other; and third, and perhaps the most significant—the rehaul of the way the company had approached business.

And this was what UTV did, some time in 1997–98, as it got out of a troubled relationship with Zee into a tougher one with Star and its Indian bosses. It was around this time that UTV decided to reorient itself and move away from a B2B model, to set up channels and platforms on its own.

There were three broad avenues for a content company to do this. Broadcasting, or setting up channels, where UTV had missed the wave not once but twice—first in 1992 and then in 1995—when Zee and then Sony had been launched; films, where Screwvala says he had 'missed the wave for the last ninety-five years'; and gaming, which no one in India really understood back then.

He decided to start with the toughest—films.

Ask UTV's founding team—Ronnie Screwvala, Deven Khote and Zarina Mehta—about their first tryst with the film-making business and each will react differently. Khote remembers all three being shocked and embarrassed. Screwvala's 'It wasn't a good start but we learnt a lot,' and Zarina's 'Frankly we didn't know whether we were coming or going. The movie was so bad that I wanted it buried,' indicate how tough it must have been.

The movie in question, *Dil Ke Jharokhe Mein*, was the first film UTV produced in 1997. It was a forgettable film that bombed at the box-office and vanished from public memory soon after its first run.

Films had not yet broken away from the tried and tested formula—the standard boy meets girl sagas with a series of song and dance numbers and irate parents—all put in place with the fervent hope that they would reduce the risk at the box-office.

'In this case, the film-maker was so careful,' Khote recalls, 'that he even had a snake thrown in for effect because apparently, someone had told him that the snake would add a dose of luck!' Both Khote and Zarina confess that while the film was an affront to their collective sensibilities, they didn't realize that Screwvala was making some big plans.

Khote says, 'It was probably just a low-cost, low-budget film done to give Ronnie a feel of what the industry was like. Having spent all these years with Ronnie, the one thing I can say is that nothing he does is without a plan in mind. He is always looking far ahead.'

In 1998, Screwvala was looking in quite another direction—film distribution—because he had learnt some important lessons from this attempt at playing producer. First, he learnt that if he wanted to enter the movie business, he had to stay away from the run-of-the-mill movies, like the one he had made and, second, he would have to start slow and in an area where he could get a quick entry. 'We started in the movie business from sub-zero, so distribution was the only option. If you had money and were willing to pay a price, everyone was willing to give you their film rights.'

There was a huge untapped opportunity here that he was quick to figure out. Former UTV Motion Pictures CEO and now MD (Studios), DisneyUTV, Siddharth Roy Kapur, says: 'The movie "business" has three basic verticals—the producers, the distributors [who market and distribute the movies and hence also determine how many prints go where] and the exhibitors or the plain-vanilla-theatre owners.' He adds, 'For the longest time, the distributors were a mass of very fragmented regional players who were forced to buy movie prints from the big producers based on nothing but face value.' He goes on to say that there was hardly any science behind it and most often, past experience, gut feeling and the producer of the film or the star's track record determined how much a distributor paid.'

This meant that often two of the most crucial determinants of a movie's success, marketing and the audience connect, were determined not by the producer of the film, who had the most at stake, but a small decrepit distributor in charge of a small territory. There was hardly any incentive to push the movie and even lesser accountability. Kapur adds, 'These problems were even more exaggerated overseas. And it was only in the beginning of the early 2000s, after movies like *Lagaan* and, more importantly, *Swades* [UTV was involved with both] were released that one even started to realize how big the revenues from there could be.'

In 1998, when Screwvala took his first tentative steps into the movie business, he walked straight into an inter-connected world where links mattered. Film-making was dominated by director-producer families who had close ties with the stars. Most film companies were like mom-and-pop shops, and the industry was fragmented and unorganized. If the distribution end was chaotic, almost every other arm was as bad. There was no pre-planning, scripts were often written on the go and productions often overshot schedules by a year.

Screwvala was quick to realize that the industry had great potential, if only one were to get some method into it. It didn't take long for him to do some quick calculations. The world's most prolific movie industry (a thousand films are produced in India each year, ten times what Hollywood does) made less than one-third the box-office of a single Hollywood studio. Screwvala also figured that the revenue from the big productions was massive there because a lot was spent on promoting films—sometimes as much as 50 per cent of the film's budget was spent on marketing it—while in India, the marketing was done by a bunch of faceless distributors and exhibitors with little or no interest in investing in the promotion of the films.

Screwvala's focus was on creating the first truly national

film distribution player in India. All the movies he handpicked were the ones he felt would work in a fast-changing urban India, which was also easy to sell to. The early movies UTV distributed were new-age ones tailor-made for urban audiences. One of the earliest, for instance, was Nagesh Kukunoor's *Hyderabad Blues*, in 1998, followed by *Fiza* and then the 2001 blockbuster *Lagaan*.

Screwvala explains how this came about: 'Our first big bet was on *Lagaan*. We took only the Mumbai territory, which spans Maharashtra and Goa. We didn't take all of India at that time and here too, we just took theatrical rights and tied up with the distribution company, Shringar.' The next few films saw him expand his distribution coverage. And as marketing around these films increased, so did the buzz—the number of people who turned up at theatres and the fact that more and more producers and film-makers were keen to have UTV distribute their films. This is because they knew that the company would spend a lot more marketing their film intelligently, by targeting the right kind of audience. A lesson well learnt from the days when the team had worked closely with FMCG companies.

All this opened up the doors to the next big step—producing films through partnerships.

With access to a deep pocket, a growing national distribution network, marketing acumen and a modern sensibility that backed new-age movies and film-makers, Screwvala's rise in the business through the early 2000s was rapid. Luck was on his side too. 'In 2002–03, we closed three films in quick succession.' And they were all very big—*Chalte Chalte*, a commercial success and a film that was co-produced by Bollywood A-lister Shah Rukh Khan [the only film he has ever co-produced), *Lakshya*, a film directed by Farhan Akhtar, who was riding high after the success of the 2001 hit *Dil Chahta Hai*, and *Swades*, made by *Lagaan* director Ashutosh Gowariker.

For someone trying to make inroads into India's movie business, the timing couldn't have been better. The six films gave Screwvala a crash course in movie distribution and production. The successes also got him the right kind of friends and potential partners, and all of this helped when, in 2006, he made *Rang De Basanti*, which catapulted him and his company into the big league of Indian cinema.

RANG DE BASANTI

The movie business in the late 1990s witnessed a lot of changes that offered a rank outsider like Screwvala entry into the industry. The first of these was a new platform for films—the multiplex, which with its multiple screens (both small and large theatres) made it possible to screen niche films which did not necessarily target a wider audience. This helped create a new kind of cinema and the emergence of new storylines and film-makers with similar sensibilities. *Hyderabad Blues* is the perfect example of a multiplex film which would have probably never found an audience in the era of single-screen theatres.

Can Screwvala's success be attributed to the fact that he was at the right place at the right time? 'I am happy to give credit to luck wherever it applies, but in this case, it wasn't so. One had to discover this generation. The viewership was there but it had to be tapped.' The reaction to *Rang De Basanti* was typical. 'Every one of them [the young guard] said, "Yeah, I liked the movie" but I didn't think it would work. The mindset was still very old.'

But it wasn't just guts that made him stick his neck out with *Rang De Basanti.* No one realized that Screwvala's decision to back the film was one of the most measured and calibrated ones he took and, in doing so, he stumbled upon a valuable evaluation tool. He decided to set up focus groups, which he had seen a lot of FMCG companies doing during this time.

When UTV decided to co-produce *Rang De Basanti* with the film's director, they put in place a diverse focus group of their target audience to give them constant feedback at every stage of the film. The feedback was very good. 'By the time *Rang De Basanti* released, we were pretty sure how it would be received. Mind you, even we didn't know how big the film would be. By day two, word of mouth had brought in so many youngsters . . . the business had never seen anything like it.'

Since the first experiment, UTV has developed the focus group concept so well that it has emerged as the biggest tool and intelligence meter within the motion picture division. This has helped the company in two ways: Knowing how competing films are faring and what kind of marketing campaigns have worked for them; and helping it to quickly course correct. For instance, a full twenty minutes of content in the 2009 release *Kaminey*, which went on to become a big box-office hit, had to be knocked off. 'Initially, Vishal [Bharadwaj], the film's director, had a lot of misgivings, but eventually he realized that it's much better to get the feedback before the release, so that you can course correct. And the feedback proved to be correct.'

Balsara puts Screwvala's achievements in context. 'Ronnie is a cowboy. He is the only guy I know who combines the creative side with the financially savvy one. He can relate to directors like one of them and he can put the brightest private equity guy to shame. I haven't met anyone who can combine the right brain and the left brain so well.' Balsara also believes that Screwvala has been a catalyst for many changes in the movie business. 'Before he came into the picture, for instance, there was hardly a concept of bound and closed movie scripts [many times, they were reworked on the go and this meant huge time and cost overruns] and marketing support for movies was mostly absent. Ronnie brought in all this and insisted on tight timelines and an almost obsessive effort to keep within budgets.' There were incentives too: if the movie was shot well within budget, the excess was given to the director, who was often the co-producer.

The admiration for Screwvala is obvious as Balsara continues, 'For far too long, the industry has been fragmented, with too many small players accounting for far too little.' He points out that even for an analyst like himself, who has tracked the media and entertainment industry for the last twenty years, the movie business remains an enigma. 'Nobody knows the real size of it. All we know is that it is prolific. India is the largest producer of films in the world and a lot of the numbers reported in terms of the size of the industry or ticket sales are still very gray.'

Balsara believes that by applying his mind to the business, Screwvala has been able to iron out some of the irregularities and has gained an advantage over the rest. First, by being one of the big corporate players in the industry, he has always been able to attract the right kind of private equity money. By focussing on the distribution end first, Screwvala did something even the biggest banners in the business had not been able to do till then—create an all-India network. And by cultivating a different, and modern, set of sensibilities, he and UTV have been able to capture the imagination of a young, fast-evolving India.

All of this is commendable, particularly because Screwvala can't speak Hindi, the language he does most of his work in, as well as he should. 'He literally taught himself the language,' Khote explains. 'It used to be hilarious. He could barely string a sentence together in Hindi, but then he virtually worked his way through the problem. Today he reads every script that comes to him and though he is still not comfortable speaking in Hindi, it's not how much but what he says that's important. During sessions, when there is a discussion on scripts, he says one word in Hindi here, one there, but he always makes the most astute comments. People hardly notice that he can't speak the language well!'

Screwvala's most acknowledged contribution to the Indian film business has been the way in which he set a template for bigger and better things. In 2006, the year *Rang De Basanti* was released, he made a splash overseas with a series of international productions including Mira Nair's *Namesake*, which was followed by Manoj Night Shyamalan's *Happenings*. *Newsweek* described him as 'the frontrunner in the race to become Bollywood's Jack Warner'.

Two years later, in 2008, *Esquire* took it to another level when it named Ronnie Screwvala as one of the seventy-five most influential people of the media industry in the twenty-first century. It said Screwvala and his UTV film unit have co-opted Western concepts like co-financing, diversified revenue models, and brand extensions to increase industry profits and improve the quality of films. Also mentioned was that he had been compared to Louis Mayer and Jack Warner.

But while *Esquire* compared Screwvala to the movie business legends of the US, what it missed out on was that he also had an important sounding board and partner in Walt Disney.

THE 'MICKEY' IN THEIR MIDST

The overall transformation of UTV was thanks to a decision made in 1998, when Screwvala and his partners decided to shift focus and create a consumer-facing company. 'We understood content and it was obvious that we needed to find scale in whatever we did if we had to be relevant,' he explains. 'So while others did things like getting into DTH and creating distribution platforms, we decided to focus on what we understood, across media platforms.' But at this juncture, having done TV content all along, wouldn't it have been easier for Screwvala to start an entertainment channel?

Farokh Balsara talks about how Screwvala moved into niche broadcasting while navigating through the movie business instead of starting an entertainment channel. 'Ronnie would have had to reduce his exposure to the TV production business whenever he set up a broadcast company and till the time movies took off, he couldn't afford to do that. That was where the bread and butter was coming from!' Instead, he waited it out and decided to set up his first channel, Hungama, for kids. He was astute. He did this only in 2004, when he was sure that movies would keep bringing him money. And that does make sense because even till the time the company was listed in the Indian stock markets, in 2005, a lot of the revenues it earned actually came from the TV business, and he didn't want to disturb that since no broadcaster would have given UTV a large chunk of business if they were competitors.

Why get into a niche kids' channel? Screwvala explains,

'When we did *Shaka Laka Boom Boom*, a very successful kids' show UTV produced for Star TV, there was a lot of resistance to start with. The channel said it wouldn't work, but they were proven wrong. The show became one of the biggest drivers for TRP [viewer ratings] in the evening band.' The response was amazing. 'When we dug a little deeper, we realized that there was no real content for children even though they constituted a huge chunk of viewership in India. The biggest testimony to this was the fact that studies had shown that the bulk of the sizeable viewership for the Zee Horror Show or even a simple programme like Antakshari came from kids.' He adds that kids seemed to be watching these programmes because they were not able to find anything made for them on television.

The result of this hypothesis was Hungama, which took its time to shape up but opened up a whole new genre of programming. It was the first home-grown kids' channel to take on the biggest names in the world, Cartoon Network and Disney, and it did this with a simple formula—local content (or perhaps regional, because Japanese cartoon characters like Doraemon were big hits on the channel) for local people.

Within a year of Hungama's success, media companies across Asia wanted to repeat the formula. The Hungama team headed by the company's COO, Zarina Mehta, was soon flying off to Malaysia and Indonesia to set up children's channels for networks there. So successful was this formula of localized content that the Malaysian channel Astro, headquartered in Kuala Lumpur, expressed its interest in picking up a stake in Hungama.

Just then, as the modalities for this were being worked out, Screwvala got a call from the Walt Disney company. They were keen not only to buy out Hungama, but also to pick up a stake in UTV. This eventually came through in 2006. 'It's a confirmation of the success we made of Hungama that this is the only Disney channel across the world that doesn't carry the Disney name,' Screwvala says proudly.

The reaction of those watching Screwvala at this time varied. Some like Balsara believe that it was a gutsy move to make since he had managed to do what no one in the kids' space had done; he had competed with Disney and proved that he could do really well in the Indian markets.

Others believed that Screwvala had sold out. He was a mercenary and he had set up the channel only to sell it and make money off it. The human fallout of the deal and takeover—the obvious lay-offs—didn't help his cause. But Screwvala defends what he did because in return for Hungama, he got a lot more from Walt Disney, especially over the next few years, when businesses across the spectrum faced a crisis such as had not been seen before.

BUILDING UP TO SELL OUT?

On a weekend in August 2007, an unlikely group of people headed out to the Sahara Group-owned resort in Aamby Valley, a ninety-minute drive from Mumbai, for a company off-site. The team members had come from all over and had little in common. There were the film sorts from Mumbai and Chennai, techies from London and San Francisco, gamers from Japan and Singapore, TV people of every hue, a clutch of entrepreneurs whom Screwvala had bought out of their respective businesses over the last year, or was hoping to buy out, and a couple of journalists.

But it wasn't just the wide array of people that stood out. It was Screwvala, who stood in the middle of it all, laughing at the jokes and nursing a glass of cold water on the rocks, as everyone else got more and more 'spirited' as the night progressed.

The next morning it was clear why Screwvala had got this rather diverse flock together. After seven years of hectic growth and riding high on a series of box-office successes, Screwvala and UTV were setting up half a dozen niche broadcast channels and expanding into the gaming and digital space in a major way. In retrospect, it might have been the wrong time to make such a move because six months later, stock markets the world over collapsed after the fall of Lehman Brothers. This was followed by a recession and turmoil.

Despite this, Screwvala and UTV managed to pull through. The channels UTV launched were an interesting mix. Perhaps there was a larger plan in mind. Taking off from where Disney left off in terms of its target audience base—that is, the preteens or 'tweens' as they are referred to—UTV launched Bindaas, an irreverent, in-your-face youth channel that was edgy and sometimes risqué. There was a movie channel as part of the same bouquet that was subsequently dropped, followed by a channel dedicated to action movies dubbed in Hindi, a channel to telecast world cinema, and finally a business news channel. Screwvala eventually got out of the last when he roped in Bloomberg as a partner and then Reliance ADAG as an investor.

Screwvala probably did get his timing right, after all. If he had launched his channels earlier, in the period 2004–07, the cost of running them would have been higher since the economy was booming and almost all the channels set up at that time were run at very high cost. Salaries were also very high. When the slowdown happened, several of these channels became unviable. If he had launched his channels later, things would have got delayed because it would have been tough to raise money during the slowdown, which was a protracted affair. This way, UTV's broadcast arm was ready to run as soon as the dust had settled. Having Walt Disney as an investor helped during this period, and, as it eventually transpired, it also gave him a ready buyer in time.

So, were these channels set up with a sell-out in mind? Was it done with UTV partner Disney in the know to create a bigger play?

First, the numbers: between 2006 and 2012, the time of the final buyout, Disney increased its stake in UTV steadily. It had first acquired a 14.9 per cent stake for about $15m in 2006. In 2008, it upped its stake to 32.1 per cent for about $203m; this also gave it a 15 per cent stake (valued at $30m) in UTV's broadcasting unit, which ran the array of new channels. Finally, in 2011, a year before the full takeover, Disney upped its stake to 50.44 per cent, leaving Screwvala and his partners holding just a 19.82 per cent stake in the company, which was also sold off to Disney eventually.

Screwvala justifies his progressive stake sales by listing what Disney brought to the table. 'I think it was great to have them through the period [2006–11] and their experience really helped. For instance, at a time when every media company was splitting up and hiving off divisions to create more market value, they advised us to keep to the course and keep all the companies under one entity. I think it was the smartest thing we could have done because it allowed us to develop scale and keep our balance sheet strong.'

Second, just when everyone was scaling down as the Indian economy took a knock in 2008, the support of Disney and the fact that they made even more investments allowed Screwvala to scale up the bouquet of niche channels that UTV had launched. If second-guessing 'what next' is the most important trait an entrepreneur can have, he seemed to be bang on in his understanding of what was happening in the media business in 2010.

Screwvala expected a massive shake-out over the next three or four years. He believed the key to survival would be creating scale: 'I think for me scale would mean companies with about $4–5bn revenue, a far cry from the story now, when despite the proliferation of media companies and channels, no one is making money.' According to Screwvala, the biggest mistake media companies made at that time was to list their shares and diversify needlessly. 'To create the kind of scale that is required, many of us are still in an investment mode and analysts just don't get it. They want quick returns and that's going to take time in coming. Most equity market analysts don't even get what we are trying to do. They want quick quarterly returns.' He adds, 'That's not happening in this business. We have to focus on investments in infrastructure, in building the business. And we need to focus on cash flows. If your channel is not making money, that's a problem. You can't go around launching new channels in spite of that.'

In 2011–12, most of India's biggest listed media conglomerates, be it the TV 18 Network, NDTV, or TV Today, began to feel the strain of stretched balance sheets. And all of them, over a period of time, were forced to get a fresh infusion of funds from some of India's well-known businessmen. Reliance chairman Mukesh Ambani virtually bought out the

TV 18 Network, promoted by Raghav Bahl, soon after Mukesh's brother Anil pumped in money into a slew of other investments—including Bloomberg UTV, and AV Birla Group chairman Kumar Mangalam Birla picked up a stake in TV Today. Screwvala says, 'Everybody is calling this a consolidation. They are saying, finally we have the shake-out in the media business we had predicted. But they are wrong. This is not a consolidation. What we are seeing is just a fresh infusion of funds. A bailout perhaps. Media businesses are still under stress. The next few years will be tough for everyone.'

So is that why Screwvala sold out to Walt Disney? Had he realized that he would need far deeper pockets, more staying power to play the game he had played for so long, or did he simply run out of patience as had been predicted by all those who saw his frenzied and almost restless journey to the top in the Indian entertainment business?

Is the sell-out his final walk into the sunset as an entrepreneur after creating one of India's most vibrant media companies? Or does he have something else up his sleeve? After all, he has sold out parts of his company before, only to come back and become even bigger than before.

THE SELL-OUT

On 1 February 2012, Screwvala made headlines in business newspapers and channels in India and the US when he announced that he was selling out his whole business across verticals to the Walt Disney Company. For Screwvala, who had taken the Indian media and entertainment world by storm over the last two decades, this was curtains down. His last bow.

That this deal was on the cards had been talked about for

some time. And those who had tracked UTV weren't surprised. But those who knew him personally, were.

In his innings as a businessman, the one tag that had stuck to him was that of a rather mercenary entrepreneur who would sell anything if the price was right. After all, in his career, Ronnie Screwvala has sold out or axed as many businesses as he has built, and he has made money on each. It started in 1997, when he sold 49 per cent of his company to Rupert Murdoch. He diluted his holding even more when he sold a stake to private equity firm Warburg Pincus. This allowed him to expand into TV and the movies. In 1998, when the call was taken to shift focus from a B2B company to a B2C company, he closed down his animation and in-flight entertainment business. He sold out Vijay TV and made a lot of money on the deal. Then he created Hungama and sold it for a profit. After this, he sold a stake in his company to Walt Disney more than once. Each deal got him higher profits than the previous one.

Despite all the sell-outs, he always made a comeback, leveraging each of these to grow further.

Screwvala, who is now the managing director of Disney in India, sold out to Walt Disney because the business landscape in the media industry has been changing and getting bigger. He knew that something that had worked in the past might not do so in the future. 'The next phase in this business has to be with scale in mind. I think the next three years will define the three or four big players who have at least $4–5bn market capital. And this next level of scale will need a completely different thought process.'

This realization was, perhaps, at the heart of his decision because the need for scale would have required all partners to put in money and Screwvala knew that as a first-generation entrepreneur with little else to fall back on, he would always face an uphill task. 'I knew, as the need for investment grew, I would have to put more money in. This would have been dilutive anyway. For instance, if we needed to invest Rs 3,000 crore, I would be asked to put in at least half of it. Then I would have had to go to firms like Blackstone or Morgan Stanley and this would have diluted our stake by half or more. My holding in UTV would come down drastically each time they did. At another level, it might have been me trying to protect my stake and scale because of this inevitability and that wouldn't be right.'

Over time, if he hadn't sold out, he would have gradually lost the company anyway as he tried to raise money through multiple rounds of funding. Moreover, the debate on whether he should let go of the control of a company he had led had been decided upon long back. 'It wasn't as though I was a 51 per cent stakeholder. I had passed that litmus test years back and it had worked well.' Each time Screwvala sold his stake, he had brought in a stronger partner with deeper pockets. This had allowed UTV to expand. On a personal level, however, there is a difference this time, as apart from the Rs 1,000 crore he pocketed with the deal, he has a hedge in place. He has a 3.5 per cent stake in Walt Disney India and a completely different charter to scale up the businesses. 'Now this, compared to a 15 per cent stake in UTV and constantly diluting, which is better?' he asks.

If the view that size is what will determine success was behind Screwvala's decision, the other consideration was the frustration of having to be a listed company dependent on the stock markets to raise money. This is something that he had often harped about in the past and it stemmed from a very basic problem he faced. 'Nobody [stock market analysts] understands this business in a new market like India. You have to have a longer view. You can't be forced to take decisions with an eye on quarterly results.' A grouse many CEOs secretly voice because constant pressure to show quarterly gains has pushed companies across sectors to expand and create 'value', a term loosely used to denote multiple verticals or businesses, and grow rapidly.

This is something Screwvala too was forced to do in the movie-making business, where, for instance, he said there was always pressure to have a certain slate or number of movies even if it meant buying distribution rights alone. With Disney in control, he hopes the game will change.

But what will happen to UTV? Will it get subsumed into Disney? Can a smaller, nimbler entrepreneur-led company be the same if it is taken over by a multinational? The media mogul probably spends most of his time thinking about these things.

After all, the first reaction to the deal, from one of the few media analysts in a brokerage firm, was, 'It's the classic case of a small entrepreneur-driven, nimble, aggressive company going and merging with the large, established behemoth, one whose tentacles are spread across the world.'

Isn't this bound to create friction and slow down decision making? Will Screwvala be okay being answerable to someone in Disney's headquarters? What happens if there are differences? Will he be able to bulldoze through differences as he has done so far? These are some of the questions doing the rounds.

'It is too early to say how things will pan out,' he confesses, 'but you must remember, I have worked closely with Disney for six years now. We were totally aligned on where we wanted to take the company. We also had common goals and visions independent of each other.'

He thinks concerns of Disney slowing down the aggressive growth that UTV has seen is the wrong way of looking at things, because as the company gains the kind of scale it will after the deal, it will require a far more measured point of view and strategy. 'Making a plan, for say, a sum of $500m [a hypothetical figure] is different. It can't be done on an impulse. It has obviously to be well thought out. That doesn't equal slowing down.'

As Screwvala justifies what he has done and figures out what next, perhaps the toughest thing for him will be the journey from being an entrepreneur to an employee, something he has never been, save for three months after college. Most are sceptical about whether he will last out the five years he has committed to Disney.

And Screwvala is also watching, it seems. 'Honestly, it is still settling in. But I think Disney is conscious that they have brought an entrepreneur into their fold and that is what they are going to get. Moreover, I guess, in fast-growing emerging markets like India, they want someone who has the entrepreneurial drive and understands the dynamics of doing business here.'

As for Disney, which has been a small player in India for the last decade, the acquisition of UTV has put it among the biggies in the Indian media and entertainment industry for the first time. This period of cooling its heels has also made it realize that the Indian media industry is different and in many ways, customization to suit the Indian context is what has worked best here.

But while Screwvala's answers are considered and the move happened after months of deliberation, in a sense, for both Screwvala and Walt Disney, all of this is new. There is still much more to do.

THE NEED FOR SCALE

Despite the fact that India is the largest producer of films—over a thousand are produced every year in twenty different languages—revenues for the industry every year were just $3bn in 2011. Even though overall film revenues tripled between 2004 and '11, it is estimated that total revenues in the industry will only touch $4.5bn in 2016. With just half this number of movies, Hollywood earned over $50bn in revenue in 2011. Part of the problem in India is the reach and the fact that a lot of the ticket sales are not reported.

The scale that Hollywood has achieved has also been thanks to its revenue model, or where the revenues originate from. In India, 70 per cent of movie revenues still come from theatre ticket sales and most of the actual numbers here are not even reported. What's more, India has just 13,000 cinemas compared to 40,000 in the US (even though the US population is one-fourth the size of India).

In the US, just one-tenth of the numbers come from theatre. In fact, most of the US studios make their money from the so-called back end: DVD sales, multi-picture output deals with movie channels, pay TV and network licensing.

As the author of *The Hollywood Economist*, Edward Jay Epstein, points out, numbers prove that the core business of Hollywood studios today is creating rights that can be licensed, sold and leveraged over different platforms including TV, gaming and DVD. All of this is evolving in India even as the role of every player in the business changes. As in Hollywood, the big studios are beginning to do a lot more than produce movies. Big directors don't just direct movies as they try to get as much revenue share as they can, and the big stars don't only act—they produce and often direct the movies that they are in.

If every piece of the pie is getting bigger and more complex in the film-making business, the screen and platforms are also fast changing.

Just before he sold his company to Disney, Screwvala's big focus was on how to push content into the mobile phone screen as handsets got smarter and users savvier. UTV's broadcast business head (now MD, Media Networks at DisneyUTV) M.K. Anand says, 'Ronnie is essentially making a conscious attempt to spread himself across platforms keeping the target group [young Indians] and essence constant. Ronnie's bet is on really capturing eyeballs across screens from the big silver one to the small mobile one.'

The plan seems bang on in a country where more than half the population is below thirty and the biggest seller anywhere on TV (40 per cent of revenues come from movies) or mobile (downloads of film songs is one of the most lucrative value-added services in India) is film content. The big bet is on when there will be a big spurt in content viewing. This will lead to the creation of new formats and a paradigm shift across categories. 'I think the young kids are going to define the second viewing screen format that has been absent in most households.' And that is an important aspect because even after two decades of cable TV, and the plethora of channels, India is essentially a single-TV-household market.

According to Screwvala, things will now change and the

youth, powered with smartphones, will determine the second viewing screen and content. To him, it will be a viewing screen but not a TV. It may be a tablet, PC or phone, but whatever it is, it will be mobile. This will also change the way content is generated. For the audience will want content at a much higher frequency and pace and probably different packaging.

The landscape is bound to change over the next few years.

Digitization will add a new dimension of business and revenue for the industry and as new telecom technologies come in, television could be just one of the many screens to view and drive content.

BEHIND THE CAMERA

Affable, astute, shrewd, even cut-throat sometimes, and canny, these are the words used most often to describe Ronnie Screwvala as a businessman, and like most other successful businessmen, he has proved that one needs a good mix of all these to succeed.

He says that what primarily worked for him were common sense and a calm head. 'You know, I think I get it pretty soon. I get situations quite fast and I work through all possible scenarios in my mind and also think about all the possible solutions based on each situation.' This cool-headed rational 'thought process', a word that Screwvala peppers every second sentence with, has always ensured a way out of any sticky situation for him. It has also helped him keep up with the times and second guess what comes next. And there has been ample proof of that.

After all, he was one of the first businessmen in the Indian media and entertainment industry to understand the opportunities foreign private equity investors could bring in, and he made sure he was ready for their arrival. So much so that over time he became the most bankable business partner anyone investing in India could hope for. Through the years, he has partnered with Star, Disney, Astro, CNN, BBC and Bloomberg.

As James Murdoch reportedly told Andy Bird, the chairman of Walt Disney International, when Bird tried to do a reference check on Screwvala before Disney invested in UTV, 'You know you can never get the better of Ronnie in a deal. But he is the most reliable guy to do business with in India.' Even if a deal or a company he has his money in seems to be on a weak wicket, Screwvala will find a good way to get it back on track.

There is also a certain quality of equanimity about the man. 'Despite having known Ronnie for years, I don't, for instance, ever remember him being thrilled or elated or even down and out. He is forever ready with a sarcastic jibe,' remarks a close associate, who has sat across the table from him for years. 'But when his patience runs out, you will see Ronnie lose it, and work everyone to the bone, being completely unreasonable in his demands sometimes.'

Someone who has worked with him closely says, 'In a business of fragile—sometimes comically so—egos, Ronnie is totally out of place. He has absolutely no qualms about talking to anyone he needs to and he speaks his mind always. He is cut and dry.' He continues, 'I know a lot of people—the most unlikely kinds—who turn to him when they want a frank opinion. He always gives it, even if it means he has to add a fair dose of sugar to soften the blow.'

If these traits have helped Screwvala cut a deal, what has driven him ahead is the ability to not just think differently but also think ahead. And one way he manages to do this is by surrounding himself with the right mix of people.

The average age of employees at UTV is thirty years. There is a reason for this. 'We are dealing with the young, around whom everything is changing—the platforms are changing. I can't have a forty-year-old who doesn't understand them and isn't like them making my business plan!' But he quickly adds, 'Ideas are of no use unless you can get them executed. And this ability to efficiently do so has helped us do what we have done so far.'

Screwvala is quite embarrassed about his reputation as a man who is in the game to sell out and make a fast buck. 'Everyone gets me wrong. I don't know where that comes from. I have only sold two channels in the past—Vijay TV, because of the bind we got into with Star, and Hungama—because Disney was also picking up a stake in UTV and I thought that would be the most attractive part. Many of my peers have sold off as many businesses as I have outside the media [internet, animation etcetera]. Why aren't they questioned? Look back at all my deals; we have always made sure when investors walk out that they are better off.'

But the last deal that he struck, the biggest one in his career as an entrepreneur, has been different. While the previous rounds were about money coming into the business, the sell-out to Disney means the money is coming to him. Screwvala shows no trace of settling down after selling out. Instead, he is brimming with plans and jokes. 'The joke in the office is that "Ronnie seems to be on steroids after the deal." Here I am constantly pushing Disney with new plans and they are like sure, let's take some time and do it.'

He also has a long list of to-dos. First, there is the question of how best to use the money from Disney, which gives UTV a longer leash, wider spread and a bigger vision. But in all probability, Screwvala won't be with Disney a few years down the line. The plan seems to be that he will set the ball rolling for the amalgamation of UTV with Disney and move on. Probably to set up a business in a totally different sphere or, who knows, even the media and entertainment industry, which as per his deal with Disney, he can enter only after five years. In the meantime, he has his hands full as the MD of Walt Disney India, and as an investor.

He has set up a foundation, SWADES, with Zarina and together they are focusing on rural development. This trust has pledged that it will adopt villages in the districts of Raigad and Ratnagiri in Maharashtra to start with and address issues of water, education and health. Screwvala and Zarina have pledged Rs 350 crore from their family foundation with plans to raise an additional 500 crore.

Through the company he started with, Unilazer, Screwvala is investing in small businesses while also mentoring young entrepreneurs.

He believes he has at least twenty-five years more before he bows out as an entrepreneur. 'There is so much one can do,' he says. 'I would have been a success in any business I did. It need not have been TV or the movies.' The money he made out of selling toothbrushes proves him right.

Over twenty years on, the journey has come full circle. But in that 'thought process' as Ronnie Screwvala would say, the journey has just begun.

RAJEEV CHANDRASEKHAR

Just after ushering in the New Year in 2010, Air Commodore M.K. Chandrasekhar (retd) sat in the cockpit during a trial flight of a Bombardier 300 in Canada. Soon after the flight in the mid-sized jet capable of flying across continents, he sent a simple SMS to his son Rajeev Chandrasekhar: *Thank you.* When Rajeev called back, his father told him that exactly fifty years ago, on the same day, he had stepped into his first plane to train as an Air Force cadet. He had never ever imagined that there would come a day when he would be sitting in his son's aircraft. But then, Rajeev has always been a super achiever with a long string of successes behind him.

By forty-eight, he was a successful techie in Silicon Valley, one of the pioneers of India's telecom industry, a billionaire, a serial entrepreneur, the head of not one but two national industry associations, a member of the prime minister's panel of advisors, a media baron and a feisty member of Parliament, now in his second term. As Rajya Sabha MP, he has been vocal on a number of issues, most famously the 2G scam, vociferously criticizing the parties to it: former telecom minister A. Raja,

Rajeev Chandrasekhar in his office

the Telecom Regulatory Authority of India (TRAI), several business houses and the government.

Rajeev's story could have been the story of anyone growing up in India in the 1970s and '80s. Opportunities were limited. Government-owned public sector companies controlled over three-fourths of the economy and placed severe restrictions on growth in the private sector.

If this was the picture at the macro level, on the ground too, private business was concentrated within a few regions and dominated by certain communities. The Marwari, Gujarati and Parsi communities collectively controlled sixty-two of the one hundred largest companies in India even as late as in 1989.

If you were a youngster like Rajeev and belonged to a regular middle-class family, you would either have to get into the government services, become an engineer or a doctor or a professional in some other field from the limited choices available, or go to the US or UK for higher studies, hoping to stay put, get a job and settle there.

By twenty-six, Rajeev had done all of the above. He was also part of the select team that built the Intel 486 processor. This was the game-changing chip or microprocessor that brought in technology which could allow a computer to execute 40 million instructions per second. The team also launched the Pentium chip in 1993. Rajeev's stint at Intel afforded him a ringside view of the creation of some of the most iconic names in the computing world, like Microsoft and Sun Microsystems. While doing this, he was rubbing shoulders with the likes of Bill Gates and Larry Ellison, and driving around in a gleaming black Porsche.

If one considers his middle-class roots, Rajeev was already a roaring success. But that's where the script turned and became a journey that is amazing not just for the highs he witnessed, but also the lows he went through. A journey that not only underlines the hopes, aspirations and potential of India but also the corruption, sabotage and politicking that is often part and parcel of doing business here.

It is rare for a businessman in India to talk so openly and with so much clarity about what he went through. Rajeev wants to make sure that others don't have to go up the same sharp and often painful learning curve that he had to. No book on Indian enterprise can be complete without a realistic assessment of the kind of hurdles a businessman faces on the ground. Hurdles that came as new sectors of the economy were opened up after 1991, when the government decided to liberalize business and invite private enterprise. This created a wave of entrepreneurs in new areas of business, such as technology and services. But it inevitably came with its own frictions. For example, in telecom, where the regulatory framework often didn't keep pace and had to be retrofitted to fix the problems faced within the rapidly evolving sector. As Infrastructure Development Finance Company (IDFC) chairman Rajiv Lall says, 'It's always painful when private enterprises grow faster than the policy framework. In India, in a sense, we put the cart before the horse.'

Rajeev was a product of these changes and they affected him deeply. His story provides an appropriate ending to this book because it reiterates that realism, along with optimism, make an entrepreneur what he is.

AN UNLIKELY BUSINESSMAN

The first thing you notice about Rajeev when you meet him is that he could well be the guy next door or the buddy you hang out and have a glass of beer with after work. He loves music, fast cars, super bikes and all those things that guys do, but his feet seem to be firmly planted on the ground. The second is that he wears his patriotism on his sleeve and when one hears him talk, one often wonders why he isn't in the armed forces, guarding the border somewhere. Both aspects are a reflection of where Rajeev comes from.

'To understand my journey, you have to put me right in the middle of the India of my childhood,' Rajeev says. His father was in the air force and life was a series of adventures and transfers to numerous new places for him, as was the case with other defence personnel kids. 'I was diagnosed with tuberculosis when I was four. While I think it must have been a wrong diagnosis, the fact is that I fell sick every time we drove up to Mohanbari [an air force station in Assam] where my father was posted. As a result, I was sent to my grandparents in Kerala to recuperate and then to a hostel. For a four-year-old, this was tough, but for the parents this was the only option. You can't even suggest that kind of life to our children today. They would have an emotional breakdown!'

But this was all part of growing up. 'Between 1971 and '84, we moved to seven or eight places and we loved it. As dad got transferred from one place to another, we would pack up our bags and take our Volkswagen for the long drive.' It was unforgettable for young Rajeev because not only did it kindle a passion for travel and cars, it also made him feel very responsible. 'Every time we took that drive, I was the guy in charge of navigation.' If the simple process of getting to a new place was exhilarating, living in cantonments, in the back of beyond (most often), was an adventure in itself! 'Growing up in cantonments was fun. I would spend my weekends in the hangars, watching planes being overhauled.'

He speaks of the many government-run schools or the ubiquitous Kendriya Vidyalayas (KVs) he studied in and how they were the greatest levellers for any kid growing up. In a small station, all kids, no matter how senior their fathers were, would study in the same school. 'The size of these KVs depended on the station or town you were posted in, and it could be really small at times. For instance, the KV in Yelahanka, on the outskirts of Bengaluru, where the city's new airport is situated, was a four-room set-up where multiple classes were taught simultaneously. The KV in Hindon, near Delhi, another air force base, was opulent in comparison, with ten rooms, two of which would switch between being biology and physics labs each day.'

If school wasn't posh, travelling to school was another story altogether. 'You would be required to take a one-tonne truck with an open back used by the army, which doubled up as a school bus and a ferry, transporting everything from students and rations to soldiers, through the day. These trucks would often not turn up and you had to make your own way back home. I remember making the trek between Hebbal and Yelahanka all too well. And we would have a great time walking back home too. Many a time, we would have no money for anything but a small packet of pickle and soda [a local delicacy].' It must have taken a long time, considering it's a half-hour drive on the highway these days.

There was a sense of adventure to the trek, nevertheless. 'It really didn't matter that you didn't have too much money. In fact, it was a frugal existence, in some ways. While you weren't poor, you understood the value of money. Even now the smell of a steaming hot plate of home-cooked mutton curry reminds me of what a luxury it was when we were growing up. I don't want to sound like an old-fashioned guy, but a lot of our ability to deliver on our dreams and achieve our ambitions comes from our hunger and desire. And the knowledge that working hard is the only way to achieve your dreams. I learnt that there is no shortcut to success and working hard is often a gruelling grind.'

This was the biggest lesson Rajeev learnt in his growing up years and it also kept him grounded in the face of the many ups and downs that followed. Like many youngsters of the time, he applied for both medical and engineering courses, and ended up getting admission to an engineering college. He went off to study in what he calls the 'Wild West', since the Wild West was what he was reminded of when he was in Manipal.

When one looks at Rajeev's photographs from his college days, it is hard to recognize the nerdy-looking, lanky guy with the Afro hairstyle. There is a world of difference in his looks and build now but the sensibilities, especially his love for music, obvious in the many autographed guitars that line his office in Bengaluru, have remained the same. As a student, his love for music resulted in periodic trips on bikes with friends (his gang was called Junk Sangh) to Bengaluru to attend rock concerts.

The gang would often be refused accommodation. Rajeev later got to know that the owner of one hotel they never managed to get a room in was a dear friend of the man who would be his future father-in-law. 'We would often go and hang out on the sidewalk near the massive BPL showroom in Bengaluru's main street. I had no clue that I would some day be part of the family.' Ten years later, he was married to Anju, the daughter of BPL founder T.P.G. Nambiar.

Another interesting episode from his student days is his first tryst with politics. Without giving away any names or party affiliations, he narrates how he and his friends were roped in for some good, old-fashioned campaigning and 'booth managing' during the elections. 'The stint involved driving through the interiors of Karnataka in a green Matador van and getting money and some liquor at the end of each day. The boys were expected to rally support for the local candidate and also go about casting votes in the booths during the elections. We didn't have a care in the world . . . We just thought it was a great adventure!'

During 1983–84, after getting an engineering degree, he hopped some forgettable jobs that saw him selling pumps to sugar companies in Uttar Pradesh, working in a seedy office in Delhi's Connaught Place area and designing software and writing codes for a small IT start-up, Softec, also in Delhi.

Working at Softec was like a breath of fresh air. One had the freedom to spend hours writing technology code, something he had started to enjoy. The company was quite a frontrunner for its time. While most firms used pirated versions of IT software, Softec decided to be among the few small Indian companies to develop compilers using computer languages like 'C' and 'Pascal'. This was no mean task. 'Compilers are amongst the most complicated software to write. I had a blast for the three or four months I was there,' Rajeev remarks.

The job and the hours spent developing software would have an important role to play in the next phase of his career.

THE INTEL DAYS

Like most upper-middle-class parents back then, Rajeev's parents also aspired to send their son to the US. His father took out his entire provident fund money to write him a cheque for a princely $9,000 to send him to study at the Illinois Institute of Technology, Chicago. On his very first day there, Rajeev got mugged as he made his way to the computer science lab.

Despite this setback, he was quick to settle in. 'In a very short time, I became one of the most prolific code-writers on campus. I was the one who handled the computerization of the entire chemical engineering lab. By the end of the first semester, I had earned a teaching assistantship and the next two years were heady.' By then he was sure about what he wanted to do—join an emerging hotspot like Microsoft and live the American dream, something he did eventually, albeit through another company.

Just as he was planning a short break before his first job, after passing out of college, his father called and insisted that he meet a person called Vinod Dham, in Santa Clara, where a small chip-making company called Intel was based. Rajeev wasn't too keen, but given that Dham was the brother of the air force doctor his parents had consulted for medical advice when he was a kid, he decided to make the trip. He ended up joining the small start-up.

What swung it for him was that they offered great money and gave him a two-month advance to shift base. 'It's at Intel that my whole life changed,' he says. When he joined three decades ago, Intel was a much smaller set-up, still tightly managed by the mercurial brain behind the success of the company, Andrew (Andy) Grove. He remembers how Grove used to stand at the door each morning to ensure that everyone turned up on time. 'Between 1985 and '91, the IT sector was in a state of flux. Companies were developing various pieces of internet architecture and no one quite knew what shape and look this rapidly evolving industry would take. Intel itself was a small outfit. Craig Barrett was the manufacturing guy and Vinod [Vin] Dham was heading the Pentium programme. Andy would be the first to come in each morning and the last to leave,' Rajeev remembers.

Work at Santa Clara was a mix of strong competition, creative freedom and a lot of discipline, and he learnt more in those years than at any other time. 'The work atmosphere was like nothing I had seen in India and sadly, that still holds true. There is a "chalta hai" attitude here. Our definition of what constitutes excellence is so casual that people get a performance rating for just showing up at work. And it all stems from not taking pride in what you do'. Rajeev tried his best to recreate the Intel management style and work culture at BPL Mobile, which he was to form later.

So he had an annual operating plan, Intel style, a set of corporate-strategy objectives and various short- and long-term incentive plans. But, the intense motivation and competitiveness that marked Intel's success was the hardest to recreate, and this led to something he confesses he didn't quite intend. 'I had to perforce become a manager who was demanding. This probably left no space for people's initiatives, but what else can one do when there is so little initiative!'

At Santa Clara and the Intel headquarters, the highs were many, the team was strong and the company amazing. 'One would actually bump into Bill Gates in the cafeteria. I remember having doughnuts at the same table as Oracle's Larry Ellison once. There was no megalomania at that time; everybody realized that technology was a work in motion and there were equal chances of it becoming a hit or totally irrelevant. Everyone was watching. Windows was coming, the internet was being built and Bill Gates did not know whether he was going to remain relevant two years down the line.'

Within Intel, first the i486 and then the Pentium chip, which would go on to transform the company and the IT world, were being worked upon. Rajeev was part of the core team that worked on both. His office has an enlarged copy of the Intel 486 processor chip, with the initials of all those who were part of its creation imprinted on it.

By twenty-six, Rajeev had truly arrived. 'I was in a cutting-edge company, driving a Porsche, I was happy planning a PhD programme in Stanford on microprocessors, I had applied for a green card, and life was set.'

It was also around this time that he met and began courting his wife, Anju Nambiar, in 1989. At that time, BPL was one of the biggest consumer-goods companies in India. For the techie that Rajeev was, this meant little. He had no plans of moving to India and Anju was anyway in Boston, studying.

Business was quite alien to him. It was Anju who painstakingly explained to him what a balance sheet looked like. He was actually made to understand why the two columns of assets and liabilities had to be balanced. While that's a little hard to believe, this was an important learning for what was to happen next.

THE TELECOM TURK

It is amazing how connections work in life and how doors open just when you least expect them to. In Rajeev's case, that is what happened when he came home, taking a year-long sabbatical from Intel after he got married.

On a trip to Delhi, he accompanied his father, who was going to meet the late Congress leader Rajeshwar Prasad Singh Vidhudi (Rajesh Pilot), then the Union Minister for Communications. Pilot, who had trained under Rajeev's dad, was a Gujjar politician from Dausa in Rajasthan. He took on 'Pilot' as his surname after he left the air force. He was the only man from his village to have become an Indian Air Force pilot, reaching the rank of squadron leader. Rajeev was impressed by the courtesy extended to him by Pilot. He wasn't just gracious, he was also persuasive. In the course of the evening, he managed to convince Rajeev that it was time that people like him came back to India.

By the mid-1980s, the first whiff of change and reforms was palpable in India. In December 1985, the Rajiv Gandhi government had, for the first time, laid out a tentative plan to boost exports, relax industrial regulation and encourage capital goods imports. What was significant was the change in 'attitude', and this was matched by an attempt to bring technocrats and experts from different sectors back to India. Computers, telephony and connectivity had become fashionable buzzwords in political circles and a refreshing new leadership was starting to inspire many to come back. With differences between India and the West being so stark, there were plenty of takers for Rajiv Gandhi's pet mantra, of ushering in an 'electronic revolution' in India, so that the country could be ready for the twenty-first century.

In this context, a techie like Rajeev, who had the right credentials, was a perfect find. He only needed a little nudge to take the decision to come back home. Once it was taken, he was also quick to decide that he didn't want to have a go at India's fledgling IT industry. 'I had already done far more exciting things in Intel. Anything else in technology would have been mundane.'

Not surprisingly, what he finally did choose was anything but mundane, a new sector that was opening up—telecom.

Like many of his contemporaries in the telecom space, he probably walked into this one blindly. There was little to go by, save the fact that in a country where a basic telephone connection took years and there were 2.5 million Indians waiting for one even in 1991, any alternative would be welcome!

Armed with nothing but the BPL brand name (which his father-in-law was happy to lend) and two partners—France Telecom and Craig McCaw—Rajeev decided to throw his hat into the ring as the government announced the opening up of the telecom sector to new technologies and private players.

For the government, it all started with the realization that it was impossible for it to meet the demand for telephone lines. The long list of applicants meant that it would have to build the infrastructure at a rapid pace. This could cost upwards of Rs 24,000 crore, and it didn't have the money. To address this, it began to invite private sector participation in a phased manner. First, value-added services like paging and cellular mobile telephone services were allowed, followed by fixed telephone services.

In 1992, the process of identifying players for eight licences, two each in India's top four metros—Delhi, Mumbai, Kolkata and Chennai—was started and, in 1994, the government announced the National Telecom Policy, which opened it up further into eighteen circles. (The Department of Telecom had divided India into circles—broadly, statewise—and this was extended by the policy to incorporate cellular circles.) Each of the winning companies had exclusive rights for a period of twenty years and they had to pay a fixed sum of money to the government every year.

It was an amazing journey. What worked in Rajeev's favour in the early stages was probably the earnestness and idealism with which he pursued his new calling. 'It may seem ironic in hindsight, but in many of my earlier presentations to investors, I actually had slides on how Indian politicians had changed and how a new, forward-looking generation had taken charge!'

In the first round, Rajeev bagged the licence for India's commercial capital, Mumbai. Soon he and his team were working out of a small office to launch their service in the Nariman Point area. Till now the going had been smooth, but gradually, by the second round of licences, things started going a little awry. A year after the launch of the first round of services, licences were granted for eighteen more circles, but the story takes an interesting turn here.

Before the licences were auctioned off, Rajeev, like all other telecom operators, was invited for a meeting with the then telecom minister, Sukh Ram. He was thrilled at the prospect of sharing his plans with the minister, and was a little taken aback when the minister listened to his painstakingly prepared presentation with little interest. 'He just listened and said, "Come back tomorrow." I went back with an even more detailed plan, and the same thing happened. Finally, after a few such meetings, the seemingly frustrated minister asked me, "Isn't there any senior person in your house I can talk to?"' But there was no one because it was a fledgling business.

Rajeev and the other new entrants into telecom worked hard to get the new idea off the ground. BPL Mobile was among the first companies to get multiple licences and, today, Rajeev is proud of the fact that he managed to get the business going despite the initial political hurdles.

In 1994, he got the Maharashtra, Kerala, Tamil Nadu and Mumbai circles. He was close to getting two more—Gujarat and Karnataka—when the first signs of politicking became visible. The minister changed the policy to restrict the number of players. The ministry claimed this was done to prevent a 'private sector' monopoly. Rajeev says, 'Do you know, BPL Mobile and I were at the centre of the first telecom storm in Parliament?'

As the story goes, when the bidding for the new circles opened up in 1995, many big Indian companies, in partnership with global majors, put in their bids for the licences. But as the results came out, it became apparent that something was amiss. The winner of most of these auctions was a small equipment manufacturer that few had even heard of, Himachal Futuristic Company Limited (HFCL). The company had won nine of the eighteen licences and its bids totalled a whopping Rs 85,000 crore.

A paper prepared jointly by the United Nations Development Programme (UNDP), National Council of Applied Economic Research (NCAER) and the Indian Institute of Public Administration (IIPA)—'Indian Telecom Reforms: A Chronological Account', in 2006, lays out what happened. It points out:

> Soon after the results of the bids were announced, the government announced that it had decided to 'cap' the number of licences. It announced that no company would be allowed to retain more than three of the category 'A' licences [for the main state circles]. This meant that HFCL had to forgo six of its licences. In effect, this also bailed out HFCL from having to pay the huge amounts it had bid.

In December 1995, MPs demanded that the telecom minister be sacked for his attempts to benefit a particular company and for causing losses to the exchequer, a charge that would be made again, many years later.

This twist in the tale affected Rajeev because he had been close to getting additional circles, including Gujarat. But he still had his hands full. BPL Mobile was on a good wicket. It was business as usual for the next two years as the fledgling cellular companies, among them BPL Mobile and Sunil Bharti Mittal's Bharti Cellular, tried to set up their network and woo new customers. But as the months passed, the excitement was tempered with a realization that they might have got things wrong. Telecom was a new sector then and many didn't understand what went into putting a network and the required infrastructure in place.

Over the next few years, they learnt some tough lessons. It was virtually impossible to make money in the sector. High licence fees and low revenues from subscribers who were still trying to get a hang of this new technology meant that costs for the telecom companies reached an all-time high. What's more, hundreds of crores were needed to get the infrastructure and system in place. This meant that one needed deep pockets or investors who would look at the long term. Nearly all the telecom companies were bleeding. Within three years of getting the licences, companies began to default on their licence-fee payments. Delays by the Department of Telecom (DoT) in clearing radio frequencies and getting permissions aggravated the problem.

As these realities became obvious, and Rajeev realized he would need far more money than he had initially estimated, he made the first of his three big mistakes as an entrepreneur who was desperate to make it in India's telecom sector. In 1995, like everyone else in the business, he had borrowed a large sum of money—Rs 250 crore—to set up his network. 'The idea was that we would eventually do a fresh round of equity funding to finance this.' The opportunity came in the form of a proposal from a famous investment banking firm's head. 'He came up with an idea I had frankly never even thought of. "How about listing BPL Mobile internationally in the US and using the money raised from these new American depository receipts [ADRs] to pay back the debt?"' Rajeev barely had time to react. The concept was alien to him and he says the biggest mistake he made was in trusting the man. Today, he is wiser. 'That investment banker wouldn't dare approach me now. The incident taught me a lot about life.'

Rajeev was sucked into the story the bankers spun for him. 'I had no clue about how to raise the money and what an ADR or a roadshow actually meant. I was just fascinated by what they were telling me. Take, for instance, the fact that as soon as the bankers came in, they demanded that the company be restructured to unlock all the value. Then they intervened and added a lot of frills to the business, including new platforms like DTH. So in 1996, BPL cellular operations wanted to go public with a DTH platform and I met the global head of PanAmSat along with many others. It was all very exciting for a thirty-two-year-old like me.'

So much so, that the young entrepreneur couldn't keep his big plans to himself. While making a sales call to a top industrialist (at this time, Rajeev used to double up as a sales manager meeting big businessmen to sell them corporate phone connections), he blurted out that he was planning to take his company to the US. He was touched when the industrialist asked to see the papers and offered to help. 'Like a complete fool I showed him everything, my prospectus, my offer document, my finances, valuations, everything! For a youngster like me, an industrialist like him was someone I could look up to.' Rajeev bought into the promise and shared details of everything he had done and every milestone of the listing process. 'Like an ass, I would keep him informed. I trusted him completely, something that came back to haunt me later.'

The problem started when he reached the India leg of the roadshow.

'We met several weather-beaten investors in Hong Kong to whom we were making detailed presentations. All was well till we reached Mumbai. That was when the first articles attacking us started appearing. Later, I got to know that every journalist had received a copy of the prospectus with highlighted points showing up the losses the company was making across its circles or the key markets it operated in. Most journalists at that time didn't quite understand what this new beast [telecom] was, and they were left wondering why a loss-making company was going for an ADR in the US.' (Listings in the US don't mandate that a company has to be profitable, like the exchanges in India do.)

Soon the stray questions turned into a tide, and by the time Rajeev completed the next leg, across the US, and landed in New York, it was evident that he had flown straight into a storm. It didn't help that at that time the global stock markets were going into a tailspin as well.

'By the last leg of the roadshow, the responses had tapered off. But even then, I wasn't quite ready for what happened next.' Days before the issue was to open, Rajeev got a message from the investment banker who had been so encouraging and gung-ho till even a few weeks back. 'It was a bland "I think we'll have to pull the offer of the ADR out." That's it. We had got only 80 per cent of the book subscribed in the pre-placement despite all the assurances. There weren't enough investors who were ready to bet on the company.'

A shocked Rajeev realized there was some kind of finality here. 'That was the first time in all this while that I felt the floor under me give. I faced a situation where I didn't know what to do. I had a Rs 250 crore debt to pay off and thanks to the leaked prospectus, there wasn't a soul in the financial community who wasn't aware that I needed that money to survive.'

He was sure his run was over. But he bounced back. 'I restarted the fund-raising efforts with the help of some bankers and in a few months raised $75m from a group of private equity funds.'

And BPL Mobile got a new lease of life.

TANGLES AND A BIGGER MESS

No other sector has been so riddled with crises like telecom, even as it is celebrated as the big success story of India. It has been witness to scams with uncomfortable regularity. Despite the ADR debacle, within BPL Mobile, the early years of telecom were thrilling. As the new sector opened up, people began to understand what a mobile could do. But with success came the questions.

Rajeev feels this was largely because the incumbents and their bureaucratic masters were not quite ready for the new rage. And it wasn't their fault, as telecom analyst Mahesh Uppal puts it in the paper on telecom reforms he co-authored:

> In an interesting twist [to the National Telecom Policy 1994], it was decided that government operators would not be allowed to bid for telecom licences. The minister argued that government resources needed to be augmented by bringing in private investments. Getting public-sector companies to bid would defeat the goal.

The result was friction on the ground and a series of litigations between the private sector, the incumbent state-owned telecom companies and DoT, with the lawsuits amounting to Rs 10,000 crore! By now there were many issues concerning tariffs and how calls should be charged as they passed through operators, be it cellular or fixed line. Adding to the confusion was the fact that there was no clear framework for the new telecom regulator, TRAI.

'In 1998, the government and the incumbent [state-owned telecom companies MTNL and the Department of Telecom that controlled the fixed-line service across the country] started making life hell. They realized there was a lot of potential here and they had missed the bus somewhere. Things got worse after 1997–98, when the market began to pick up and they realized they had lost out because they didn't have any cellular circles. It was almost as though it became their life's mission to try and make us unviable and force us to shut down.' These are serious allegations but, perhaps, a telling sign of the discord between private players and the government was the number of litigation cases from both ends.

A litigation meant delays and for private telecom companies, burdened as they were by heavy duties and high interest rates and roll-out costs, it looked like the end of the road. The numbers reiterate the point. At this stage, despite the four years of roll-out, the total subscriber base in India was just 5 lakh. Also, private players like Bharti and BPL, among others, had invested about $2bn.

As the crisis festered, the government stepped in and decided to empower the independent regulator, TRAI. Things started moving after a long wait. 'The regulator started pushing back the monopoly and passed a number of orders that began to make our lives slightly better.'

The big turning point for the private telecom players came in 1999—the new telecom policy that year removed the crippling yearly licence-fee regime. The policy, instead, mandated that companies would have to pay only a portion of their revenues to the government each year. As a compromise to allow the state-owned incumbents entry into the lucrative sector, the government also did away with the duopoly for twenty years that the earlier regime mandated, allowing a third entrant, the state-run MTNL and ITI's new entrants across circles, and ushering in competition in the telecom sector. Court cases were dropped and the players focussed their energies on the ground, on growth and expansion. Between 1999 and 2000, Rajeev saw 'a honeymoon period with cellular operators growing rapidly'. Success attracted money and, in 2001, foreign direct investment in the sector doubled. By this time, demand for phones was also going up and TRAI gave its recommendation on opening up the sector further with the introduction of a fourth licence to allow yet another entrant into a telecom circle. This way, existing telecom players would be able to expand into the cities or circles that they didn't have licences for, provided they had the money.

But, by now, another battle was brewing. After a lot of resistance even within the government, in January 2001, the stage was set for the entry of a new group of operators, who until now had had only fixed-line licences, into mobility, though in a limited way.

Rajeev was at the forefront of the battle against what GSM players claimed was the back-door entry of fixed-line players into mobile telephony. The frustration in his voice is evident even today when he explains how the lines became mobile. 'The regulation allowing wireless in local loop was the most complex work of wordplay you could have seen and despite a "no" from the Department of Telecom, there was a complete turnaround. Within thirty to forty days, the regulator gave a recommendation allowing limited mobility and it was so ambiguous, it could be easily exploited. It was really a loophole that changed limited mobility to full mobility.'

For the Global System for Mobile (GSM) communications players, especially BPL Mobile, this was a setback. Wireless in Local Loop (WLL) allowed the entry of fixed-line players like Tata Telecom and Reliance Communications into mobility without having to pay the high licence fee the cellular players had to pay. Also, it allowed them to make a quick switch at a minimal cost.

In Bengaluru, just back from a leadership programme at INSEAD, in Paris, Romal Shetty, director and head of the telecom practice at KPMG, who has advised some of the biggest telecom players across the world, gives his version of what happened over a decade back: 'The reason the government first allowed limited mobility to players like Reliance and Tata who had fixed-line [landline] facilities was because they didn't have the money to set up the physical infrastructure for the last-mile connectivity and they wanted to attract private investments here. The idea of limited mobility was simple; it was to ensure that landlines could connect to the local exchanges without the need for wiring, basically like a cordless phone. While the idea was simple, what the government missed out on was how this could be interpreted.'

Shetty continues, 'The fixed-line players, including MTNL, simply used this concept as a relay and using the "call-forwarding" technique—which connects different local area exchanges—made the basic telephone line go mobile. Soon they were offering mobility in their circle or area of influence, however large it was. This had huge ramifications for the actual "mobile" companies.'

GSM players like BPL Mobile took a knock. With much lower costs and overheads, without having to pay any kind of licence fee, instead enjoying some subsidies and having a ready pool of users, the WLL players could offer services at a fraction of the price charged by the GSM players. For the GSM players, who had begun to get their finances in place, the timing couldn't have been worse. They still had to invest and to grow into national mobile providers and they were hoping to bid for the fourth licence. Rajeev, who was head of the cellular players' lobby, the Cellular Operators Association of India (COAI), led the battle. He had the most to lose. The COAI took the battle to the court.

THE BATATA MERGER

When problems come, they usually come in droves. This was what happened in the case of telecom companies in early 2000. If the introduction of WLL threatened to sweep the market and drop tariffs and hence profits drastically (which it did), there were a series of other issues that threatened BPL Mobile.

When the bids for the fourth licence were invited it was clear to all players that they would have to bid aggressively if they wanted to expand and keep competition out. Bidding required money and BPL Mobile once again faced a crunch.

'We were at a heavy investment stage and my partners weren't in a position to invest money.' At this point, making matters worse was the fact that both of Rajeev's foreign partners, France Telecom and US West, were in trouble. 'France Telecom was broke and US West had changed owners so many times that India was the last thing on their minds.' Rajeev now decided to look east at a potential partner, SingTel, the Singapore government-owned telecom giant. Hectic meetings and negotiations later, both parties agreed to sign up. And confident about the next step, he returned to India.

'It seemed as though it was all done, but the moment I came back, I saw a report hinting that we were talking to SingTel. Within days, the deal was off and the company signed with Bharti. The rug was again pulled from under my feet.' And this time too, it could not have happened at a worse time. The proposals for the fourth licence in each circle were out and to survive, he had to find a partner, raise money, or look at a possible merger or acquisition and grow inorganically.

The last route seemed the most exciting. Most players were

facing the same level of stress; there was nervousness around the entry of MTNL and Reliance. 'Nobody had the money for acquisitions, be it of circles or competitors.' It was around this time, when Rajeev was talking to a whole lot of possible players, including the Tatas, who had Kolkata under them, that he was approached by investment banker Nimesh Kampani with a proposal that apparently came highly recommended from the office of then Tata Group chairman Ratan Tata.

'When I met Kampani, I was confronted with the need to grow. My partners [foreign] were dead or missing. I had lost the SingTel deal to Bharti Airtel. There was a need to bid for the fourth licence and that is when Nimesh Kampani came to me with his proposal.' The Birlas had already merged their joint venture with AT&T and the Tatas to form BATATA. It was proposed that Rajeev merge BPL mobile with the combine to create what could be the biggest telecom company of the time.

There was immense excitement around the prospect of this mega deal. Rajeev says, 'My principal hook was Ratan Tata. I liked him, and for all practical purposes, Kumar [Kumar Mangalam Birla] was a young guy and Tata's friend, and they had a tie-up in BATATA already. So I had no reason to doubt them.'

In a hurriedly organized press conference on 28 June 2001, Ratan Tata, Kumar Mangalam Birla and Rajeev Chandrasekhar provided the perfect photo-op at the Tata headquarters, Bombay House, as they announced the merger of their businesses. The media and the financial markets were taken aback by the news and for weeks the headlines were all about how the three were creating a giant that would be valued at a whopping $2bn. The deal was simple. As the bigger entity, with a subscriber base of nearly 9 lakh, versus the BATATA combined base of 8 lakh, BPL Mobile and its partners would own a 49.32 per cent stake in the company while Birla, Tata and AT&T would hold 50.68 per cent. Other potential problem areas were also covered. 'There was an agreement that we would have a neutral management and no one would be a controlling shareholder. Since I was the closest to telecom in terms of everyday operations, I told both my partners that I would meet them every week and give them a detailed presentation. My team created the first draft of the "Idea" branding,' Rajeev explains.

But the merger was far from smooth. Even before the team could group together and work out a strategy, there were hurdles. First, there was the contentious issue of Maharashtra and the clash of interests because both BPL Mobile and BATATA were competing in this circle. BPL had to hive off its operations in Mumbai into a separate company before the deal was announced. After the announcement, one of its key investors, the UK-based Commonwealth Development Corporation (CDC), which held a 3 per cent stake in BPL Mobile, took it to court, accusing it of ignoring its voting rights while finalizing the deal with BATATA. The case dragged on for a year and BPL Mobile finally won in the Supreme Court a year later.

While these modalities were being worked out in Mumbai, Rajeev was caught in a far bigger battle that was brewing in Delhi—the one between the cellular or GSM operators and the new players, the Code Division Multiple Access (CDMA) technology-driven WLL players, who were waiting to enter.

Not surprisingly, the much-in-the-news Rajeev, the biggest and perhaps most voluble player in the telecom sector, was asked to lead the charge as the president of the Cellular Operators Association of India, representing the GSM lobby.

Rajeev is critical of his decision to take on the battle, even though he justifies it by saying, 'Being the biggest player and having the most money invested on the ground, I had the most to lose from the entry of WLL. I was far too naïve and trusting. I simply got carried away.'

He minces no words: 'When the other cellular operators came together and asked if I would lead the battle at COAI, I agreed. Anyway, I was fearless and didn't care what I did. Also, I thought, everyone likes me, everyone is counting on me, so I took on the job, not realizing that they were actually setting me up, making me look like the bad guy. I was pulled into it and I didn't realize it was a ruse.' Evidently, this second mistake Rajeev made as a businessman still hurts. 'I got carried away by what would later turn out to be double talk,' he claims. 'They said, "You know you are young, you are dynamic, you should do it." So I said fine.' Although, he still justifies taking up cudgels against the government because it was the right thing to do. 'But I didn't realize that behind my back, they were benefiting from it by cutting private deals with the government.'

It became obvious to him only in 2003 that despite the victories that the cellular operators were gaining, none of them wanted to take on the fight. 'By this time, I had picked a fight with almost everyone in the government. I had become the bad guy.' Just then another problem surfaced, and it was even more damaging. By the time Rajeev realized this it was far too late.

A year after signing the MoU to merge under the BATATA banner, BPL Mobile had gone easy with expansion in Mumbai and not applied for the fourth licence. This was as planned because it was believed that expansion would be driven by the combined entity. But what this inadvertently meant was that BPL Mobile was on the wane, and BATATA was gaining at its expense. While this was according to plan too, Rajeev didn't quite anticipate the next step. 'The Birlas demanded a revaluation of the business, thereby indicating that they no longer saw me or BPL Mobile as a dominant partner in the merged entity.'

While Rajeev refused to budge, he was quick to realize what had happened. He had been elbowed out, almost made irrelevant, even as he was fighting the system alone. He acknowledges today, 'My mistake was I trusted so easily.' Within a year after the big announcement, a battle-weary Rajeev was left with a falling market share, the wrong end of the deal after the proposed merger fell through, lots of enemies in very powerful places and a business in shambles.

But, here too, he learnt a crucial lesson. 'Between 2001 and 2003, I learnt a lot about Indian businessmen. I learnt that nobody wants to be a Mr Bad Guy with the government. But they don't mind a patsy being the bad person, someone they can control with a remote and wind up. They did that with me at COAI and they gave me the unprecedented honour of being the COAI chairman for two years back to back, so I fought it out. I took the government to court and we made some serious progress. In the process, I took on successive ministers, souring my relations with them. I think they also got back at me through my bankers, who cut off my lines of credit.'

Even as foreign investors and partners were getting into the ring, the foreign investors in the holding company, BPL Communications, CDC and American Insurance Group (AIG) filed a court case for control of the company, claiming that a dividend had not been paid. In 2002, he spent 40 to 45 per cent of his time in litigations with foreign investors, 45 per cent fighting over WLL as president of COAI and just 10 per cent looking into the workings of his own company.

'I was upset, but I wanted to fight back, and in the next two years I simply got back to trying to build my business from scratch. It was tough, I had loans to repay and important investments to make, and my bank had clamped up, refusing to give even what was due to us.' Rajeev, who by now had learnt some hard lessons, finally went looking for help, knocking on the doors of the finance minister, Jaswant Singh.

Here, too, he almost didn't make it. 'The start was a disaster. I opened the conversation by saying, "Sir, the banking system seems to be gunning for me." An imperious Singh took great offence at this and called in his team. The moment I said it, I was like, I have done it again, now it's over! But it wasn't. Jaswant Singh interrupted as I was speaking and sent the entire presentation I was carrying with me to the RBI. And India's central bank stepped in.' (The RBI, which sets lending norms for banks, had provisions to make it easier for banks that had lent to companies like BPL restructure loans.)

Funds started coming in then and Rajeev was able to focus on the business. Suddenly, there was a lot to do. By now, BPL Mobile had gone from being a dominant player in Mumbai to a much smaller one. Competition was tough and for over a year, no money was put together, nor any effort made to get things back on track.

The exercise of reviving BPL Mobile and ensuring that it got back on its feet was dubbed 'Project Clawback' internally. 'We had not worked like this for years. For one and a half years, we worked like dogs, marketing, networking, reworking equipment contracts to improve margins, and by the end of 2003–04, we were humming and back in business. By March 2004, I had made money,' Rajeev says.

Project Clawback worked, things were getting back on track, but BPL Mobile had missed the bus. At the crucial stage where it should have been aggressively looking at expansion—the entry of the WLL players and the resultant crash in telecom tariffs had created a boom in telecom—it was busy sorting out its internal mess.

Rajeev knew his company could never become the biggest player from here on. So after July 2005, he announced his decision to sell out. The buyer was the Essar-Hutchison Group. The deal was valued at roughly $1.2bn and Rajeev is estimated to have made upwards of several hundred crores from it, after clearing all the dues.

For Rajeev, the period marked an amazing transformation in his life as he realized that exiting a business or walking out was no big deal any more. He had also learnt other lessons. 'I was clear that I was done with the sector. I knew that from here on, the story was going to be about getting new licences. This would require totally different sets of skills and I wasn't willing to go down that path.' He was so bitter about what had transpired that he made a resolution. 'I decided that I wouldn't invest in anything that had anything to do with the government.' His time as a businessman was over.

Romal Shetty says Rajeev's biggest problem was that he couldn't manage to get the long-term investors needed for a business like telecom. 'He was simply unlucky with his investors. There was no one who was looking at the longer term. They weren't willing to take a ten- or fifteen-year bet.'

Rajeev's contemporary, Sunil Bharti Mittal, had the

advantage here. He managed to rope in Singapore's SingTel and Warburg Pincus. Both were willing to give Bharti the money and the space to build itself into one of India's biggest telecom networks and go overseas. According to Shetty, Rajeev made two big contributions to the telecom space. First, at the most crucial moment, at the time of the entry of WLL players, he fought an important battle for the GSM operators. It was a battle for survival, quite literally, because they had so much at stake. Second, he created a great pool of talent within BPL Mobile. Today, most of those who worked there are in senior positions in the sector.

For Rajeev himself, the stint was a game changer. 'I could deal with anything after this. I had faced every problem that I could have faced and entrepreneurship didn't have the same kick and excitement after this.' In ten years, he had met with stupendous success. He was feted as one of the stars of the fledgling telecom sector, but if the highs were great, his fall was as sharp. He faced corporate sabotage, he stared bankruptcy in the face, he was pushed to the wall and he had bounced back, rebuilding his business from scratch.

BPL AND STRAINED RELATIONS

While Rajeev did not use more than the name of his father-in-law's company to set out and make a mark in a new sector like telecom, it did help. Leading up to the late 1990s, BPL, originally the British Physical Laboratories, started by T.P.G. Nambiar, Rajeev's father-in-law, to make panel meters for the defence forces in Kerala's Palakkad district in 1963, had become one of India's biggest consumer goods companies.

The company that essentially made TVs and refrigerators

lorded over a quarter of India's market and was a familiar brand name. It helped Rajeev establish his credentials. But over the years, relations within the family soured, something that wasn't evident in the beginning. In fact, articles and profiles written on the BPL group till as late as 1999 show how the young guard, Ajit (Nambiar's son) and Rajeev were rewriting the rules of the game. *Business India* dubbed them as 'BPL's bold new face(s)', working together, shoulder to shoulder, in the company.

It was evident from the beginning that Rajeev was the telecom man while Ajit handled the core business. It was probably because of the growing pressures on the telecom side that Ajit pushed for a clearer division. Though Rajeev doesn't mention it, the first strains in the relationship were manifest even before the many cheery interviews of 1999.

At a time when a company's financial dealings could impact others in the group, the high debt at the mobile division and the ADR debacle had probably started hurting. And as early as 1997 and '98, the two divisions had become separate entities.

Rajeev claims there were other factors. 'Since my views were at variance with my father-in-law's, I said I want to do only telecom, and all my money was anyway sunk in the business. As long as the business was doing well, everything was okay, but then as the telecom business became sick and came close to default in 2001–03, Ajit wanted to understandably protect his business.' The division now became even more pronounced and the two groups split more than just functionally, as two different unrelated verticals that had been under the same banner.

'When the turnaround happened and the money was obvious, eyes suddenly turned to the business. By now BPL had begun to go into a tailspin and that put even more focus on what was working. However, I wanted to make sure no one dipped into the honeypot.'

That's when the next battle started for Rajeev, and this one was at home. The next few years after the turnaround were tough. He doesn't want to talk about it, except to say that he won in court and has moved on since then.

DOUBLING HIS MONEY!

Within two years of selling his stake in BPL Mobile and pocketing upwards of $250m or nearly Rs 1,200 crore, Rajeev managed to double his money through a series of strategic bets and new businesses he ventured into.

Today, he spends most of his time managing the portfolio of private equity investments that he has done well with. He set up Jupiter Capital the day he sold BPL Mobile. The same year, in 2005, he invested in a railway freight transportation company in India, Linx, a joint venture with the largest shipping company in Asia.

The next investment was in a Malayalam channel, Asianet, based in Kerala. 'My only connection with the channel was watching my staple Sunday afternoon movie on it. Suddenly, I heard that one of the shareholders, Raji Menon, wanted to sell out. I grabbed the chance and became a majority owner of the company.'

Rajeev was quick to infuse a sizeable chunk of cash into the company and with the Rs 160-odd crore he put into the channel, a staple with the large Malayali expat community, it showed a fast turnaround. He remembers how the merger of Asianet with Murdoch's Vijay TV created the only network that could take on Sun TV's clout in the south.

'Sometimes a merger does work. Even though I failed to pull it through in telecom, I did manage it in regional TV.' He is sure that if the BATATA merger hadn't fallen through, BPL Mobile would have been the biggest player in the country. But lessons have been learnt and Rajeev is sure he will not repeat the mistakes he made. He confesses he has become much more dispassionate and hands off with the businesses he is in. He would rather view them as pure investments. 'I studiously and strictly avoid getting into management. I love mentoring and brainstorming on ideas and strategies, but I am adamant that I will remain nothing more than an investor.'

Today, Rajeev has investments in sectors like infrastructure, hospitality and aviation, and is enjoying life. The period between 1997 and '03 had taken a toll on his health and family. All through those years, he hardly spent time at home with his wife and kids. 'The hard work and long hours made me unhealthy. There was a time when I weighed 123 kilos.'

After the telecom stint, Rajeev has got back to being fit. He says, 'I do nothing that I don't want to, and everything I want to!' And these days he wants nothing more than to be a political activist, putting the spotlight on public policies that are holding the country back.

So much so, he has over time exited most of his investments. He has only two businesses left—Asianet News and an FM Radio service, Indigo, which plays the kind of music he loves, and this is a conscious decision. 'You can't be an activist and a businessman. You have to pick one.' And he has. 'I have chosen public life and I want the flexibility of criticizing the government or supporting it as the case may be.'

Rajeev believes that few people in business can do both, and at the heart of this view is another cynical one. 'There are too many headwinds to start a non-technology-driven business in

India today. It is not a satisfying or happy process. There is really no incentive for me to do anything more than regular short-term investments.'

The cynicism at the heart of Rajeev's observation is unmistakable. It has made him resolute in his decision that he will never invest in any business that is heavily dependent on government policy.

POLITICS AND BEYOND

Today Rajeev is proud to be an MP. He believes he can make a difference by leading the discourse on public policy. He is emphatic about why he is doing this. 'We can't be cynical about politics and governance and sit at home till the problem comes all the way to our doorstep.' His way of doing his bit is to take pains to understand policy ramifications and bring up significant and far-reaching issues.

Perhaps the best chronicled is the one around the infamous 2G scam. The scam raised the question of how the telecom ministry had handed out telecom licences to companies in 2008 on a first-come-first-serve basis. The rules were manipulated so that the first-come-first-serve policy would be functional, but not on the basis of who applied first for a licence. It was on the basis of who first acted in accordance with the conditions. The comptroller and auditor general of India (CAG) came out with a scathing report and created a furore when it pegged the loss to the exchequer at Rs 1.76 lakh crore, a fact the government vehemently denied.

Having watched the telecom sector evolve since it first opened up in the mid-1990s, Rajeev believes that what is being seen now is symptomatic of a larger problem—a classic example of policies not keeping pace with rapid transformation and change. 'Every country and every sector in it goes through a maturity curve and maturity doesn't just mean maturity in the market, it also means maturity in policy and ensuring that public good is at the heart of it. The mistakes and scams we are seeing today are because policies and regulations haven't kept pace with the growth in the market.'

This is a vicious cycle that has plagued the most crucial sectors and that is where the maximum problems lie. For example, statistically speaking, a bulk of India's GDP growth right now comes from three sectors—infrastructure, housing and mining—which are growing at a much faster rate than the average sectors. With growth has come wealth and this has attracted a fair bit of interest, often of the wrong kind.

What's wrong is that often the interest is not because of the actual potential of the market or the entrepreneurs' zeal for making a difference. It is because of an opportunity of a different kind. 'Those who enter the fray are mostly businessmen who are far more aggressive and better at the "game" than their predecessors. The entry of such players unravels a deeper nexus between them and politicians, leading to excesses,' Rajeev remarks.

In telecom, the judiciary's intervention in the 2G case at multiple levels and its eventual cancellation of all the 122 licences that were dished out are a severe indictment of the executive and an indication of the collapse of governance. This can have far-reaching repercussions.

If Rajeev's logic is to be believed, the biggest failing of the government was its failure to ensure that the sector was overseen by independent, knowledgeable experts. Instead, there were bureaucrats. And with no real vision statement of how policy should evolve, it was left wide open for loopholes and interpretations.

This is something experts have also pointed out. As the authors of the UNDP-commissioned report on telecom reforms say, 'The absence of a well-thought-out initial plan comes through clearly as the main reason for many of the problems that arose in India's telecom reforms.'

'While the stakes have risen manifold with growth and opportunity in the private sector and it has become as sophisticated as the most evolved companies, the politicians haven't evolved so fast, the 2G scam being a point in case,' Rajeev says. He realized this when two communist party MPs walked up to him and expressed their shock at the magnitude of the scam. 'They had dealt with scams that were small—to the tune of Rs 50 lakh or Rs 1 crore. That a scam could run into a whopping Rs 100,000 crore was a shock for them.'

But amidst this gloom, Rajeev also sees hope. He believes that if anything, 2011–12 showed an awakening of the media and the citizenry to the deep underlying corruption and policy paralysis that have festered for so long in the country. He is proud of his role in fanning the flames of dissent that have gone far beyond telecom.

Even before the 2G scam came to light, as president of the Federation of Indian Chambers of Commerce and Industry (FICCI), he had steered the debate towards corporate governance and the need to keep an arm's length between corporate India and the government so that there was no scope for a nexus or friction between the two. Since then he has consistently, within Parliament and outside, focussed on 'governance', on the need for clear, transparent policies that look ahead and across. In many ways, what Rajeev is talking about also echoes elsewhere in the sentiments of citizen activists who want to steer the debate beyond the 'noise' of politics and politicking to issues that matter.

Of the many battles he has fought, this is the one that he is most passionate about and it's also the toughest. Rajeev has always worked around ten-year plans. The first was from 1995 to '05, when he wanted to make $25m. He went on to make ten times that amount.

The next ten-year plan was about influencing policy and making a difference, and who knows, there could be a clearer target beyond that too.

CONCLUSION

It is not easy to hit the pause button and capture the essence of a story in a constantly moving picture, but I tried my best to do so as I pieced together these seven stories.

The timing couldn't have been more perfect. Each of the men in the book found themselves at a crossroads in the years after 2010. Some self-created, as in the case of Ajay Piramal and Ronnie Screwvala after they sold their core businesses to script a new chapter in their journey, and others by circumstances they didn't have any control of, be it a slowing world economy that forced Gautam Thapar to scale down his transnational plans or the crises and controversy at home that forced Ajit Gulabchand and G.M. Rao to recalibrate theirs.

But as the dust settles and this book concludes, I can't help but look ahead at what is in store for these men as they script the next chapter of their life.

First, of course, is Ajit Gulabchand, who has had the toughest three years possible. Just when he thought his old company would cash in on the great opportunity that infrastructure in a new, open India offered, he, like many businessmen in his space, was forced to slow down. Today his company is debt-ridden and it will take more than a few years for him to get it back on track. Sad, given the time Gulabchand already believes he, HCC and India have lost. He has spent far too much time waiting for things to change. In his mid-sixties now, he knows he hasn't got the decades he has already put in. He needs to plan his succession and HCC is far too closely associated with one man—himself. It will take more than his passion and vision to ensure that the company lives up to its potential.

Succession is an issue that is foremost in Baba N. Kalyani's mind too, especially since he has taken his forging company way beyond the comfort of the automotive segment he and his team of engineers were so familiar with. In his case, the slowdown in the power sector and infrastructure in India due to policy issues have come just when he had put in place his plans to be a significant player in both these segments. Over the next few years, he will have to ensure that the investments and bets he has made bear fruit and his son Amit and his team are capable of managing things the way he has always done.

That is something Gautam Thapar too, seems to have assiduously worked towards over the last few years. In many senses, this scion of the Thapar family is quite unlike the heads of other family-owned companies in India, perhaps because his group is not technically a family-owned one. He is the man in charge and his lookout, even as he navigated his increasingly outward-looking group through the slowdown in key markets—Europe and the US—over the last two years, was to build a team of leaders who could manage the business so that he could get more free time to live a simple life, teach his kids, play eighteen holes of golf as often as possible, and look ahead.

GT withdrew from the day-to-day work at the two companies that are core to his group—BILT and Crompton Greaves—years ago. Since then, he has been silently working to build a new business empire. Away from the limelight and the media glare, at home in London and whenever he is in India, it is very much a work in progress. It will be interesting to see what shape Avantha takes.

One man whose plans have been delayed, if not waylaid, is G.M. Rao. Rao's inspiring journey onto the international runway of success has had more than its fair share of setbacks. His ambitious T3 project in Delhi's Indira Gandhi International Airport is bleeding and the Male airport, which he lost to politics in the island state, has been a major setback. All this happened just when he thought he would retire to his town in Rajam and hand over the reins of the company he had built to his two sons and son-in-law.

But succession, as per the rules laid out in the 'family constitution' that Rao is so proud of, is the last thing that should be on his mind these days. There are bigger concerns that only a businessman, who has been as audacious and ambitious as Rao, can handle. And the future of the group will depend on how well he does that.

But there is a lot to look forward to for each of these men as well.

According to government estimates, India will require investments to the tune of $1 trillion to meet its 'building-up' requirements over the next ten years. Over the next twenty, this amount will triple. A bulk of these investments will be needed in power, roads, airports and bridges, businesses all these men have their fortunes tagged with. Even if a part of the plans fructify, each of the men could have their fortunes increase manifold.

If the biggest challenge for Ajit Gulabchand, Baba N. Kalyani, Gautam Thapar and G.M. Rao will be to stick to their plans and ensure that the course they set out on is followed, the challenge for the other three—Ronnie Screwvala, Rajeev Chandrasekhar and Ajay Piramal—will be to improve upon what they have already done. Ajay has probably got the clearest line of vision for this. Like in his meticulously and patiently charted journey so far, the building blocks are slowly falling into place, be it in the form of the companies he has bought or the key drugs his R&D teams are working on. If things go according to plan, you could see Ajay do what no other businessman in the vibrant Indian pharmaceuticals industry has done before—discover a blockbuster drug. If it happens, he will be propelled onto the big league on the world stage.

Ronnie Screwvala is perhaps the toughest man to figure out amongst the lot. There is a detachment about him that is quite unusual in an entrepreneur. Has it been just a gamble, a game? What drives him? What are his plans for the future? These are some of the unanswered questions and yet, over the last few months, Screwvala has been in the headlines for the small investments he has made. He wants to make a difference, use his business acumen to develop ideas and businesses that can make a change. But philanthropy is just one part of the story he is scripting. He seems to be biding his time with a clear picture in his mind about the next big wave he is going to ride. After all, he has age on his side, a decade at least. That's more time than he has given to any of the businesses he became so famous creating! He will probably make a success of whatever he does. But what is the legacy he leaves behind in the world of cinema? How will he be remembered on this stage of make-believe? These are questions that will remain.

The man with the longest runway ahead of him is Rajeev. In his late forties, in an arena—Indian politics—where the average

age is seventy, he has a long way to go and much to do, no matter how convincingly he says he doesn't want to make politics his career. Those close to him believe that despite everything he has done, he hasn't fulfilled even half his ambitions!

Each of these men has had a fascinating run in business. Mostly because of the hard work they have put in and a vision that has kept them ahead of their times. A fair dose of curiosity, ambition, acumen and humility have helped them to attempt the impossible, overcome unbelievable odds, and they continue to do what they do best, follow their heart and ride the wave.

BIBLIOGRAPHY

AJIT GULABCHAND

BOOKS

Lalvani, M., '*Sugar Co-operatives in Maharashtra: A Political Economy Perspective*', Department of Economics, Mumbai University, 2008.

Piramal, G., *Business Maharajas*, New Delhi: Penguin, 1996.

Piramal, G., *Business Legends*, New Delhi: Penguin, 1999.

Sadhu, A., *The Pioneer: Life and Times of Vitthalrao Vikhe Patil*, Pune: Rohan Prakashan, 2011.

ARTICLES

Adhikari, A., 'Brick by brick', *Business Today*, 19 August 2012.

Ashar, S., 'CM favours regularizing Lavasa's illegalities', *TNN*, 15 June 2011.

Bavadam, L., 'A movement in decline', *Frontline*, 12–25 March 2005.

Chandawarkar, R., 'We could have made some mistakes in Lavasa: Chairman', *DNA*, Pune, 8 January 2011.

Cherian, D., 'The return of the raiders', *Business India*, 4 April 1988.

Roy, S., 'Rama Prasad Goenka: A saga of empire building', *Business India*, 11 January 1988, pp. 38–48.

Shanker, S., 'PE firm Xander picks up stake in HCC', *HT*, 29 September 2011.

Thekaekara, T., 'The Great Urban Juggernaut', *New Internationalist*, 1 May 2010.

Vaidya, A., 'Sharad Pawar's Lavasa is about conflict of interest', *DNA*, Pune, 9 January 2011.

'Constructing growth', *Business India*, 7 March 2010.

'End of a legacy', *Business India*, 25 August 1997.

'HCC making it big', *Business India*, 16 August 2004.

'HCC rebuilding its strength', A Corporate Report, *Business India*, 16 April 1990.

'HCC leapfrogging to the future', *Business India*, 5 February 2001.

'India's infrastructure builders', *Business World*, 6 December 2010.

'Lavasa project controversy: Pawar forces Jairam on backfoot', *DNA*, 1 December 2010.

'Lavasa controversy a question of height', *HT*, 29 November 2010.

'Ajit Gulabchand wants PM to intervene in Lavasa', NDTV, 14 October 2011.

'Environment Ministry refuses green clearance to Lavasa', *PTI*, 14 October 2011.

'Open for dialogue with MoEF', *PTI*, 21 January 2011.

'Oxford's Lavasa tamasha', *Sunday Times*, 30 August 2009.

'Contest of the century: India vs China', *Economist*, 21 August 2010.

REPORTS

HCC Annual Reports and Chairman's Speech, 1999–2011.

HSBC Global Research Report on HCC, 29 July 2011.

Institutional Equities Report, Nirmal Bang Institutional Equities Research Desk, 26 September 2011.

See interview on Future Dialogue with Dr Shirish Sankhe, Director, McKinsey & Company, 6 August 2011.

PINC Research Report on HCC, June 2008.

'Sustainable Cities: Mastering the Challenges and Opportunities of Rapid Urbanisation', A Background Paper, Economist Intelligence Unit for Future Dialogue 2011.

GAUTAM THAPAR

BOOKS

Anand, I.P., *A Crusader's Century: In Pursuit of Ethical Values*, New Delhi: K.W. Publishers, 2010.

Dasgupta, A., *The Life and Times of Karam Chand Thapar*, Mumbai: Archive Publishers, 1998.

Succeeding for Generations, Ernst & Young.

Jalan, B., *India's Economic Policy*, New Delhi: Penguin, 2008.

Piramal, G. and M. Herdeck, *India's Industrialists: Volume 1*, Washington, DC: Three Continents Press, 1986.

ARTICLES

'BILT appoints JP Morgan, Citi for Dutch units listing', *Economic Times*, 2 July 2010.

Layak, S., D. Chattopadhyay and A. Subramanian, 'The Empire crawls back', *Business Today*, 15 February 2010.

Mitra, M., 'Gautam Thapar taking Avantha to greater heights', *Economic Times*, 3 June 2011.

Malhotra, S. and S. Dobhal, 'The outsider', *Financial Express*, June 2011.

'Indian Co., US varsity innovate clean energy', India Blooms News Service, 29 June 2009.

'Avantha Group's Gautam Thapar', Knowledge@Wharton, February 2009.

'Fitch revises outlook on India's BILT', *Reuters*, 23 July 2012.

'Questions and Answers: Gautam Thapar', *Wall Street Journal*, 6 October 2009.

'Avantha's advance: A sprawling family business charts a course for its rivals to follow', *Economist*, 8 April 2010.

'Indian CEOs see bigger opportunity in China', *TNN*, 29 June 2010.

REPORTS

DBS Cholamandalam Securities Report, Company Update on Crompton Greaves, July 2009.

Ambit Research Report, 'Crompton Greaves: The Great Unravelling', August 2011.

Emkay Research, Report on Ballarpur Industries, 2009.

WEBSITES

Indian groups $20M NanoCollege pledge; http://www.timesunion.com/news/article/Indian-group-s-20M-NanoCollege-pledge-562463.php, 26 June 2010, Albany.

Vaknin S., 'Analysis: The demise of the Mittelstand', 29 January 2003, United Press International.

BABA N. KALYANI

BOOKS

Cappelli, P., H. Singh, J. Singh and M. Useem, '*The India Way: How India's Top Business Leaders are Revolutionizing Management*', *Harvard Business Press*, 2010.

Church, P., *Added Value: The Life Stories of Indian Business Leaders*, New Delhi: Lotus Roli, 2010.

Kumar, N., '*India's Global Powerhouses: How They Are Taking on the World*', *Harvard Business Press*, 2009.

Rajan, R.G., *Fault Lines: How Hidden Fractures Still Threaten the World Economy*, New Delhi: HarperCollins, 2010.

Srinivasan, R. (ed.) *The New Indian Industry: Structures and Key Players*, New Delhi: Macmillan, 2005.

ARTICLES

Cover Feature, *Business India*, December 2006.

'Bullish on China Shop', *Business India*, February 2003.

'Diversification Dreams: Will Bharat Forge Become India's Newest Conglomerate', Knowledge@Wharton, January 2010.

'Germany's Mittelstand: Slipped Disc', *Economist*, 13 December 2001.

WEBSITES

Raghunathan, A., 'Forging Ahead', Forbes.com, 26 December 2005.

AJAY PIRAMAL

ARTICLES

Jain, A., 'NPL bound for British Columbia in search of biotech bounty', *Financial Express*, 13 November 2003.

Rajwadkar, K., 'Indian pharma cos to be partners of choice for multinationals', *Financial Express*, 11 May 2003.

Ramaswamy, E.A., 'Ugly lessons from the textile strike', *Business India*, 26 June 1989.

'Advantage Piramals', *Business Standard*, 29 October 1996.

'Battling new ailments', *Business Standard*, 19 April 2003.

'Can we succeed in drug discovery?' *Economic Times*, 12 February 2003.

'Expanding its portfolio', *Business India*, 4 November 1996.

'Garrotting the Girangaon', *Business Standard*, 17 April 2000.

'Gujarat Glass set to acquire US firm', *Financial Express*, 13 May 2003.

'Indian pharma cos eye acquisitions', *Financial Express*, 14 November 2003.

'Meet Mr Right Timing', *Economic Times*, 22 May 2010.

'Morarjee Goculdas to use five-year Rs 25 crore IDBI loan for update', *Financial Express*, 6 November 1998.

'Morarjee revamping Devanagere unit', *Business Line*, 15 October 1998.

'Morarjee sets sights on designer garment market', *Economic Times*, 18 July 1998.

'Nicholas Piramal signs pact with Teva', *Business Standard*, 1 November 1996.

'Nicholas-Boehringer boards approve merger', *Pioneer*, 1 November 1996.

'NPL acquires ICI India's unit for Rs 70 cr', *Times of India*, 26 January 2002.

'Nicholas acquires ICI India's pharma business', *Free Press Journal*, 26 January 2002.

'Nicholas Piramal forms new holding company', *Business Line*, 14 June 2003.

'Nicholas Piramal raises $10m by ECBc', *Asian Age*, 13 June 2003.

Obituary of Samant, 'End of Samant', *Business India*, 27 January 1997.

'Pharma Industry to raise fake drug issue with Centre', *Financial Express*, 10 May 2003.

'Piramal Group poised for dominant role in pharma industry', *Afternoon Despatch & Courier*, 1 November 1996.

'Pharmaceuticals in India', *Economist*, 7 December 1996.

'Piramal enterprises poised for a leap', *Business World*, 13 November 1996.

'Piramals plan housing complex in Parel mill', *Economic Times*, 18 March 2003.

'Pharma cos hike R&D spend to gain global edge', *Economic Times*, 9 June 2003.

'Restructuring Piramal style', *Express Investment Week*, 2 March 1998.

'Spinning a profitable yarn', *Business Standard*, 25 February, 1991.

'States of strategic alliances in India', *Strategist*, July 1997.

'Survival of composite mills depends on the export market', *Independent*, 23 April 1990.

'Takeover Tycoon', *Afternoon Despatch & Courier*, 1 March 1998.

'The art of acquisition', *Business India*, 4 November 1996.

'The future is in the present', *Marwar India* magazine, September-October 2010.

'BMIL plans merger with Nicholas Piramal', *Times of India*, 29 October 1996.

'Top designers lend their touch to Morarjee mills', *Afternoon Despatch & Courier*, 18 July 1998.

'Woman of vision', *Financial Express*, 3 August 1996.

WEBSITES

'Pharma uppers and downers of 2005', Rediff.com.

G.M. RAO

BOOKS

Church, P., *Added Value: The Life Stories of Indian Business Leaders*, New Delhi: Lotus Roli, 2010.

ARTICLES

'Wheels of Progress', *Engineer* magazine, 1971–72.

'One Step up, Two Steps down: The Story of G.M. Rao. The Story of Indian Infrastructure', *Forbes India*, 17 June 2011.

'India, US moot $10bn infrastructure fund', *Economic Times*, 9 November 2010.

'Turning Points', Interview on *Moneylife*, June 2007.

REPORTS

Jain, R., 'Airport Privatization in India: Lessons from the Bidding Process in Delhi and Mumbai', IIMA Research and Publications, 2007.

Tongia, R., 'The Political Economy of Indian Power Sector Reforms', Working Paper, Stanford University, December 2003.

'Airport investment encouraged but uncertainty remains', CAPA Report, May 2008.

GMR Infrastructure Limited Annual Reports, 2006–12.

WEBSITES

Das Gupta, S., 'The Story behind GMR's success', Rediff.com, 23 April 2005.

RONNIE SCREWVALA

BOOKS

Chopra, A., *First Day First Show*, New Delhi: Penguin, 2011.

Epstein, Edward J., *Hollywood Economist*, Brooklyn: Melville House Books, 2009.

Ghosh, P., 'Indian cinema at 100', *International Business Times*, 3 August 2013.

Khanna, T., *Billions of Entrepreneurs: How China and India are Reshaping their Futures and Yours*, New Delhi: Penguin, 2009.

Padamsee, A., *A Double Life*, New Delhi: Penguin, 1999.

Paul, R. and L. Monica, *Inside Rupert's Brain*, New Delhi: Penguin, 2009.

Pinto, Jerry (ed), *The Greatest Show on Earth*, New Delhi: Penguin, 2011.

ARTICLES

Rai, Saritha, 'Profile: Ronnie Screwvala', *Global Post*, 6 April 2009.

Subramanian, A., 'Behind Ronnie Screwvala's Rs 2,000 cr Walt Disney deal', *Business Today*, 28 July 2011.

Subramaniam, A., 'UTV Production', *Business Today*, 2 November 2008.

'Hooray for Bollywood', newsweek.com, 30 November 2011.

'Leader Speak with Ronnie Screwvala', *Business Today*, 23 January 2011.

'A large part is marketing', *Business World*, 9 October 2010.

'Dancing with the idea of change', *Mint*, 5 March 2011.

'India's biggest movie icons', *iDiva*, April 2012.

'Star, Zee join hands for distribution', *Mint*, 24 May 2011.

'UTV's Ronnie Screwvala', Knowledge@Wharton, June 2008.

'Why Rs 100 cr is the biggest star in Bollywood', *Economic Times*, 12 February 2012.

'Would Scrooge approve?' *Business Today*, 9 March 2008.

REPORTS

UTV Ltd, Draft Red Herring Prospectus, 2005.

E&Y Report, 'Poised for Digital Growth', 2010.

E&Y Report, 'The New Market Shehers', 2010.

E&A Report, The M&E Quarterly, 2010.

E&Y Report, 'Tune in to emerging entertainment markets', 2009.

WEBSITES

Bali, A., 'An Interview with Ronnie Screwvala', Tech2.com, 8 October 2009.

Wadia, Shirin K., 'Ronnie Screwvala: Bollywood to Hollywood', 25 June 2008, Parsikhabar.net.

'UTVs Ronnie Screwvala: Took all the pains but no gains?' Wordpress.com, 11 August 2011.

RAJEEV CHANDRASEKHAR

BOOKS

Sanghvi, V., *Men of Steel*, New Delhi: Roli Books, 2007.

ARTICLES

Badrinath, R., 'Jupiter Capital mulls $150m joint PE fund', *Business Standard*, 25 August 2008.

'A false ring to it', *Hindustan Times*, 18 May 2010.

'A giant is born', *Business India*, July 9, 2001.

'BPL's bold new face', *Business India*, 1 November 1999.

'CAG likely to probe 2G spectrum issue', *DNA*, 2 December 2009.

'CBI questions Rajya Sabha MP Rajeev Chandrasekhar', *Indian Express*, 15 June 2011.

'Chandrasekhar claims Sibal's claims bizarre', *Hindu*, 12 January 2011.

'Clawback Kid', A Corporate Report, *Business India*, 15 March 2004.

'DoT chalks out priority list for 2G spectrum', *Financial Express*, 10 December 2009.

'DoT-MoD 3G spectrum row', *Economic Times*, 27 October 2009.

'Govt gets SC protection in 2G spectrum tangle', *Times of India*, 16 December 2009.

'Hindustan Infrastructure bids for all weather port in Karwar', *Livemint*, 12 November 2007.

'Indian court cancels contentious wireless licenses', *New York Times*, 2 February 2012.

'It's not a scam, it's a crime', Rajeev Chandrasekhar's interview, *Tehelka*, 4 December 2010.

'Jupiter gets Vijaydurg Project', *Livemint*, 16 July 2007.

'News spectrum policy may see further delays', *Livemint*, 7 December 2009.

'Rajeev Chandrasekhar to invest Rs 1,300 crores in Maharashtra Port', Agency reports, 3 May 2007.

'Rajeev Chandrasekhar buys 51% in Asianet', *Economic Times*, 30 October 2006.

'Rupert Murdoch set to acquire majority stake in Asianet', *Economic Times*, 5 August 2008,

'Star and Jupiter form JV to tap south Indian market', *Livemint*, 15 November 2008.

'SC hauls up telecom dept over arbitrary 2G cut off', *Financial Express*, 16 December 2009.

'Supreme Court scraps UPA's illegal 2G sale', *Hindu*, 2 February 2012.

'Tata slams Rajeev Chandrasekhar and GSM operators', *Live India*, 9 December 2010.

'Telecom: The cup, the lip and the slip', *Business India*, 23 July 2001.

'The Raja-Radia tapes', *Outlook*, 18 November 2010.

'The X Tapes', *Open*, 20 November 2010.

'3G spectrum auction on schedule', *Economic Times*, 27 October 2009.

'3G auction govt pares its revenue expectations', *Livemint*, 16 December 2009.

'3G auction may be delayed', *Economic Times*, 8 December 2009.

'3G spectrum, SC frowns at the Govt', *DNA*, 17 December 2009.

'Why Open Ran the Radia Tapes', India Real Time, *Wall Street Journal*, 26 November 2010.

'Radia Tapes Controversy', Karan Thapar's show on CNN IBN.

REPORTS

Uppal, M., S.K.N. Nair and C.S. Rao, 'India's Telecom Reform: A Chronological Account', UNDP Study, 1995.

TRAI recommendations on Spectrum Management and Licensing Framework, 11 May 2010.

TRAI recommendations on review of licence terms and capping number of access providers, 28 August 2007.

'2G spectrum scam: MOCITs claims versus facts', Rajeev Chandrasekhar's report as member of Parliament, 21 January 2011.

Rajeev Chandrasekhar's open letter to Ratan Tata, 9 December 2010.

WEBSITES

'Government ignored my warnings on 2G scam', Rajeev Chandrasekhar's interview, Rediff.com, 15 November 2010.

'Telco's requests for 2G spectrum after cut-off not rejected: Govt', Indian Express.com, 16 December 2009.

'The Great Telecom Crime', Rajeev Chandrasekhar's blog.

INDEX

ACKNOWLEDGEMENTS

I have a lot of people to thank. First, of course, are the men in this book for their time and help during the last three years. I am forever indebted to them for sharing their experiences and narrating their stories.

A dear friend, Srinjoy Chowdhury, for leading the way and encouraging me always; my publisher from HarperCollins India, Krishan Chopra, for his wisdom, insight and tremendous patience; the editor, Bidisha Srivastava, for sharing my excitement over this book and burning the midnight oil to help make it happen; Shravani Dang, Arun Bhagat, Jimmy Mogul, Sarita Iyer, Mr Kutty and the teams at Avantha, HCC, Bharat Forge, Piramal Healthcare, GMR, UTV and Jupiter Capital.

Additionally, M.K. Anand and Vivek Law for allowing me to take the crucial little breaks needed from work to write this book; Rahul Bajaj, for being so supportive; Dr Swati Piramal and Alyque Padamsee, for their time at such short notice; Mr and (late) Mrs B.M. Thapar, for their warmth and hospitality; the experts—Farokh Balsara, Manish Agarwal, Vinayak Chatterjee, Kumar Ketkar, Sujay Shetty, Mahesh Uppal, Romal Shetty, Jagannadham Thunuguntla, Lulu Raghavan, Vikas Dandekar; and many others—for their insights.

My first boss, Ashok Advani, for allowing me to access the *Business India* library; the old UTV team—Zarina Mehta, Deven Khote and Siddharth Roy Kapur—for their time and help; Prof. Tarun Khanna and A.M. Naik for their encouraging words; my mom-in-law, Valsa Williams, for all her insights about the tech world; and finally, everyone at home for giving me the time, support and space to do this.

ABOUT THE AUTHOR

Mini Menon is executive editor of Bloomberg TV India, where she oversees news and features programming. She has led the coverage of financial and corporate news with award-winning documentaries and cutting-edge shows, including a popular mini-series, *Inside India's Best Known Companies*, with India's top CEOs and businessmen.

Mini has worked with some of the other leading names in Indian news broadcasting, including Times Now and CNBC TV 18, over the last fifteen years.

In 2013, Mini was recognized as one of the ten most influential women in Indian media, marketing and advertising by *Impact* magazine. She has won awards like the Rajiv Gandhi Excellence Award as a young achiever and the Zee Astitva Award for Journalism. She was adjudged the Best Business News Anchor by the Indian Broadcasting Federation in 2009.

An alumna of St. Stephen's, New Delhi, Mini was a Chevening scholar and has trained in broadcast journalism from India and the UK.